TRANSFORMATION OF LIFE AND LABOR IN APPALACHIA

Journal
of the
Appalachian Studies Association

Edited by
Ronald L. Lewis

1990
Volume II

The Appalachian Consortium was a non-profit educational organization composed of institutions and agencies located in Southern Appalachia. From 1973 to 2004, its members published pioneering works in Appalachian studies documenting the history and cultural heritage of the region. The Appalachian Consortium Press was the first publisher devoted solely to the region and many of the works it published remain seminal in the field to this day.

With funding from the Andrew W. Mellon Foundation and the National Endowment for the Humanities through the Humanities Open Book Program, Appalachian State University has published new paperback and open access digital editions of works from the Appalachian Consortium Press.

www.collections.library.appstate.edu/appconsortiumbooks

This work is licensed under a Creative Commons BY-NC-ND license. To view a copy of the license, visit http://creativecommons.org/licenses.

Original copyright © 1990 by the Appalachian Consortium Press.

ISBN (pbk.: alk. Paper): 978-1-4696-3699-3
ISBN (ebook): 978-1-4696-3701-3

Distributed by the University of North Carolina Press
www.uncpress.org

Journal of the Appalachian Studies Association

Volume 2　1990

Transformation of Life and Labor in Appalachia

TABLE OF CONTENTS

**Preindustrial Jackson County
and Economic Development**.. 1
　Gordon B. McKinney
　Western Carolina University

**Folk Tradition and Industrialization
in Appalachia**... 11
　Jean Haskell Speer
　Virginia Polytechnic Institute and State University

Signs of Civilization: *The Trail of the
Lonesome Pine* **as Colonial Narrative**... 21
　Rodger Cunningham
　Sue Bennett College

**Household Composition and Early Industrial
Transformation: Eastern Kentucky 1880-1910**........................... 47
　Thomas A. Arcury
　University of Kentucky

**Bringing Modern Notions of Childhood and
Motherhood to Preindustrial Appalachian:
Katherine Pettit and May Stone, 1899-1901**................................ 69
　Rhonda England
　University of Kentucky

**Four Perspectives on Appalachian Culture
and Poverty**... 76
　Roger A. Lohmann
　West Virginia University

Organized Medicine and the UMWA Welfare and Retirement Fund: An Appalachian Perspective on an National Conflict..................92
    Richard P. Mulcahy
    University of Pittsburgh-Titusville

The Roving Picket Movement and the Appalachian Committee for Full Employment, 1959-1965: A Narrative..................110
    Kate Black
    University of Kentucky

Community Mobilization: The Tug Hill Landfill Site..................128
    Beth Degutis
    University of Tennessee

The Bitter Creek Appalachian Symposium..................143
    Garry Barker
    Berea College

A Bridge or a Barrier?: Assessing the Usefulness of Public Education for Individual Success in an East Tennessee County..................155
    Roberta Campbell and Alan J. DeYoung
    University of Kentucky

"Never Met a Man Who Made a Basket ... Never Saw My Daddy Cane a Chair"..................175
    Bobby Ann Starnes
    Harvard University

Appalachian Studies Association Membership..................187

These articles are based on presentations made at the 1989 Appalachian Studies Conference.

1989 Appalachian Studies Association Officers

Loyal Jones ....President
Doyle Bickers ....Vice-President
Ronald Lewis ....Conference Program Chair
Sallie Miller................................Newsletter Editor/Secretary
Alice Brown...Treasurer

Steering Committee

Loyal Jones, Chair
Doyle Bickers
Barry Buxton
Roberta Herrin
Parks Lanier, Jr.
Grace Toney Edwards
Gordon McKinney
Rosemary Goss
Eliot Wigginton
Wilburn Hayden

Program Committee

Ronald Lewis, Chair
Dwight Billings
Kate Black
Rebecca Hancock
John Inscoe
Nancy Joyner
Jane Shook
William Turner

Local Arrangements

Mary Beth Pudup, Chair
Staff of Regional Research
Institute of WVU

Ronald L. Lewis, the 1989 program chair of the Appalachian Studies Association and guest editor of the *Journal of the Appalachian Studies Association*, is professor of history and chairman of the department of history at West Virginia University. He has published extensively on the coal industry.

Preindustrial Jackson County and Economic Development

Gordon B. McKinney

The presence of a growing number of community studies of preindustrial Appalachia allows us the luxury of taking a broader look at this most important part of the mountain past. The number of studies has increased rapidly and has been of very high quality (Waller, 1988; Dunn, 1988; and Pudup, 1989). The results suggest the need for a major revision of our understanding of the traditional world of the highland farmer. This change in perspective will then require a modification of our interpretation of the role played by industrialization in the years between 1880 and 1920. This more realistic understanding of the foundations of preindustrial society will inevitably undermine some of our more cherished notions about the responsibility for the economic problems that followed. This is a small price to pay for increased knowledge and a sounder conceptual base upon which to base our analysis of present conditions.

One of the most difficult tasks for historians to deal with is the baneful effect of perfect hindsight. Knowing that the mountain region was to be industrialized, has led most of us to deal with the previous time as nonindustrialized Appalachia instead of approaching it on its own terms. This has allowed us to create a virtual 'Garden of Eden' waiting to be despoiled by insensitive and greedy outsiders and capitalists (Eller, 1982; Billings et al. 1986). This has encouraged most of us to ignore or repress such historical developments as the dispossession of

Native Americans, African slavery, the exploitation of women, the misuse of the environment, elitist politics, rampant drug use, and reluctance to support education as part of preindustrial life. This convenient memory lapse has allowed us to center our attention on the formation of an agricultural society characterized by communal and kinship ties that limited the impact of impersonal economic relationships. A study of Jackson County, North Carolina, in a broader context will allow us to examine the validity of even this limited vision of the mountain past.

One concept associated with the traditional mountain lifestyle that has survived the onslaught of recent scholarship is that of community. The new studies agree that the nuclear family homestead was the most basic economic unit. They point out, however, that the families were never individually self-sufficient (Loehr, 1952; Shammas, 1982; Puritt, 1984). In fact, many of those who lived on the land were not themselves landowners. A study of several north Georgia counties concluded that as many as 40 percent of the farmers in that region were tenants (Bode and Ginter, 1986). This conclusion is partially confirmed by the work of my colleagues on the Jackson County project (Blethen and Wood, Jr., 1987). Steven Hahn's innovative work on the Georgia upcountry strongly suggests that despite these differences in the relationship to the land that personal contacts and concerns dominated a community based economy (Hahn, 1983). The point being that all residents of a locality required the skills of craftsmen like millers, blacksmiths, joiners, coopers, and wheelwrights to survive. Hahn concluded that this community agricultural economy was not deeply influenced by the market economy. Several studies of twentieth-century mountain people document that this sense of personal relationship persisted despite the impact of industrialization and change required by Federal policies (Dunn, 1988; Hall et al. 1987; and McDonald and Muldowny, 1982).

Another school of interpretation suggests that the presence of a community-based economy does not mean the absence of market pressures. Among the most significant of the scholars proposing this perspective is James T. Lemon. Lemon (1972) argues that the early settlers in southern Pennsylvania were deeply influenced by commercial motives. Many of these individuals ultimately migrated to Virginia and North Carolina and became the first settlers in the Appalachian highlands. If Lemon is correct, the original mountain settlers came not to escape the competition of the market economy, but to find a better opportunity to succeed in it. Nor is Lemon alone in his assertion that community economies were part of a broader market economy. A variety of traditional and Marxist scholars have concluded that American farmers had strong commercial ties by the early 19th century (Clark, 1979; Appleby, 1982; Merrill, 1977).

For example, Winnifred Rothenberg (1981) has analyzed the convergence of market-center prices and local prices and concluded that by 1820 at the latest Massachusetts farmers were part of the market economy.

Analysis of preindustrial Appalachia confirms both the role played by the community in the economy and the importance of the market. The traumatic events of the Civil War illustrated the interdependence of mountain families. Since there were relatively few slaves in Jackson and other mountain counties, the absence of husbands and sons in the army left most families at risk. One Jackson County woman reported that the families of Cherokee soldiers were "living on weeds and the bark of trees ...."[1] Since their neighbors were little better off themselves, the state and local governments were forced to turn to a formal welfare program to try to insure that soldiers families had food (Escott, 1984). The Confederate draft not only took farmers, but the army needed highly skilled craftsmen to equip and maintain itself. The result was that Jackson and most other mountain counties were stripped of millers, joiners, blacksmiths, tanners, and shoemakers. The loss of these men was disastrous in the extreme and desperate appeals went out to government officials to return some of these essential workers to mountain communities.[2] Thus, the stress of war conclusively demonstrated the dependence of mountain families on their neighbors.

Despite the community structure of the mountain economy, there is increasing evidence that the farmers of the region were integrated into a broader series of regional relationships. While local residents may have appeared to take part in a series of barter exchanges, their transactions were based on monetary values being assigned to each item. For example, one western North Carolina farmer made the following offer to a local merchant: "We received a note from you stating that you was anxious to swap beef hides for leather. We will swap at the old prices if that will suit.[3]" Jackson County farmer and businessman, William Holland Thomas, was typical of this type of mountain store owner. During the years between 1820 and 1850, Thomas secured furs, hides, livestock, butter, and ginseng from his neighbors. In return, he provided them with liquor, salt, gunpowder, hardware, and dry goods (Blethan, p. 74-75). Advertisements in the Asheville News in 1860 offered a wide variety of products for sale. These included such luxuries as piano fortes, personal photographs, and hooped skirts. Clearly, the mountain people had access to the broader American economy.

There were other indications of the mountain people's participation in the regional and national economy as well. Not only was cash the basis for commodity exchange, but it was also the measure of value for the most basic of goods—land. Unlike real property in other parts of the South where it was treated as a disposable resource—an attitude found among some in the highland as well—land was usually the measure of a mountain farmer's wealth and a source of speculative investment (Wright, 1986; Blethen, p.77). William Holland Thomas not only ran a number of stores, but he invested in hundreds of thousands of acres of western North Carolina land. While part of Thomas' reasons for doing this was to protect the homeland of the Eastern Band of Cherokees, he used most of the land for his own personal gain. His own holdings were smaller, however, than those under the control of the Love family—his in-laws (See Inscoe, 1984; Crawford, 1986). Of course, the value of slaves had a regionally determined monetary value as well—prices in Texas and Arkansas determined values in the mountain counties. A report in the Asheville paper noted that five slaves were sold for an average cost of $1,150—a very good price for the time—in early 1859. As a result, all aspects of a mountain farmer's life including his land, crops, livestock, and labor were computed in monetary terms.

Thus, we seem to have a contradiction in our analysis. Jackson and other mountain counties were the home of a community economy that functioned through a series of interdependent local relationships. At the same time, all items in the economy were valued in monetary terms determined by broader regional and national markets. The confusion seems to rest on the assumption that the people at the time sensed that these two conditions were not consistent. Apparently they did not. Certainly in western North Carolina, there was a strong push by local leaders to encourage increased economic development outside of agriculture. The problem as Mary Beth Pudup has convincingly demonstrated was the absence of local capital to finance the desired changes. Thomas, although a member of the anti-development party in North Carolina, was an outspoken proponent of the extension of the Western North Carolina railroad into the mountain counties (Jackson County Journal, 1912). His stand was endorsed by the entire political opposition and by most voters who willingly accepted higher taxes in return for access to the outside world (Kruman, 1983; Asheville *News*, 1959).

Using the small amount of state aid available, western North Carolina county governments provided the first major roadways in the region. The Buncombe Turnpike—laid out north and south—connected East Tennessee with upper South Carolina through Asheville. This route provided an avenue for most of the livestock trade of that part of the mountain region. At one point in the 1850s more than 100,000 hogs a year moved across this route (McDonald and McWhiney, 1975). The state road cut across the mountains from east to west and was maintained by local labor. The importance of this road was demonstrated when it fell in disrepair during the Civil War and goods could not be shipped to Jackson County.[4] Even government officials were forced to admit that the normal pattern of transport to western North Carolina had been destroyed. The North Carolina salt commissioner at Saltville, Virginia, could not ship his precious cargo to several mountain counties.[5] Obviously, these problems would not have been so crucial if the region had not needed to trade with other parts of the South.

The impact of the breakdown of mountain transportation during the war further illustrated the dependence of mountain families on the outside world as well as their communities. Abundant evidence indicates that most western North Carolina families had stopped producing their own cloth. Many households lacked even the basic cotton cards and wood cards needed to start the process of preparing the fibers to make thread and yarn.[6] Others refused to consider starting from that basic level and insisted upon obtaining finished thread and yarn ready for weaving.[7] Even those who tried to do it themselves found the old skills difficult to learn.[8] Still others disdained the use of the loom and would purchase only the finished product.[9] The demand for cloth was so great in the western counties that one group wanted to construct a textile factory there.[10] As conclusive as the above example is of market involvement, the expectation of farm families that they would have to purchase food during the war is equally convincing. Those involved did not find the practice unusual or unexpected. While the numbers involved were relatively small, the appeals to the government for direct assistance were done with the expectation that food could be directly purchased.[11] It is clear that many mountain families had become dependent on the market for products that scholars have assumed were produced at home.

The investigator must confront the question of why contemporary observers were convinced that the mountain people lived in a different world from the rest of the country. This perception would seem to be based on the assumption that the relative isolation of the mountain people was a matter of their own choice. They chose to live apart and to live at the subsistence level. Mary Beth Pudup's recent work suggests otherwise. Looking at economic developments in Eastern Kentucky, she demonstrates that the mountain population actually lost contact with the market economy in the latter part of the nineteenth century. As railroads opened up the adjacent lowlands, trade routes moved away from the mountains, and the resulting economy was more isolated than had been previously the case (Pudup, 1988). When outside capital perceived the opportunities provided by the natural resources of the region, the state governments and large corporations provided the rails that opened up the region. These investors fulfilled not only their own visions of development, but those of many mountain businessmen who had little access to capital.

Thus, one can argue that the creation of the community-based agricultural economy of the Southern mountains was not an escape from the market economy. Instead, it was a reflection of the geographical realities and economic resources of the region. This does not mean that the mountaineer did not live in relative isolation. Nor does it mean that the families in Jackson County produced many manufactured goods or commercial farm products. But it does indicate that this was not the result of a commitment to an ideology that opposed economic expansion and industrialization. When the railroads arrived in Sylva and Dillsboro, the farmers left their relatively unprofitable farms to work in town or for timber companies. Even the great depressions of the 1890s and 1930s did not stop this flow of people off the farm.

Our new understanding of the preindustrial world of Jackson County must, therefore, contain the following points. The acknowledged isolation of the mountain people was relative and did not shield them from the workings of the market economy. Many in the county and in the region worked hard to maintain connections to the outside world. Individual slaveowners, merchants, stock drovers, craftsmen, and farmers were already directly involved in a cash economy in which prices were determined outside of the region. The failure to expand commercially and to industrialize was not due to hostility directed against that type of activity, but was due primarily to an absence of local capital necessary to finance large scale enterprises. When the capital was made available by outside sources, the mountain middle class eagerly participated in the economic revolution that followed. Many mountain farm families also exchanged their dependence on the neighbors for the dependence on the large companies that exploited the resources of the region. Large landowners like William Holland Thomas were replaced by large landowners like Champion Paper Company.

Viewed from this perspective, the industrialization that followed the coming of the railroads was an acceptable change. While many residents of Jackson County would decry the loss of intimacy in personal contacts, few desired to return to their previous way of life. In addition, they were able to maintain contact with large numbers of their children who would have had to migrate if industrial jobs had not provided opportunities near the homes of their parents. By looking at the preindustrial period as free from commercial influences, scholars have overemphasized the changes brought by economic development. In addition, they have been able to portray the mountain people as unwilling victims of a world they did not understand. While many of them did not comprehend or endorse the totality of the changes, they did welcome the opportunities presented and recognized that the region had irrevocably changed. It is now time for Appalachian scholars to make the same discovery.

Letters

Adkins, William. Statement, n.d. Eller, Jas *et al*, to Zebulon B. Vance. 8 November 1862. Callaway, R.F. *et al*, to Vance. 11 November 1862. Reel 15: Shell, J. F. to Vance. 3 March 1863. Reel 16: Conley, Elizabeth *et al*, to Vance. 10 July 1863. Reel 18: Shoop, D.C. to Vance. 24 March 1864. Reel 22: Love, R.E.A. to Vance. 22 April 1864. Reel 23: Coxey, John A. *et al*, to Vance. n.d. Reel 26. In McKinney and McMurry, *Vance Papers*.

Atkinson, Thomas to Zebulon B. Vance. 27 November 1863. Reel 20: Bowen, N. to Vance. 6 January 1864. Reel 21: Erwin, J.J. to Vance. 1 February 1864. Murdock, [W.] to Vance. 7 February 1864. Reel 3: Reagan, J.A. to Vance. 15 February 1864. Welch, R.V. to Vance. 20 February [18]64. Reel 22: Warren, J.M. to Vance. 16 March 1865. Reel 26: In McKinney, *Vance Papers*.

Cummings, A.W. to Zebulon B. Vance. 14 April 1863. Reel 17: Walker, R.T. to Vance. 2 March 1865. Reel 4: McKinney, *Vance Papers*.

[Deaver], Mary to _____. 30 March 1863. "Mary Cansler is here learning me how to spin, but finds it a rather hard job." *Gash Family Papers*, North Carolina Division of Archives and History.

Henry, Wm. L. to Zebulon B. Vance. 16 May 1864. Reel 23: McKinney, *Vance Papers*.

Lankford, Wm. to Zebulon Vance. 14 April 1863. Reel 17: Summey, A.T. to Vance. 20 May 1863. Reel 7: McKinney, *Vance Papers*

Love, Margaret E. to Zebulon B. Vance. 10 May 1864, Reel 23. In McKinney, Gordon B. and Richard M. McMurry, eds. 1987. *The Papers of Zebulon Baird Vance*. Frederick: University Publications of America.

McClelland, H. T. to Zebulon B. Vance. 22 February [18]63. Reel 16: Lonon, John to Vance, n.d. Reel 26: McKinney, *Vance Papers*.

Miller, S. H. to Zebulon B. Vance. 23 March 1863. Reel 16: In McKinney, *Vance Papers*.

Spicer, H. and H. J. to J. and C.J. Cowles. 26 January [18] 63. *Calvin J. Cowles Papers*, North Carolina Division of Archives and History.

Woodfin to Zebulon B. Vance. 1 October 1863. *op.cit.*

Works Cited

Appleby, Joyce O. 1982. "Commercial Farming and the 'Agrarian Myth' in the Early Republic." *Journal of American History LXVIII*: March 1982, 833-849; Merrill, Michael. 1977. "Cash is Good to Eat: Self-Sufficiency and Exchange in the Rural Economy of the United States." *Radical History Review III*: Winter 1977, 42-71.

Asheville, N.C. *News*. 6 January 1859.

Asheville, N.C. *News I*. 1 November 1860.

Billings, Dwight *et al*. 1986. "Culture, Family, and Community in Preindustrial Appalachia." *Appalachian Journal XIII*: Winter 1986, 154-170.

Blethen, H. Tyler and Curtis W. Wood, Jr. 1987. "The Pioneer Experience to 1851." In Max R. Williams ed., *The History of Jackson County*. Sylva, N.C: The Jackson County Historical Society, 83.

Bode, Frederick A. and Donald E. Ginter. 1986. *Farm Tenancy and the Census in Antebellum Georgia*. Athens: University of Georgia Press.

"Campaign Broadside," reprinted in *Jackson County Journal*, 12 June 1912.

Clark, Christopher. 1979. "The Household Economy, Market Exchange, and the Rise of Capitalism in the Connecticut Valley, 1800-1860," *Journal of Social History XIII:* Winter 1979, 169-189.

Dunn, Durwood. 1988. *Cades Cove: The Life and Death of A Southern Appalachian Community, 1818-1937*. Knoxville: University of Tennessee Press.

Eller, Ronald D. 1982. *Miners, Millhands, and Mountaineers: Industrialization of the Appalachian South, 1880-1930*. Knoxville: University of Tennessee Press, 1-37.

Escott, Paul. 1984. "Poverty and Government Aid to the Poor in Confederate North Carolina," *North Carolina Historical Review LXI:* October 1984, 462-480.

Hahn. 1983. *The Roots of Southern Populism: Yeoman Farmers and the Transformation of the Georgia Upcountry, 1850-1890*. New York: Oxford University Press.

Hall, Jacquelin D. *et al*. 1987. *Like a Family: The Making of a Southern Cotton Mill World*. Chapel Hill: University of North Carolina Press.

Inscoe, John. 1984. "Mountain Masters: Slaveholding in Western North Carolina." *North Carolina Historical Review LXI*: April 1984, 143-173; Crawford, Martin. 1986. "Wealth, Slaveholding and Power in the Southern

Mountains: Ash County, North Carolina, in 1860-1861." Appalachian Studies Conference: unpublished paper.

Kruman, Marc W. 1859. *Parties and Politics in North Carolina, 1836-1865.* Baton Rouge: Louisiana State University Press, 10; Asheville, N.C. *News,* 9 June 1859.

Lemon, J.J. 1972. *The Best Poor Man's Country: A Geographical Study of Early Southern Pennsylvania.* Baltimore: Johns Hopkins University Press.

Loehr, Rodney C. 1952. "Self-Sufficiency on the Farm," *Agricultural History XXVI*: January 1952, 41.

McDonald, Forest and Grady McWhiney. 1975. "The Antebellum Herdsmen: Reinterpretatio." *Journal of Southern History XLI:* May 1975, 161-162.

McDonald, Michael J. and John Muldowny. 1982. *TVA and the Dispossessed: The Resettlement of Population in the Norris Dam Area.* Knoxville: University of Tennessee Press.

Pudup, Mary Beth. 1988. "The Limits of Subsistence: Agriculture and Industry in Central Appalachia." Unpublished paper: 11-13.

Pudup, Mary Beth. 1989. "The Boundaries of Class in Preindustrial Appalachia." *Journal of Historical Geography, XV*: 1989, n.p.

Puritt, Bettye Hobbs. 1984. "Self-Sufficiency and the Agricultural Economy of Eighteenth-Century Massachusetts," *William and Mary Quaterly XLI*: July 1984, 338.

Rothenberg, W. 1981. "The Market and Massachusetts Farmers, 1750-1855." *Journal of Economic History XLI*: June 1981, 302.

Shammas, Carole. 1982. "How Self-Sufficient was Early America." *Journal of Interdisciplinary History XIII:* Autumn 1982, 252-253.

Waller, Altina L. 1988. *Feud: Hatfields, McCorys, and Social Change in Appalachia, 1860-1900.* Chapel Hill: University of North Carolina Press.

Wright, Gavin. 1986. *Old South, New South: Revolutions in the Southern Economy Since the Civil War.* New York: Basic Books, Inc., Publishers, 30-31; Blethin and Wood, "Pioneer," 77.

Wright, Gavin. 1978. *The Political Economy of the Cotton South: Households, Markets and Wealth in the Nineteenth Century.* New York: W.W. Norton & Company, 144-154.

Footnotes

[1] Love, Margaret E. to Zebulon B. Vance. 10 May 1864. Reel 23. In McKinney, Gordon B. and Richard M. McMurry, eds. 1987. *The Papers of Zebulon Baird Vance*. Frederick: University Publications of America.

[2] Adkins, William. Statement, n.d. Eller, Jas *et al*, to Zebulon B. Vance. 8 November 1862. Callaway, R.F. *et al*, to Vance. 11 November 1862. Reel 15: Shell, J. F. to Vance. 3 March 1863. Reel 16: Conley, Elizabeth *et al*, to Vance. 10 July 1863. Reel 18: Shoop, D.C. to Vance. 24 March 1864. Reel 22: Love, R.E.A. to Vance. 22 April 1864. Reel 23: Coxey, John A. *et al*, to Vance. n.d. Reel 26. In McKinney and McMurry, *Vance Papers*.

[3] Spicer, H. and H. J. to J. and C.J. Cowles, 26 January [18]63. *Calvin J. Cowles Papers*, North Carolina Division of Archives and History.

[4] Miller, S.H. to Zebulon B. Vance. 23 March 1863. Reel 16: In McKinney, *Vance Papers*.

[5] Woodfin to Zebulon B. Vance. 1 October 1863. *op.cit.*

[6] Atkinson, Thomas to Zebulon B. Vance. 27 November 1863. Reel 20: Bowen, N. to Vance. 6 January 1864, Reel 21: Erwin, J.J. to Vance. 1 February 1864. Murdock, [W.] to Vance. 7 February 1864. Reel 3: Reagan, J.A. to Vance. 15 February 1864. Welch, R.V. to Vance. 20 February [18]64. Reel 22: Warren, J.M. to Vance. 16 March 1865. Reel 26: In McKinney, *Vance Papers*.

[7] Cummings, A. W. to Zebulon B. Vance. 14 April 1863. Reel 17: Walker, R.T. to Vance. 2 March 1865. Reel 4: McKinney, *Vance Papers*.

[8] [Deaver], Mary to _____. 30 March 1863. "Mary Cansler is here learning me how to spin, but finds it a rather hard job." *Gash Family Papers*, North Carolina Division of Archives and History.

[9] Lankford, Wm. to Zebulon Vance. 14 April 1863. Reel 17: Summey, A.T. to Vance. 20 May 1863. Reel 7: McKinney, *Vance Papers*.

[10] Henry, Wm. L. to Zebulon B. Vance. 16 May 1864. Reel 23: McKinney, *Vance Papers*.

[11] McClelland, H. T. to Zebulon B. Vance. 22 February [18]63. Reel 16: Lonon, John to Vance, n.d. Reel 26: McKinney, *Vance Papers*.

Gordon B. McKinney is a program officer with the National Endowment for the Humanities. He recently edited *The Papers of Zebulon Vance*.

Folk Tradition and Industrialization in Appalachia

Jean Haskell Speer

Folklore, like Appalachia, is one of those words that is usually misunderstood. Both words are mystified and mythologized in the popular media and popular parlance. For many people, the words "folklore" and "Appalachia" do not belong in the same sentence with the word "industrialization." So, I want to begin this paper with a definition of terms, then give an overview of the transformation of traditional culture in Appalachia through increased modernity and industrialization, and finally examine in detail some specific traditions to illustrate the changes.

Some people dismiss what they consider to be "just folklore" as the quaint and trivial parts of the culture of a group. Folklore, they believe, is the remnant of some earlier, more primitive level of culture found only among rural and/or illiterate persons. Folklore is unreliable belief or practice, always on the verge of dying out. These are common misconceptions.

Folklore, in fact, is found in all cultures, and at all levels of society. It is not a mark of, nor a lack of, sophistication. Folklore is not a sign of the uncultured—folklore *is* culture. Folklore may not be reliable in the same way that historical fact, legal documents, or scholarly studies are, but it is an accurate indicator of the shared aesthetics, philosophy, values, and identity of a group. Folklore creates both communities and families and may inform us more about culture than do dates, names, events, or prominent leaders.

Folklore and folklife consist of received traditions passed on by those who have gone before us, or, with whom we share some community. It is our *traditional* culture: all that we learn informally, orally, by observing, or by imitating. Tradition is part of all lives; our folk traditions create the distinctive sense of us that we share with our families, friends, work groups, regions, and so on. In folklore, the groups in which people participate express their values and worldview in traditional ways.

Folk traditions do reveal some of the past to us; but folk traditions are, in fact, more revealing of the present than the past. While folklore does conserve patterns and some specifics of language, belief, or behavior, folk traditions do not persist unless they are dynamic as well as conservative. While folk processes are recognizable across time and space by some unchanging features, traditions disappear when they do not make dynamic adaptations to changes in people's cultural circumstances. We only maintain those traditions that are meaningful to us in the present and adaptable to our current needs. So, some traditions do die out; others remain vital and viable, while still others are revived when circumstances change. This is not to suggest that all folk traditions serve us well; some are dysfunctional. Often people are hidebound by what we may call the tyranny of tradition, but this too is a symptom of their current lifestyle as much as it is an indication of the past. Folk traditions will reveal, however, what we think we need from our past.

When we study folk traditions, we examine the processes by which culture is expressed in verbal art such as stories, ballads, jokes, curses, and the like; things made by hand, or material culture (barns, fences, clothing, baskets, tombstones); and the things people do or customary lore (beliefs, gestures, music, celebrations, work processes, rites of passage). Many of the folk traditions we study, of course, are complex and encompass all these categories at once: an Appalachian hog killing, for example, combines traditional patterns of work, food preservation, weather lore, verbal art, and much more.

One way to see the dynamism of folk tradition is to observe the adaptation of traditional forms and practices to new necessities of life. Periods of rapid change in a society are peak times for observing this adaptive process. In Appalachia, the transformation from a more stable, agrarian lifestyle to an industrialized, modernized, and fragmented life, particularly in the early part of this century, transformed traditional culture in the mountains as well as the economy. The story of the industrialization of Appalachia has been told with insight by Eller (1982), Kirby (1987), and others.

These researchers document rapid and wrenching social and economic changes that occurred in the mountains in the period from 1880 to 1960. In the first major period of industrialization at the turn of the century, the development of timbering, mining, and tourism changed the physical landscape of Appalachia, as well as the economy and the social structure. A people who had been largely independent, subsistence farmers became urban, industrial, or service workers. While some cultural traditions most assuredly disappeared with these changes, the process of tradition remained unchanged. Many older folklore forms were adapted to new themes, contexts, and functions; new traditions developed from changed patterns of living.

One of the clearest examples of this adaptation of traditional forms is the use of folksong and ballads as vehicles for expressing the emotional experience of coal mining. There were songs about explosions ("The Dream of the Miner's Child"), songs about labor struggles ("Coal Creek Troubles"), songs about heroes ("The Death of Mother Jones," "John Henry"), and Blues like "Black Lung Paycheck." Older folksong and ballads have often been adapted to songs of protest on the picket lines; such songs combine continuity and change in an effort to keep the protesting group cohesive and aligned with their cultural roots.

Jack Kirby, in his book, *Rural Worlds Lost*, cites another example of a traditional Appalachian practice that changed, but persisted, with the industrialization of the mountains. He writes:

> That the collapse of mountain lumber and coal industries and the onset of the Depression coincided with national Prohibition made moonshining and bootlegging all the more logical as a strategy for coping with misery and overpopulation. And just as country people took their liquor-making skills and habits to coal camps, migrants to textile towns also cooked whiskey for succor. During the mid-1930s a physician making house calls in the squalid Piedmont Heights section of Burlington, North Carolina, saw a man distilling spirits on his kitchen stove. Another factory hand sold corn whiskey from his mill village shack, hiding his supplies under the house next to the Chimney base. No adult (including the police) could squeeze into the crawl space, so the bootlegger's four-year-old son did the fetching. Thus were rural ways adapted to urban scenes (1987: 205).

One phase of Appalachian industrialization began during World War II and postwar years, when changes in the industrial economy sent thousands of mountain folk to live in urban centers outside the mountains; the process of tradition migrated along with them. Although fictional, Harriett Arnow's, *The Dollmaker,* charts changes in tradition memorably. Gertie Nevels, a mountain carver of wooden figures, moves with her family from the mountains of Kentucky to a large, industrial city in the north. The transformation in her family's relationships, values, and lifestyles are embodied in the changes in her traditional carving. As her carvings become popular among her new neighbors, and the commercial potential of her carving becomes clear, her husband, Clovis, and her children urge Gertie to "mass produce" her wood figures by using an electric saw and make them more commercially appealing by painting the figures. Gertie resists until she must face the choice between her old ways of craftsmanship and feeding her family. Because her dolls are "folksy" enough for her urban customers, she gets a large order for her work:

> She told Clovis of the doll order when she went indoors, and he was pleased. "You could have a little steady income—if you can make the things cheap enough but nice enough that a lot of people'ull want em."
>
> "Yes," she said, but with no enthusiasm, studying now the thumb of the uplifted hand in the block of wood [the figure of Christ she has been carving for years]. She held her own just below her breasts, then dropped it quickly; her hand would never be like that; she had two hands now, one reaching out making people drop into it money that might have gone for down payments [on land back in Kentucky]. She felt heavy and tired and old (Arnow 1954: 507).

Arnow uses Gertie's carving as a central metaphor in the novel to show the devastating effects of industrialization, and to point out the resilience of traditions.

In Jim Wayne Miller's poem, "The Brier Losing Touch With His Traditions," he, like Arnow, captures the changes that traditions often undergo, but that many people find unacceptable:

The Brier Losing Touch With His Traditions
Once he was a chairmaker.
People up north discovered him.
They said he was "an authentic mountain craftsman."
People came and made pictures of him working,
wrote him up in the newspapers.

He got famous.
Got a lot of orders for his chairs.

When he moved up to Cincinnati
so he could be closer to his market
(besides, a lot of his people lived there now)
he found out he was a Brier.

And when customers found out
he was using an electric lathe and power drill
just to keep up with all the orders,
they said he was losing touch with his traditions.
His orders fell off something awful.
He figured it had been a bad mistake
to let the magazine people take those pictures
of him with his power tools, clean-shaven,
wearing a flowered sport shirt and drip-dry pants.

So he moved back down to east Kentucky.
Had himself a brochure printed up
with a picture of him using his hand lathe.
Then when folks would come from the magazines,
he'd get rid of them before suppertime
so he could put on his shoes, his flowered sport shirt
and double-knit pants, and open a can of beer
and watch the six-thirty news on tv
out of New York and Washington.

He had to have some time to be himself. (Miller 1980: 44)

Miller astutely demonstrates how much people prefer their own perception of folklore and folklife rather than the realities of the traditional process in an urbanized, industrialized age.

As a folklorist who primarily studies oral traditions, I find it interesting to see how traditional story forms are adapted to changing cultural circumstances and needs. A story we collected in Patrick County, Virginia, a few years ago as part of a grant project, illustrates the evolution of such a traditional story. The county still appears outwardly to be rural and serene. In reality, most of the residents no longer live off the land, but commute outside the county to work in textile plants, furniture plants, or similar industries. The young people generally leave the county to find employment after schooling.

Since the beginning of this century, the changes in this community have been profound, and we documented these changes in our project.

Not surprisingly, the traditional culture, or folklore, of the community also has adapted to, and expresses, the changes. Anthropologist Victor Turner (1977: 76) has said that the texts of a community are special reflexive mechanisms for mirroring and monitoring behavior in a culture. These cultural performances, such as stories, legends, ceremonies, rituals, and so on, help us to learn our own culture, give our lives meaning beyond the immediate present, confront our fundamental values, and help us discover the principles for right living within our own culture. The stories and other cultural performances that we studied in Patrick County functioned as just such reflexive mechanisms for commenting on life in the community.

One story we collected was a traditional ghost story. The story roughly goes this way: a man spends the night in a haunted house or cabin. An apparition appears and speaks to him (in some versions the apparition is only seen and does not speak). The man runs, and, after some distance, stops to rest. The apparition again appears beside him and says, "We had a pretty good race, didn't we?" The man replies, "Yes, and we're fixin to have another one." The story is a traditional one found throughout the Appalachian mountains and contains two traditional motifs: "Fear test: staying in haunted house," *H1411; and "Ghosts scare people deliberately," *E293 (Baughman, 1966).

In most of the tellings we recorded, the story was told for its entertainment value, as a story of the way wit, construed as creative intelligence, can outweigh greater power and serve courage. This seems to be the performance tradition of the story. But, in one version of the story, we can see how this traditional form is adapted to the changed circumstances of the social and economic life of the community.

The storyteller is Mrs. Ada Martin, about 85 years old, and living alone (see appendix for her version of the story). Mrs. Martin is concerned about the ability of her community to carry on correctly: to live in a "right relationship" to one another. A dominant theme in the oral history interviews conducted with her is her fear of the fragmentation of community. She expresses a deep sense of loss for the communal caring of earlier days, and a belief that such continued loss will lead to the disasters that God visited on Pharaoh to save the culture and community of the Israelites. Mrs. Martin says, sadly:

> Well, life was really wonderful in those days, when you'd think about it ... we, uh, all the people look like, uh, was just united together in a way, because they would just love each other. And they'd try to do what they can, for each other, in sickness, troubles, anything that come upon them. And uh ... I felt like that at the time that people would, uh, had more love in their heart, or something, I

don't know ... than they do these days because people's too
busy now ... they have to work too hard ... and they don't
feel well. I feel like in those days when we done our work,
we went to the field and done a little, got our crops laid
by, and put away, and we had time to entertain each
other. To get around, and have a good time together. But
people now don't ... and nowadays, seems like they all, is
just nervous, full of nerves ... and, uh, I feel the difference
(Patrick County Project, 1981).

Mrs. Martin echoes the sentiments of many in her community, young and old, and she, at the least, clearly believes that loss of community is both spiritually and physically debilitating. Personal and community health depend on interdependence.

In her performance of the ghost tale, the protagonist is not a local person; indeed, he comes to the community as a stranger and, "he couldn't find anywhere that he could stay." He gets discouraged by this lack of warmth and hospitality, and asks for "an empty house" to stay in. The community sends him to a haunted house, and he accepts this rebuff and the challenge they have given him with bravado, "I don't care anything about that ... just tell me where the house is." Mrs. Martin's tale reverberates with echoes of earlier traditions—the sacredness of guest-host relationships as old as the Greeks, Biblical rejections of strangers, especially "no room at the inn."

Part of what makes this story memorable for Mrs. Martin is pleasant recollection of the interaction that produced it. There was a sharing of gifts, a story for a song between herself and her uncle, the kind of sharing she remembers as more typical of her community years ago. In the oral history interview that produced this performance, Mrs. Martin goes on to tell seven 'haint' tales in succession, warming to the friendly interchange with the interviewer.

She says all the ghost tales she knows are old—"I don't understand that, unless they uh, spend the days at the time that people just enjoyed talking ... people like to tell things ... sit around the fire and talk, you know, in those days." She particularly recalls a woman in whose home people gathered to hear her tell ghost tales. Mrs. Martin, sighs, "She was a good woman and a good neighbor."

For Mrs. Martin, ghosts tales are less about the supernatural and more about the natural order of things. This folk tradition she knows from the past becomes her vehicle for expressing her needs and concerns in the present. It reveals what she needs now from her past.

It is interesting to note, too, that "more sophisticated" people will believe that collecting a ghost tale from an Appalachian resident proves that mountain folk are still a primitive, superstitious, unsophisticated lot who believe in the supernatural. This elitist attitude demonstrates an ignorance of the serious business of storytelling and of folklore in general.

At the conclusion of Ron Eller's book about the industrialization of Appalachia, Eller quotes a letter from a mountain farmer in 1938 gripped by the frustration of watching his lifestyle change from one of contentment to despair. The farmer writes:

> Now what are we going to do, move on and try to fit in where we do not belong or undertake to face the situation and gradually starve to death? In the little mountain churches where we once sat and listened to the preaching of the gospel with nothing to disturb us, we now hear the roar of machinery on the Sabbath day. After all I have come to believe that the real old mountaineer is a thing of the past and what will finally take our place, God only knows (Eller, 1982: 242).

The farmer agonizes over the gut-wrenching changes he sees in the rapid industrialization of the mountains. Rightly so, for many of the damaging consequences of the environmental and economic disturbance have come to pass. He fears the loss of mountain culture as a "thing of the past." On this front, he underestimates the persistence of tradition. Certainly it evolves, adapts, and reshapes itself, but the essence of a given tradition remains recognizable. The "real old mountaineer" used the process of tradition and some of his repertoire of cultural traditions to cope with, comment upon, resist, and encompass the situations of industrialized life. The real old mountaineer is not a thing of the past but has evolved into the resilient mountain people of contemporary Appalachia.

Works Cited

Arnow, Harriette. 1954. *The Dollmaker.* New York: Avon Books.

Baughman, Ernest W. 1966. *Type and Motif Index of the Folktales of England and North America.* The Hague: Mouton.

Eller, Ronald D. 1982. *Miners, Millhands, and Mountaineers: Industrialization of the Appalachian South, 1880-1930.* Knoxville: University of Tennessee Press.

Kirby, Jack Temple. 1987. *Rural Worlds Lost: The American South, 1920-1960.* Baton Rouge: Louisiana State University Press.

Miller, Jim Wayne. 1987. *The Mountains Have Come Closer.* Boone, N.C: Appalachian Consortium Press. Used by permission.

Patrick County Project: Continuity and Change in a Rural Community. 1981. Apppalachian Collection, Virginia Polytechnic Institute and State University Library, Blacksburg, VA. Martin Tape 1, Accession 81. Transcript, p.10.

Turner, Victor. 1981. "*Social Dramas and Stories About Them,*" *On Narrative.* ed. W.J.T. Martin. Chicago: University of Chicago Press.

Appendix

(Mrs. Ada Martin, Star Route, Stuart, Virginia)

"Um, we, we enjoyed that, us kids—the older people, was older than we was you know, they had learned lots of ghost tales and they just really enjoyed it, I could tell one
that my uncle
told me when I was just about
six or seven years old.
And he told this, to me
and, if I'd sing a song for him
And so I said
"What do you want me to sing?"
He says sing "At the Cross."
So I sang that song for him
He says, "well now, I—I tell you a ghost story.
Says, "It's true now,"
that's the way he said it
He says, "It's true now."
Said one time was a man travelling,
and he come to a community
and he wanted to spend the night
and he couldn't find ANYWHERE that he could stay
Finally he got discouraged and he said, well could you tell
    me about uh is there any empty house anywhere around
    that I could stay in.
And uh, they said yes
Says uh, we know of a house
but they say it's haunted.
He says, I don't care anything about that
He says just tell me where the house is.
So they told him where the house was
And he went on to it
And that night he'd, he'd went in
got him some wood
and put in
put it in the fireplace and built him a little fire.

And he pulled his shoes off
warming his feet,
All at once the uh door came open
and a big cat come in.
And this old cat come on in
sit down by the fire
And uh, seemed like he sit there a little while
and uh he said, the cat said to him—says,
"well"
says, "it's uh real
cold tonight."
And uh
He says

And he looked around
Said, "there's a cat
a-talking?"
And uh, he got a little bit afraid.
He says, "we—says, I tell you,
Says, wait till I get my shoes on"
And says "you can have this fire by yourself."
And so he got his shoes on
He ran out the door,
and begin running.
And he run for about,
quarter of a mile,
and he stopped.
And he says uh,
looked around
and someone had come up too,
just about out of breath
Says, "we had a pretty good race, didn't we?"
He says,
well, just let me get my breath a minute or two
Says we'll have another one.
(gentle laughter)
                              March 30, 1981

Jean Haskell Speer is director of the Appalachian Studies Program at Virginia Polytechnic Institute and State University and a faculty member in humanities and communication studies. She is author of *The Appalachian Photographs of Earl Palmer* and former president of the Appalachian Studies Association.

Signs of Civilization: The Trail of the Lonesome Pine as Colonial Narrative

Rodger Cunningham

The relation between Southern Appalachia and America as a whole has been described in third-world and colonial terms for two decades. Early works in this vein concentrated on the economic and political aspects of this analogy (e.g. Dix, 1970). Building on this groundwork, other writers were soon exploring social and psychological parallels with equally productive results (e.g. Lewis, Kobak, and Johnson, 1978).

The year 1978 will go down as a pivotal year in Appalachian studies, since it saw the publication of four widely differing books, deeply relevant to the region, even though two of them make no mention of Appalachia. These are Henry Shapiro, *Appalachia on Our Mind*; Helen Lewis, *Colonialism in Modern America*; Edward Said, *Orientalism*; and Malcolm Chapman, *The Gaelic Vision in Scottish Culture*. Shapiro's book was a groundbreaking study of the construction of the image of Appalachia in the American mind. In spite of the conceptual inadequacies with which it is riddled, it brings together invaluable documentation needed to broach the topic: what it is we talk about when we talk about Appalachia. One of the many defects of the book, however, is that it deals with America's idea of Appalachia in terms of a purely intellectual response to a cognitive problem, largely divorced from considerations of power. In contrast, the volume edited by Lewis, et al., richly explores many aspects of the power-relations between Appalachia and America, but few of the essays deal systematically with the effects which those relations have had on the language used to describe the region.

The link between these two approaches to the region is made by the two books which make no mention of it. Said's book discusses another intellectual construct, namely the Western idea of the Muslim East, within a conceptual framework much more adequate to such a task than Shapiro's naive realism, especially in terms of the discursive relation between knowledge and power. No Appalachian scholar can read *Orientalism* without being irresistibly reminded that "Appalachia on America's mind" is a function of "Appalachia in America's hands." Chapman's book, finally, discusses still another such case of domination, and one closer to the roots of Appalachia, emphasizing how the discourse of power can mute the voice of opposition by covertly defining the terms in which the latter expresses itself.

The synthesis of these and other approaches into a general theory of colonial/hegemonic discourse in the domination of Appalachia has been gaining ground in the past decade. In this essay, which I hope may become the germ of a booklength study of colonial discourse in Appalachian and Appalachianist literature, I propose to examine John Fox, Jr.'s bestseller, *The Trail of the Lonesome Pine* (1908), as a potent reflector—and creator—of middle-class American attitudes toward Appalachia during the first period of rapid modernization.

Set in the 1890s, during the first great industrial penetration of the mountains, Fox's novel is built on the love affair between Jack Hale, a coal developer from the Kentucky Bluegrass, and June Tolliver, a mountain girl whom he "civilizes" and eventually marries. This plot is played out against the background of coal mine boom-and-bust, and a feud between June's family and their neighbors, the Falins. The framework of the novel is, I shall show, structured according to a developmental-historical emplotment embedded in a hegemonic sentimentalist discourse which serves the power-interests of modernizing elites. Though the novel has often been praised for showing the ambiguities of "progress" in the mountains (Coles, 1985),[1] I intend to show that Fox's ambivalences toward Hale's (autobiographical) project pull against the basic discourse of the book, and that this discourse eventually wins out in a way which causes the book to end in a cascade of false resolutions as Fox's own opposing voice is muted by his own dominant discourse.

The beginning of the novel foreshadows the clash of visions and viewpoints which informs it and briefly gives it life. The novel is told from a third-person-limited viewpoint, divided between the two main characters. The major focus is on Jack Hale, but in the opening scene we see through June's eyes. The young girl, in her red dress, sits at the foot of the Lonesome Pine, in the gap (based on Big Stone Gap but never named) above her home in Virginia, and she looks down into the first valley in Kentucky. The pastoral scene is broken only by her own curiosity toward the outside world, for she knows rather than sees, that the "trailing blue mists" below are the smoke of a "shrieking monster that ran without horses like the wind and tossed back roaring black plumes all streaked with fire" (1-2). Her perception is like that of a cliche Indian, for her preindustrial perspective, in the terms of gilded-age America, is equivalent to savagery or barbarism (Cunningham, 1987: 105). This young savage is also repeatedly described in terms of wildness and 'nature': "The little creature ... like something wild ... lay, like a crouched panther-cub, looking down. For a moment, all that was human seemed gone from her eyes" (3), as she first sees Jack Hale approaching from the shrieking monster's direction.

We then see the same scene through Hale's eyes as he contemplates the Pine, which to him is not a neutral piece of the world but an esthetic object of "nature" with which he nevertheless feels a kinship (Fox, 1908: 6). Then he spots June, whom at first he had mistaken for "a flaming bush of sumach" (7). From this point on, the novel is dominated by Hale's viewpoint, for we do not return to June's until he has transformed her into the image of his desire. At that point, to be sure, the ambiguities of her viewpoint, and Hale's awareness of her reciprocal view of him, play a large role in lifting the middle portion of the novel out of its one-dimensionality by opening spaces of dialogue which threaten to overwhelm the coherence of Fox's representations of "civilization's" march. But, as we shall see, these apertures are not maintained.

The bluegrass coal developer's growing relationship with this 'child of nature' occupies a particular, familiar site in the West's discourse over its subject territories. In the traditional mountain culture as described through Hale's eyes, certain features are consistently emphasized. The terms of its contrast with "America" are articulated in a set of dichotomies which will be familiar in its outlines to any student of colonial discourse. These may be set forth conveniently in a familiar table:

SAVAGERY	CIVILIZATION
Nature	Man
Animality	Humanity
Childhood	Adulthood
Female	Male
Solitude	Society
Chaos	Order
War	Peace
Violence	Reason
Personal Loyalty	Abstract Duty
Mountains	Lowlands
Appalachia	America

And this synchronic schematism is laid out diachronically, as well, in terms of a historical-developmental emplotment which assumes a development as inevitable and desirable as the growth from childhood to adulthood—a development from "savagery" toward a "civilization" which will continue growing more "improved" and rational forever. Thus Fox glowingly assumes, eight years after the beginning of the hopeful new century and six years before the tensions arising from the saturation of the non-industrialized world by Western "civilizing" power were to be ignited by the spark of Sarajevo.

If the terms of Hale's/America's perception of Appalachia occupy a basically familiar semiotic and ideological space, nevertheless they also occupy a distinctive site in that space, one corresponding to the distinctive site occupied by Appalachia in "a curious inner division of the WASP identity" (Snyder, 1982: 130). And the thematics of Fox's novel are governed both by the universalities of this discourse and by the distinctiveness of this site within it. Paraphrasing Foucault, Manthia Diawara notes:

> Western man, in defining himself, finds it necessary to link himself to the African as his negation. Insofar as the Western ratio is constituted through the negation of the African, Africa can only serve as the testing ground for what the Westerner can know about himself. Ethnology is not so much the story of cultures without history, as it is the region where the Western ratio seeks its unity through the duplication of its narratives and theories (1988: 67).

And, insofar as "Appalachia" is also constituted by the discourse in America, it is also a testing ground for what America can know about itself. Furthermore, insofar as such a dominant subject constructs an 'other' which is a projection of that subject's self, that quest for self-knowledge will be conditioned by narcissism—by that "increasingly obscene narcissism" of which Frantz Fanon accused the Western mind (Fanon, 1961: 313).

This, I shall show, is a strong feature of Jack Hale's relation to Appalachia and in particular to June Tolliver, in a novel whose subtest is essentially a quest for his and America's self-knowledge. And this narcissistic drive is only strengthened by that "curious inner division of the WASP identity" which constitutes Appalachia as both other to America and as peculiarly self to it—as what a noted anthropologist of Fox's time called "a peculiar type which has been developed by environment and isolation into something distinctly American, and yet unlike anything to be found outside the southern Alleghenies."[2] The encounter with what W. G. Frost called these "long lost Americans" (*New York Times*, 1914) is thus an encounter with the long-lost parts of the self—an encounter made necessary by that self-alienation which is at the root of narcissism. And the great contemporary popularity of Fox's work—it spawned a play, a film, and a popular song—is a measure of how deep was the chord it struck in the self-alienated heart of middle-class America.

And this fact also illuminates the strength of the bond of discourse between Appalachia and America—illuminates even the fact that, to this day, denigration of Appalachians is the one remaining ethnic prejudice expressible in polite company among those middle-class Americans. The status of Appalachia vis-a-vis America as both peculiarly "self" and strangely "other" means that the Other is muted by being *identified with the self* in a very direct way—denied *any* identity of its own other than what the speaker (the one endowed with voice) perceives as *his* identity. Furthermore, this relation is not only one between regions in space, but is temporalized by the characterization of Appalachia as an arrested, early form of America—as a sort of 'contemporary ancestor,' in Frost's well-known phrase. And this temporalization tightens the grip of the discourse of American power upon the region. For, thus invested with the appearance of static changelessness—since any non-static feature of the 'contemporary ancestor' is defined out of the equation—Appalachia becomes not a parallel development, a potentially threatening reminder of unlived possibilities and, hence, a real agent for self-discovery, but rather a pure potential, ready to be given actuality through 'the' developmental process. Hence, it is precisely the peculiar "Americanness" of Appalachia which gives American hegemonic discourse such a strong hold on the region.

Christopher Miller notes that in Conrad's *Heart of Darkness*, "the temporal and the spatial are conflated in such a way that physical travel will take one 'back to the earliest beginnings of the world'" (1985: 172). Even so, the colonial narrative of Appalachia executes just such a conflation, so that Jack Hale's journey, like Marlow's, is into his own heart. And if the journey is less dark than Marlow's, this is only a measure of the depth of Fox's self-knowledge as compared to Conrad's.

In the Trail of the Lonesome Pine, this discourse is explicitly imposed on the Appalachian region in a long expository speech by the Hon. Sam Budd, a "lawyer and budding statesman" (Fox: 89) who has come to Hale's coal-boom town and who "as a recreation ... was an anthropologist" (89) as well as being "an ardent disciple of Sir Walter Scott" (90). This combination of positivism and romanticism, which Don Askins notes as typical of Fox's work (Askins, 1978: 253), informs the Hon. Sam's long speech in which he expounds the classic environmentalist explanation of mountain otherness as a consequence of isolation. Budd actually uses Frost's phrase, "our contemporary ancestors" (97), to refer to what he also calls "the natives" (95) and, uniting both images, "the closest link we have with the Old World"—people who "live like the pioneers" and whose "feud business is a matter of clan-loyalty that goes back to Scotland" (97). "They were Unionists because of the Revolution," he adds, "as they were Americans in the beginning because of the spirit of the Covenanter" (97).

This last sentence is the key to the meaning of what Fox, in order to cushion the awkwardness of the exposition, makes Budd ironically call his "anthropological drool" (97). It ignores well-known historical reasons for Scots-Irish attachment to the Revolution, and for Appalachian opposition to the Confederacy. It implies, instead, that Appalachian mountain people not only retain old customs, but somehow live literally in the past—that their minds exist in some time-warp in which they are incapable of responding to what is actually in front of them, but instead go around seeing what was there a century or so earlier and bumping like zombies into whatever has changed in the meantime. This characterization, which, in fact, is typical of traditional "scientific" accounts of Appalachia, is immensely significant in view of the occasion giving rise to the speech—to wit, the gathering of a militia composed of outsiders in order to put down a strike of "native" workers.[3] There is no suggestion that the workers might have legitimate grievances against their new masters, or that these "malcontents" (94) could indeed be responding to anything in the present at all. It is all a matter of a "war between civilization and a lawlessness that was the result of isolation, and consequent ignorance and idleness" (98). If the mountaineers' reality is different from the hegemonic construction of it, then it is deemed unreal, or rather a part of the past they seem to be 'really' living in. 'Yesterday's People,' indeed.

But in fact, of course, the tables are turned on Hale and his troops: it is they and their "drooling" ideologue who cannot see what is in front of them in the present. It is they who have fallen prey to their own mystification of the reasons for what is happening when a mountaineer puts a bullet through a sign (48), counterphallically challenging the commanding discourse, or when other strikers "[puncture] the chromos in their boarding-house" (94), taking action against the imposition of cheap Victorian middle-class taste in a context of regimentation. "They won't understand," avers Budd; ". . . they'll look on us as a lot of meddlesome 'furriners' who have come to run their country as we please" (96-97). If so, they seem to understand all too well. But in this master-discourse, to understand means to see things as the master sees them, which in this case means not to see them at all. Edward Said characterizes Western anthropology as "a partner in domination and hegemony" (1989: 225) in which "someone, an authoritative, explorative, elegant, learned voice, speaks and analyzes, amasses evidence, theorizes, speculates about everything—except itself" (Said: 212), in "the almost total absence of any reference to American imperial intervention as a factor affecting the theoretical discussion" (Said: 214).[4] Clearly no better description of Sam Budd's "anthropological drool" could be found.

And yet, Budd's speech reveals not only the straightforwardly hegemonic character of the American discourse of Appalachia, but also certain ambiguities inherent in the dualism of Appalachia/ America as an "inner division" of a single identity. Budd begins by calling the militia "the vanguard of civilization—'crusaders of the nineteenth century against the benighted of the Middle Ages'" (Fox: 96). How paradoxical to think of 'crusaders' going forth *against* "the Middle Ages"—as paradoxical as the other rhetoric, occurring repeatedly in the book, in which Hale and the other outsiders are described as "pioneer(s)" (40, 98, etc.) waging war on "natives" who themselves are described as "pioneers" and "frontiersmen." These images reflect complex, paradoxical crossings and interlacings inside 'the WASP identity' and its perceptions of self and other.[5]

Indeed, even when inscribing motifs which represent the mountaineer as a "savage" and the American industrial invader as the "pioneer of civilization," Fox maintains the underlying identity of the two. He always denied the view, common in his time and maintained by some well-meaning Honorables even now, that the mountain population as a whole represented a genetically inferior "stock" drawn from the slums of London and the like. Instead, he held that the "better sort" of mountain people were the same in 'blood' and inherent "gifts" as the more "fortunate" lowland population, and that environment alone accounted for the former's "deficiencies."

And on this very point of essential identity, oddly enough, Fox's attitudes paralleled those of his ancestors toward the first 'savages' they had encountered. Fox, whose ancestors had come to the Bluegrass in 1790 from Virginia (Titus, 1971: 17) and (in the person of another John Fox) to Virginia in 1649 from England (Brosi, 1988: 6), was glowingly proud of both connections and liked to compare the Bluegrass itself to "merry England" (Askins, 1978: 255). Thus, it is informative to recall that in seventeenth-century Virginia, according to Karen Kupperman, "English colonists assumed that Indians were basically similar to themselves and that savagery was a temporary condition which the Indians would quickly lose. The really important category was status" (1980: 2), and in that regard the contemporaries of the first John Fox made careful distinctions between the "better" Indians and the "baser" sort: "Indians, like base or humble English people, were expected to be of service in the [English] society. Indians of the 'better sort' were not expected to be of service" (Kupperman, 1980: 140). Just so, in Fox's novel, Jack Hale's eroticized identification with his contrasexual and countercultural other/self, June Tolliver, is predicated on the superiority of her "stock." Immediately after Sam Budd's "drool," Hale notes of June that she was "so intelligent" as to constitute evidence that the Hon. Sam is right:

> that the mountaineers were *of the same class* as the other westward-sweeping emigrants, ... that they had simply *lain dormant* in the hills and ... that the children of that day would, if given the chance, wipe out the *handicap* of a century in one generation and would take their place *abreast* with children of the outside world. The Tollivers were *of good blood*; they had come from *Eastern Virginia*, and the original Tolliver had been a *slave-owner*. The very name was, undoubtedly, a *corruption* of Tagliaferro (Fox: 100-101, emphasis added).

The emphasized words sharply expose the episteme in which Fox's distinctions among mountaineers are inscribed, an episteme which posits one-dimensional progress along one conceivable line, and in which "goodness" is equated with wealth and domination. More particularly, they show that to John Fox and Jack Hale, goodness means being as much like John Fox and Jack Hale as possible.

This example leads to another strong parallel between Fox/Hale's view of mountaineers and his ancestors' view of Indians. Bernard Sheehan notes:

> Although the barrier between the civil and savage conditions seemed impenetrable, most commentators allowed for movement between the two. In one mood Europeans sought a return to original innocence. In another they were convinced that they had once been mired in savagism and had managed by dint of hard work and the blessings of Providence to reach the civil stage of life..... This assurance, however, did not obviate the possibility of a slide back into the savage state. The ignoble savage always loomed as an external threat to Europeans and as an internal danger because he represented primal urges that, although subdued, remained part of the human condition. In the eighteenth century this relationship between savagism and civility would be transformed into a formal theory of staged development (Sheehan, 1980: 2).

This formal theory, derived from white-Indian contact, is what Fox and Hale project upon mountain people at a time when, as I have shown elsewhere, the entire set of representations of the relation white/Indian was being inscribed upon the relation American/Appalachian (Cunningham, 1987: 102-112)[6]—a time when, in addition, an exhausted late Victorian/Edwardian bourgeois culture was tiring of, and becoming disillusioned with, its repressions and was searching eagerly but anxiously for a regenerating contact with 'primal urges.' With this in mind, therefore, let us examine the development of the relationship between Hale/America and June/Appalachia.

As Hale has established 'benevolent' control of June's community, so also he establishes an equally 'benevolent' domination over June herself. Finding that when she reads aloud she already approximates standard English quite well (Fox: 27), Hale begins by working on her language so as to standardize her speech as well. In so doing, he literally initiates and inserts her into a master-discourse to which he holds the key. Furthermore, though in persuading her to change in this way he pretends to relativism, saying simply that "the way people in the mountains dress and talk is different from the way most people dress and talk" (113), he is soon narrowing the choice to *her* adoption of *others'* customs ("you will want ..."), and then using the word *ought*. Hale is sincerely trying not to privilege his own speech, but his discourse drives him to do so. At this point June responds with anger, and Hale recalls to himself "the sensitive pride of the mountaineer" that makes it so hard for him "to make her understand" (114). These are the same terms with which Sam Budd, just earlier, has noted "a pride that is morbid" (96) as the cause of the mountaineers' resistance to outside imposition of others' notions of order, and has assured Hale that "the natives won't understand" (95)—when it is clear enough to the modern reader whose understanding is at fault in either case. Thus, this talk of "morbid pride" (still often heard in "enlightened" quarters) is simply a discursive ploy which labels a universal reaction with a special name in order to mystify the situation which is being reacted to—which attaches that special name to the Other as a mark of that otherness in order to turn an attempt at communication into the opposite.

But eventually June acquiesces to being engulfed in Jack's discourse. He literally appropriates her voice as she learns standard English verb forms (170, 175) and the standard English names for flowers (161-65). She has had a playhouse, but now she abandons it for a flower garden—one made for her by Hale (194-95). The playhouse had already been a middle term between Nature and Civilization, as June had already been 'above' her environment; the flower garden is a piece of civilization itself, an ordering of natural life which has been explicitly identified with a logocentric linguistic and discursive field, ordered and fertilized by Hale's own male force. Hale goes on to teach June the Latin names of flowers, and even imagines her one day learning that language after she masters standard English (211-12), thereby mastering a second stage of the master-discourse of Western civilization. "[L]aurel (she used to call it 'ivy') and rhododendrons (she used to call them 'laurel') ... were her old and fast friends" (257). She calls her old friends by new, "real" names. And why should she not, since she is entering a world where she is not privileged to know her own "real" name:

> "Who's that?" Hale turned—it was the Honourable Samuel Budd, coming home from Court.
> "June Tolliver."
> "June Taliaferro," corrected the Hon. Sam with emphasis (280).

Thus, with her very identity emphatically "corrected" by outsiders, June is reduced to an abject, an interlocutor who is muted precisely as she takes on the master's voice—as her dialogue with Hale is inexorably entrained into America's discourse.[7]

Thus, we see *The Trail of the Lonesome Pine* winding through a familiar colonialist discursive space in which the relation of other to self is expressed in terms of the relations child/adult and passive female/ active male. This discourse, furthermore, here interlocks with the archetype of the hero's quest into the strange land, a quest in which he finds his own self through union with the contrasexual Other. Thus, it is not surprising that the relation between Hale and June is distinctly eroticized from the beginning. Even in their earliest scenes together, it is evident that the preadolescent June is special to Hale in more than one way. He learns her name when her stepmother calls her, and he reflects that it is "a queer name for the mountains" (12). Jack and June's names not only are the same length but alliterate, as do both with her father's and with their creator's: she is an aspect of all these males, and their Js are the hooks by which he eventually purposes to pull her out of her otherness altogether. In a moment he will refuse to tell Judd his name, and only June saves him from being shot by telling her father his name as he has told her. The relation among the three of them is reflected in this interchange; and as Hale feels gratitude toward June, and wonders why she has done this, he begins musing on her beautiful eyes and on her hair, which is "exactly like the gold-bronze on the wing of a wild turkey that he had shot the day before" (16). His love for this bit of wild Nature is already eroticized and already tinged with aggression, just as, not long afterwards, he contemplates a beautiful valley and murmurs, "Such a drainage!" (46) and sees it as "the heaven-born site of the unborn city of his dreams"—the dark Satanic mills inscribed in the rhetoric of Jerusalem—as "his eyes swept every curve of the valley lovingly" (44).

This eroticism is, of course, treated in a conventional Edwardian way, which is to say that it sometimes reveals more than it must intend to. Thus, for example, in the flower-lesson mentioned above:

> With the next look she found a tiny bunch of fuzzy hepaticas.
> "Liver-leaf."
> "Whut's liver?" [Has this mountain child never seen the insides of a hog?]
> Hale, looking at her glowing face and eyes and her perfect little body, imagined that she would never know unless told that she had one, and so he waved one hand vaguely at his chest:
> "It's an organ—and that herb is supposed to be good for it."
> "Organ? Whut's that?"
> "Oh, something inside of you."
> June made the same gesture that Hale had.
> "Me?"
> "Yes," and then helplessly, "but not there exactly" (162).

This vague, tentative and anxious approach to June's corporeality occurs during a lesson in which Hale is teaching the names of flowers to "the loveliest flower of them all—little June" (165). (We have seen that she eventually learns the "correct" name for that too.) Later expressions of June's corporeality are no stronger, even when the erotic element in Hale's attraction for her is allowed to become more explicit as she matures.

June at this point is at the edge of puberty. In subsequent chapters, her sexual maturing parallels her "growth" into bourgeois American civilization, at the same time that it deepens and complicates her relation with Hale as the two fall in love. She "develops" indeed, in a variety of senses; but her "growth" makes her, not a more independent adult, but a more suitable object for Hale's desire--or at least this is so on the level in which the primary discourse operates. She abandons her fairy tales for *Paul and Virginia* (173), a classic in the romantic fusion of love of Nature withsentimentalized eroticism. In the following year she passes fully over the threshold of puberty, and in another of those remarkable Edwardian locutions:

> Her nature had opened precisely as had bud and flower that spring. The Mother of Magicians had touched her as impartially as she had touched them with fairy wand, and as unconsciously the young girl had answered as a young dove

to any cooing mate. With this Hale did not reckon, and this June could not know. For a while, that night, she lay in a delicious tremor ... and, as had all the sleeping things of the earth about her, she, too, sank to happy sleep (Fox: 181).

At this point she is about to be sent off to school—on Hale's money, though she does not yet know this. When she returns, "the little fairy-cross dangled at a woman's throat. Her figure had rounded, her voice had softened. She held herself as straight as a young poplar and she walked the earth as if she had come straight from Olympus" (239). Her middle-class posture—one of the first things she had noted about Hale was that he did not slouch like a mountaineer (4)—is here presented as one more part of her growth into a woman. It makes her, indeed, a figure from Olympus: a Europa (cf. note 7) fit to consort with Hale's Zeus, though in the same breath she can still be compared to a forest tree.

The specific mutual attraction between June and Hale becomes more and more explicit. Hale develops more esthetic appreciation of the mountains' beauty, and "June was the incarnate spirit of it all" (252). As for June: "If she saw a bass shoot arrow-like into deep water, if she heard a bird or saw a tree or a flower whose name she had to recall, she thought of Hale" (288). Hale, for her, is the name-bearer, the primary signifier even of her own native world; he is knowledge, and more and more that knowledge is eroticized. He haunts her as a specter constituted by the voice he has given her, "a ghost ... so like a human presence that she felt sometimes a strange desire to turn and speak to it" (288)—a presence particularly evoked by the new middle-class furniture of her room. Here, too, we learn that "her once-favorite picture" is that of "the lovers clasped in each other's arms—'at last alone'" (288). There is a potent irony here, for the actual title of the painting, mentioned elsewhere in the book, is *Enfin Seul*. As well as being a sad commentary on Fox's artistic taste (cf. Agnes Repplier in Titus, 1971: 90), the painting has a title which in the original refers to only *one* of the two lovers, viz. the man: That is, it is not *Enfin Seuls* or *Seule*, but *Seul*. Thus, this popular Victorian genre painting embodies a discourse in which everything, even a pair of lovers, is seen solely from the man's viewpoint. And, in admiring it, June longs for the total muting of her own presence—for absorption in Hale as she has already become absorbed, her authentic presence muted, in a world now constituted for her by his significations.

At the same time that June is becoming absorbed in Hale's world, she is becoming alienated from her own, and this, too, is presented as if it were a natural result of her growth. Her family's table manners begin to inspire her with "a vague newborn disgust" (Fox: 200); the slurping of coffee is "painful to June's ears" (199). But this process is not smoothly carried out, for the division passes not only between June and her family, but through June herself. Hale "saw that while her body was at home, her thoughts rarely were" (215). This division between body and thoughts is common in adolescence, which here is equated with assimilation in the developmentalist paradigm.

But, as June's adolescent identity crisis begins to intersect with her crisis of cultural identity, the result begins to shake the paradigm on which the book's simple plot line is based. As June becomes 'better' from her experience in New York City, Hale becomes 'worse' from his stays in the mountains, until finally the day comes when a long-awaited reunion is soured as *she* looks with distaste upon *him*. This is the main plot development of the middle part of the novel, and, thus far, all it amounts to is a straightforward demonstration of Fox's simple environmental theory. But Fox's knowledge of the situation is so detailed, and his two main characters have taken on so much roundness, that this simple paradigm generates within itself elements which complicate and subvert it, threatening to undo Fox's obvious conscious intentions for the book's scheme.

As June matures, she becomes more consciously aware of the strains in her being. Returning to the cove from New York, she experiences the flowers as "her old and fast friends," but all the works of man, and even the people themselves, appear dismal to her. It is with a shock that she realizes that "they were *her* people" (258)—a shock of self-alienation and yet of self-recognition. The ultimate result of this process is revealed in a long episode immediately following her above-quoted reflections on Hale and his painting. In this episode she attends a bean-stringing: a traditional mountain community work-gathering. Her very appearance is hybrid, a combination of city and mountain dress, but she goes to work on the beans "as one of them" (292). *As*: does this mean that she *is* one of them or that she is merely *like* one of them? This ambiguity is sustained throughout the episode, which is a minor masterpiece of social drama. Her neighbors pay "unconscious tribute to a vague something about her" (292)—not to *her* but to something that has gotten on or in her; and she pays her own tribute to them by *"dropping consciously* into the vernacular" (292) in her speech. Both words I have emphasized are significant in an interlocked way. She is a *conscious* agent, in contrast to their "unconscious" reactions, because she is *higher*, and the higher subsumes the lower—englobes its discourse—but not the reverse. At her neighbors' request she exhibits her new professional singing skills, and when her aunt remarks, "She shorely can holler some!", she "flushed and then smiled with quick understanding" at this ironic mountain style of humor (295). "Quick," but not immediate and unconsidered: her "consciousness" is starting to get in her way.

A particularly interesting manifestation of June's hybridity is embodied in her meeting with her uncle, the feudist Bad Rufe Tolliver. "Something in June's bearing made him take off his hat" (295)—once more, not she but something which has gotten into her. She, however, does not respond to this deference. She had been afraid of Rufe as a child and, though he is much changed in appearance, his eyes are still the same as they were and still inspire that fear. He, then, responds to something that has gotten into her; she, to his own inner being manifested in spite of his physical changes. Those eyes, the windows of his soul, are both the baffled agents of his knowledge (he has had to be told who she is) and the effective agents of her fear based on her own knowledge. But this fear is simply a revived childhood fear, not based on anything in the present (as far as she now knows). It is the child in her that is the mountaineer. In this interesting crossed relationship, his gaze is at first baffled and then friendly; hers is fearful insofar as she has gone back "down" to the mountain world.

June "had conquered birth and speech and customs and environment" and "become ... the woman of the world" (352). She has "conquered" her "environment"—including parts of herself which she has learned not to identify with herself—and by this act of self-amputating self-colonization she has joined the real "world," the world of the "pioneers" and "conquistadors" who are subduing her land and people. But there is a cost. This self-characterization occurs in a subordinate clause within a question: "Was she really the June Tolliver who had ...?" She has, in fact, lost her secure sense of her own identity altogether. She is alienated not only from her people but from herself.

And it is this alienation that a counter-discursive space begins to open up within the novel; it is within this self-doubt that a voice of doubt begins to question the very discourse which informs the novel. For as June's consciousness has become a facet of Hale's, so her alienation has become the site of a growing skepticism on Hale's part, and even at some level on Fox's.

Immediately after the scene in which she looks on her family with "a vague newborn disgust," comes a passage describing "the cruel, deadly work of civilization" (201-02) as it brings pollution to her world. The creek is full of sawdust, coal dust and dead fish; a circle saw is described as a "buzzing monster ... biting a savage way through a log, that screamed with pain as the brutal thing tore through its vitals, and gave up its life each time with a ghost-like cry of agony" (202). Much earlier, Hale is described as seeing "nothing alive but an occasional bird" (75); the trees are not yet alive to him. Here, though, they are not only alive but sentient. Thus, the tables are turned on "civilization," which equally with "barbarism" can be described in terms of savagery, brutality, and defilement.[8] The description of the trees as alive further recalls the comparisons of June with a "young poplar," and indeed the two are connected explicitly: "A strange spirit pervaded the Cove.... What was the matter with everything—what was the matter with her?" (207). Thus, we are invited to see what is happening to June—her very "refinement"—as itself a "cruel, deadly work of civilization."

These ambiguities can be seen in retrospect as early as the first page, when June imagines a locomotive as a "shrieking monster" (1), but they begin to become more than dismissable childish perceptions only—and abruptly—when June begins to enter into dialogue with Hale to grow by the process. Even in the scene, examined above, in which he tries to change her speech, June speaks for herself and for her culture so eloquently, and Hale shows such ambivalence, that a way is opened for dialogue and for a complexity and self-subversion which are developed more a bit later in the book. In that scene, as we have noted, he succeeds in foreclosing the dialogue by englobing her communication in words like "sensitive pride"; but as June matures, and as their relationship deepens, spaces of dialogue open which are more difficult to paper over.

What is happening is that as Hale "civilizes" June—makes her an "adult" of the only kind he can really recognize as such—she starts to transcend Hale's, or even Fox's, intentions for her. Rather than simply a more suitable object for Hale's desire, she starts to become a real adult, and her ambivalences toward her upbringing start to insert themselves into the text in a way which fissures the seamless, one-dimensional master-narrative that Fox evidently presupposes for it. Hale has been fashioning June in his image, giving birth to her through his signifying discourse. (In his image, or in the image of his desire; for the disjunction between the two is one of the apertures through which a genuine dialogue begins to squeeze.) Feminists have criticized the modern scientific/technical spirit as a fantasy of male birth, and have pointed out a trenchant critique of that fantasy in Mary Shelley's compelling allegory to which Hale alludes when he says: "The truth was he was building a lovely Frankenstein and from wondering what he was going to do with it, he was beginning to wonder what it might some day do with him" (241). One may well suspect that the uneasiness is also on the part of Fox himself, as his characters (and June in particular) begin to develop their own life, or to show a life separate from the life he is constantly trying to insert into their lifeless matter. Fox's master-discourse becomes infected with counter-discourse, and hence with the dialogue between June and Hale as well as between the different parts of Hale, and the romance, in consequence, struggles to become a polyphonic novel which threatens to do something serious (in more than one sense) to Fox's intentions for it.

For Hale, meanwhile, has been changing in a different direction. "Deterioration is easy in the hills" (249), says Fox, and though he immediately qualifies this deterioration as "superficial" and lists simple reasons for it, he quickly draws this fact into a paradigm in which "the little niceties of life" are equated with "civilization" (250) and the deeply environmental-determinist implication is made that it is impossible to be "civilized" *in* the mountains:

> Hale's life, since his college doors had closed behind him, had always been a rough one. He had *dropped* from *civilization* and had gone back into it many times. And each time he had *dropped*, he *dropped* deeper, and for that reason had come back into *his own life* each time with more difficulty and with more indifference. The last had been his roughest year and he had *sunk* a little more deeply just at the time when June had been *pluming* herself for *flight* from such *depths* forever (250; emphasis added).

What is most notable about this "deterioration," however, is that Hale undergoes it largely as a result of his "civilizing" activities. On the page after the above, a great deal of his roughness is attributed directly to his function as captain of the Police Guard, the organization which imposes "law and order" on a population whose 'lawlessness' in the first place is partly a matter of perception and partly a result of the disruption of their way of life.[9] June shrinks from kissing him when they meet because "he was as rough and dirty as the chain-carrier opposite him, who was just in from a surveying expedition in the mountains, as the sooty brakeman who came through to gather up the fares" (265). A bit later it is reported that "Hale had been raising Cain in Lonesome Cove—'a-cuttin' things down an' tearin' 'em up an' playin' hell generally'" (281). The fact, presented in the very next sentence, that "[t]he feud had broken out again" is left unconnected with this. For indeed, Fox fails to make the (to us) obvious connections in all of what he describes here. Just as Altina Waller has shown that the feuds of the period were an aspect of modernization and not of "backwardness"—a fact visible intermittently between the lines of Fox's narrative[10]—so the facts of Hale's "deterioration," as Fox shows them, are very different from what he seems to want to say about them. For in both cases, Fox imposes a simple developmental scheme which contradicts his own words—and especially the words put in the mouths of the main characters. A result of what Hale is doing to Appalachia is projected as a result of what Appalachia is doing to him. The deep ambiguity which is visible in the thematics is inexpressible in the exposition, which is trapped inside a discourse that mutes it. This becomes the main problem with the book from here on, as Fox's own sense of ambiguity is trapped in a one-dimensional episteme conditioned by the discourse of power between Appalachia and America.

We have seen things heretofore mainly through Hale's eyes, but the complications enter as we begin to see Hale seeing himself through June's new eyes. He has given her these eyes; but in spite of his intentions, they are not his eyes. Thus, a binocular view develops, one in which the images of Appalachia and America suddenly stand out in a depth which unsettles the narrative. What happens in the rest of the book, however, is a betrayal of this depth, a determined flattening of it as Fox retreats in an almost palpable panic from its implications. Hale shaves, resumes his "civilized" demeanor—"There was nothing of the mountaineer about him now" (275)—and goes to meet June, rising to encounter her from below (274). Then the two discuss matters. He expresses his doubts as to whether he has done the right thing in taking her out of the world in which she can no longer be content. Then he shifts the topic to their relationship, while showing no awareness of the shift: "I would not have married you as you were .... And now you have gone beyond me and you do not want to marry me as I am. And it is all very natural and very just" (276-77).

All very natural and very just. The main function of this crucial conversation is to reconcile Hale and June by muting the ambiguity of their situation. Neither of them moves out of their now-shared system of one-dimensional valuations. Before Hale approaches, June has been contemplating with horror the prospect of descending again to the "lower ... standards" (274) of her home community. She never questions Hale's corresponding view of the matter; she never questions the assumption that she is being 'freed' by being englobed in his discourse. That assumption is self-contradictory, of course, and the irony here and the subsequent tangles of the plot result from an attempt to untangle this paradox without cutting at the root of it. For indeed, by the end of the scene June has suppressed her very adulthood for Hale's sake: "Like a child she obeyed him" (278), and he repeatedly calls her "little girl" (277, 278). The eyes he has given her are once more becoming simply his eyes; the eyes of the image of his desire are becoming simply the eyes of his desire, leaving him *enfin seul*.

In subsequent scenes, June is further reduced to an object, her voice returned to muteness, as Fox assumes monologic control. Her Uncle Billy "was the one unchanged soul to her in that he was the one soul that could see no change in June. He called her 'baby' in the old way, and he talked to her now as he had talked to her as a child" (297). Thus, June is comforted by seeing her identity entirely in other's gaze, and, specifically, in the gaze of men who see her as a child. Furthermore, this confining yet comforting gaze forecloses the possibility of her being an adult member of her own society—it conflates time and space in accordance with Hale's perceptions.

At this point, the plot is drawing to a climax. Of the conventional savage/civilized oppositions which function in the novel, two are especially important for the plot. One, as we have seen, is childhood/adulthood; the other is personal loyalty/abstract duty. The conflict between these two has an honorable history in the thematics of Western literature as far back as Sophocles' *Antigone*. But in Fox, this conflict is, like everything else, assimilated to the colonialist paradigm: "The average mountaineer," he avers, "has little conception of duty in the abstract, but old Judd belonged to the better class—and there are many of them—that does" (152). This theme begins to be struck early on (129) and is brought up repeatedly from then on (151, 184, 221, etc.); and, in general, even the class distinction among mountaineers is not as carefully made as in the passage quoted.

June's uncle, Bad Rufe Tolliver, has returned to the mountains at the same time as she. He is, therefore, in some sense her contrasexual mirror-image, and we have already seen the crossing of mutual reactions which occurs when they meet for the first time in years. If June is the quintessentially "good" mountaineer, Bad Rufe is the quintessentially "bad" one, and he establishes this identity by shooting a policeman: one of the outside representatives of "law and order." Before he commits the act, though, June overhears him stating his intention to do so. Thus, when she is called to testify at his trial, she must choose not only between her family and her conscience, but between personal loyalty and abstract duty, and thus between two different civilizations—or rather between Savagery and Civilization.

But what actually happens at this crucial juncture? Though the issue seems clear-cut, its execution is in fact fatally blurred. When June had overheard her uncle saying, "I'm goin' over to kill me a policeman" (296), at first she had agonized at the thought that the intended victim might be Hale—such is her love of Civilization, the identification of the latter with Hale, and the labeling of traditional Appalachia as its violent enemy for the crime of defending itself. Later, at the climactic moment in the courtroom—a few seconds spread over a whole page—June's first thought is only of duty: "Would she lie for him—would she lie for him?" she wonders as "Rufe's black eyes"—those eyes which have awakened her childhood fears—"held her with mesmeric power" (320-21). But she also feels upon her "the blue eyes of a man for whom a lie was impossible and to whom she had never stained her white soul with a word of untruth…. Not a soul in the room knew where the struggle lay—not even the girl—for it lay between the black eyes of Rufe Tolliver and the blue eyes of John Hale" (321). And then, as "her dark eyes swerved suddenly full on Hale," she tells the truth which dooms her uncle.

In this scene—the pivotal climax of the novel—the issue with which it ostensibly deals, and with it the whole thematic structure of the novel, are all at once sharply skewed. June's decision between personal loyalty and abstract duty is collapsed into a matter of two conflicting personal loyalties. Worse yet, June does not even make a clearly free and voluntary choice between the two loyalties. "[T]he girl" becomes a passive object, pulled between the two powerful adult male figures, as unaware of her own real thoughts as she is of her 'real' nature. Her choice is not only personalized but emotionalized and eroticized to the point where her individual will is erased. From being a rounded character she is suddenly flattened into a female stereotype, ruled by emotion and sexual desire and incapable of thinking "above" the personal level. The thematic development of the book is wiped out by a decision which ignores that theme while ostensibly acting it out and June's personal development is also wiped out by an act in which she herself is unaware of the real locus of her struggle—an act which is explicitly located outside of her; it is located in the two men whose intersecting gazes constitute her as an object, and whose real struggle is to possess her.

This dishonest treatment of the climax shatters whatever artistic integrity the book had managed to achieve. From here on, the plot itself falls apart. It founders in the same way the developmentalist emplotment founders on the ambiguities of development. Since these ambiguities are not foregrounded, nor the contradictions dealt with creatively and dialogically, the book breaks down in a series of schematic denouements and *deus ex machina* resolutions as Fox pulls his characters and situations back into line with his preconceptions.

The first order of business is to dispose of Hale's rival for June's affections, her cousin Dave. He fits into the semiosis of the book as a young male mountaineer, therefore not amenable to the master-discourse. His identification with the mountain code of personal loyalty (137, 221) both places him on the "savage" side of the epistemic dichotomy and provides a plot motivation for his lethal hatred of Hale when June rejects Dave—and does so speaking to him, to her own family and people, in Hale's voice, that is in standard English (359).

The matter eventually comes down to physical combat between the two men. Hale wins, of course, by technique over the brute force of an opponent whose actions are repeatedly described in terms of savagery, animality, and madness—"savagely" (374), "a grunt of rage and pain... crazy rage...bellow" (376). But, before the fight, Dave has given Hale a shrewd and accurate account of their respective power-situations: "D'ye think I'd fight you hyeh? If you killed me, you'd be elected County Jedge; if I killed you, what chance would I have o' gittin' away? I'd swing fer it"

(373-74). Hale's way of winning the combat he has forced on his opponent only underscores this relation, but Hale simply avers that "I've never done anything to you that I hadn't to do" (374). His self-righteousness comes from his self-enclosure in his own discourse of power which justifies his dominance as an inevitable part of "progress."

Dave, humiliated, moves west. So do all the Tollivers, in a group, as the Tolliver-Falin feud heats up. Hale, too, leaves, having failed to halt the collapse of the coal boom in the Gap, but he returns for one last visit to a scene of human desolation. At the Lonesome Pine, where the book began, he spots Dave's horse and assumes that his old enemy has set an ambush for him. But, instead, the person who comes into view behind the horse is June, who has providentially returned to the Cove at the same instant. She is the substitute for Hale's rival for her, and, so, her appearance (at which Hale nearly shoots her) is a kind of bride-capture, a sentence in a language of patriarchal exchange in which she functions as a kind of serious pun, emphasizing and emphasized by her contrast with what she replaces. The scene also recalls, with reversed roles, the pair's crossed perceptions of each other on the same spot at the beginning of the novel.

It develops that Dave has been shot out west (405) and has given June his horse as a last token of his affection. Thus, his 'frontier' violence (Hale's negative side) is exorcized, and he awards June the good part of his own male energy. Judd has died, but not before telling June that Hale, not he himself, had been the source of the money which paid for her education: "It was all you, you, *you*, and there was never anybody but you" (405). Hale has thus deprived her family of agency in their love of her.[11] Yet, the words are ambiguous: they sound like a confession of love, and they could, in fact, be either a complaint or an expression of gratitude. Hale replies: "[Y]ou mustn't feel that way.... [Y]ou mustn't rob me of the dearest happiness I ever knew in my whole life" (406). "I knew you would say that," replies June "like a submissive child" (406). Thus she submits to his injunctions and he smilingly takes her over, having reduced her to what she always has been in relation to him.

She pledges him her undying love, and it develops that since Judd had managed to reacquire his cabin and its surrounding two hundred acres (369-70), these now belong to June as sole surviving heir. This further *deus ex machina* cuts the last strand of the Gordian knot, and the way is clear for Hale to marry June and for both of them to move into the cabin, which is "just as she had always kept it" (410). June is wearing "the last crimson dress of her young girlhood—her sleeves rolled up and her hair braided down her back as she used to wear it" (412). She is, in fact, as much as possible exactly as Hale first saw her. This wildly improbable bit of schematism (how can she possibly still fit in that dress?) not only emphasizes the erotic element in Hale's relation to June from the beginning[12] but shows that she has never been more than a child in his eyes—those eyes which at her uncle Rufe's trial reduced 'the girl' to a passive object. June had first appeared to Hale as a "keen-eyed, sweet-faced child" (35)—the eyes sharp, penetrating, perhaps dangerous in the assertive gaze, but set in a face that is an object of pleasurable consumption; the eyes active, the face passive. Now the passive sweetness is all as she looks at Hale "with parted lips and great shining eyes wide" (421)—the eyes as receptive as the lips, which in turn exist as organs of speech only to say 'yes' to his proposal of marriage. Hale's gaze, no longer binocular, flattens June so that Fox with his single vision may flatten them both. For, thus, they plan their double fantasy:

> "Even if we do go away, we'll come back once a year," said Hale.
> "Yes," nodded June, "once a year."
> "I'll tear down those mining shacks, float them down the river and sell them as lumber."
> "Yes."
> "And I'll stock the river with trout again."
> "Yes."
> "And I'll plant young poplars to cover the sight of every bit of uptorn earth along the mountain there. I'll bury every bottle and tin can in the Cove. I'll take away every sign of civilization, every sign of the outside world."
> "And leave old Mother Nature to cover up the scars," said June.
> "So that Lonesome Cove will be just as it was."
> "Just as it was in the beginning," echoed June.
> "And shall be to the end," said Hale.
> "And there will never be anybody here but you."
> "And you," added June (415-16).

Thus, in this cascade of female affirmations, the happy couple plot an escape from history, time, and society. In June's "Yes...Yes...Yes" we hear the click of locks as her counterdiscourse shuts down utterly and dialogue is finally foreclosed altogether. This speech, and the red dress, express the whole spectral, fantasticized quality of the union between them. There is not a word about reclaiming the rest of the mountains or their people, or about doing anything to stop the process which is getting under way to destroy them. Hale and June's utopia is literally inscribed in the absence of the real Appalachia existing in history—and of the real "America" as well. The ambiguities of the midsection of the book, with its talk of the "cruel, deadly work of civilization," is tied to an ambiguity:

Hale's attitude toward June and toward the patriarchal/capitalist enterprise in general. But this fundamental and threatening self-criticism, this real self-discovery through inner dialogue, must be rejected or the entire enterprise—Hale's, Fox's, and by implication America's—will collapse. So reconciliation takes place in the usual patriarchal way as the feminine discourse is englobed within a little, impotent space of its own—with "every sign of civilization" borne *just* out of sight. Insofar as the book is "about" Hale's/America's self-discovery through June/Appalachia, the ending fails when everything returns to its initial state, including Hale's own state of self-knowledge. (A failure as art, if a perfect success as cultural reflection, hence the story's enduring popularity.) And indeed, the pressure that has made the creative fissures close up and the novel collapse—which has forced Fox to take monologic control—is the nearly-fulfilled threat of self-knowledge leading to consequences which Fox never intended and which America would have rejected.

Then, out of nowhere descends the last *deus ex machina* as Uncle Billy comes riding along to marry the pair. As he is about to do so, the book ends. Hale's anticipated sweeping and garnishing had turned Lonesome Cove from the "narrow grave" (352) which June has feared—since woman, in patriarchal discourse, is dead and barren without man—into a bridal bed; from a locus of absence into one of presence generated by the hegemonic discourse (Said, 1978: 208). Yet it is the locus of a presence which can only be achieved in the absence of the historically constituted world as we know it. The reality of the "civilization" Hale represents is, in the form of its waste residue, literally evacuated.

Thus, once more, Hale's true self-discovery is short-circuited into standard patriarchal-romance terms of Redemption by Woman, a paradigm whose limitations are commensurate with those of the tiny area being "saved" from "civilization." June has lost her individual humanity and become wholly assimilated to the anima-archetype, which, being transpersonal, depersonalizes her (Cunningham, 170)—just as the semiotic appropriation of Appalachia by America takes place hand in hand with political and economic takeover and absorption.[13] June even promises to smooth Hale's wrinkles away (415) through her acceptance of them (417)—to erase his experience through her reciprocal gaze from eyes which have ceased to be anything but the reflection of Hale's desire. Once more he fits his early description: "With the vision of a seer, he was as innocent as Boone" (41).

Thus, Hale's self-discovery collapses into that self-gazing narcissism which Fanon attributed to Hale's civilization, here among the precipices of Appalachia. Hale has engulfed June as America engulfs Appalachia.

He has taken back her eyes and made them his again as America reappropriates its "gifts" to Appalachia. He has reduced her to absolute receptiveness in a sort of rape, surrounded with the glowing rhetoric of love, as America rapes Appalachia. Thus, the dialogue finally completes its perfect collapse into a monologue without interlocutors. Jack Hale, like John Fox, like American and Western civilization, is indeed *enfin seul*.

Works Cited

Askins, Don. 1978. "John Fox, Jr., a Re-Appraisal; or, With Friends Like That, Who Needs Enemies?" Lewis, Johnson, and Askins, ed., *Colonialism in Modern America: The Appalachian Case*. Boone, NC: Appalachian Consortium Press, 251-257.

Brosi, George. 1988. "John Fox, Jr.," *Appalachian Mountain Books* 4: 7, 6-7.

Chapman, Malcolm. 1978. *The Gaelic Vision in Scottish Culture*. London: Croom Helm; Montreal: McGill-Queen's.

Coles, Robert. 1985. "Review of *The Trial of the Lonesome Pine* by John Fox, Jr. *Appalachian Journal*:12, 265-267.

Cunningham, Rodger. 1987. *Apples on the Flood: The Southern Mountain Experience*. Knoxville: University of Tennessee Press.

Diawara, Manthia. 1988. "The Other(s') Archivist." Review of *Blank Darkness*, by C.L. Miller. *Diacritics* 18: 1, 66-74.

Dix, Keith. 1970. "Appalachia: Third World Pillage?" *People's Appalachia* 1: 4, 9-13.

Fanon, Frantz. 1961. *The Wretched of the Earth*. Translated by Constance Farrington, 1968. New York: Grove.

Fox, John, Jr. 1908. *The Trial of the Lonesome Pine*. Revised 1984 by University Press, Lexington: Kentucky.

Gaventa, John. 1980. *Power and Powerlessness: Quiescence and Rebellion in an Appalachian Valley*. Urbana: University of Illinois Press.

Kupperman, Karen Ordahl. 1980. *Settling with the Indians: The Meeting of English and Indian Cultures in America, 1580-1640*. Totona: Rowman.

Lewis, Helen Matthews, Sue Easterling Kobak, and Linda Johnson. 1978. "Family, Religion and Colonialism in Central Appalachia, or, Bury My Rifle at Big Stone Gap." Edited by Lewis, Johnson, and Askins, 113-39.

Lewis, Helen Matthews, ed., with Linda Johnson and Don Askins. 1978. *Colonialism in Modern America: The Appalachian Case.* Boone: Appalachian Consortium Press.

McKinney, Gordon B. 1977. "Industrialization and Violence in Appalachian in the 1890's." J.W. Williamson, ed. *An Appalachian Symposium: Essays Written in Honor of Cratis D. Williams.* Boone: Appalachian State, 131-144.

Miller, Christopher L. 1985. *Blank Darkness: Africanist Discourse in French.* Chicago: University of Chicago Press.

The New York Times. 26 April 1915. VIII 15: 1; in Shapiro, 1978, 352.

Parker, John. 1979. "Religion and the Virginia Colony, 1609-10." K. R. Andrews, N.P. Canny and P.E.H. Hair. *The Westward Enterprise: English Activities in Ireland, the Atlantic and America. 1480-1650.* Detroit: Wayne State, 245-270.

Pearce, John Ed. Foreword to Fox,.1908. vii-xvi.

Said, Edward W. 1978. *Orientalism.* New York: Random House.

——. 1989. "Representing the Colonized: Anthropology's Interlocuters." *Critical Inquiry* 15: 205-225.

Shapiro, Henry D. 1978. *Appalachia on Our Mind: The Southern Mountains and Mountaineers in the American Consciousness, 1870-1920.* Chapel Hill: University of North Carolina.

Sheehan, Bernard W. 1980. *Savagism and Civility: Indians and Englishmen in Colonial Virginia.* Cambridge, Eng.: Cambridge University Press.

Snyder, Robert. 1982. "Image and Identity in Appalachia," *Appalachian Journal* 9: 124-33.

Titus, Warren I. 1988. *John Fox, Jr.* New York: Twayne.

Waller, Altina. 1988. *Feud: Hatfields, McCoys, and Social Change in Appalachia, 1860-1900.* Chapel Hill: University of North Carolina.

Footnotes

[1] Cole's characterization of the book as "utterly contemporary in its lack of sentimentality," (206) is as accurate as his statement that Fox, a native of Paris in the Bluegrass, "spent his early years in the mountain part of" Kentucky (265). His review is notable largely as an especially glaring example of the limitations of liberalism on the part of this great friend of the mountains.

[2] Mooney, James. 1889. "Folk-Lore of the Carolina Mountains." *Journal of American Folklore* 2: June 1889, 95-104, in Shapiro, 245.

[3] Fox's description of the activities of this group is largely taken verbatim from an earlier nonfiction piece of his titled "Civilizing the Cumberland" (Titus, 1971: 62-63). For a quite different view of this "civilizing" process, see McKinney, 1977.

[4] Fox also draws another science into partnership with domination: Cumberland Gap "would have to be tunnelled. So said Geography" (42). So, of course, says the personified intersection of 'objective' science with a particular intention toward its subject; but geography as a 'science' has never in fact been free from that intention.

[5] The British agents at Cumberland Gap (like Big Stone Gap, not named, but unmistakable) are called "helmeted Englishmen" three times (88, 232) and once "conquistadors from Albion." One is evidently intended to visualize Renaissance soldiers in morions, which, of course, is as accurate an image of the agents of the American Company as is Fox's general image of their doings, for a truer account of which we are indebted to John Gaventa, 1980.

[6] Indeed, Hale's and Budd's attitude closely echoes that of an early English writer on Virginia: "Our intrusion into their possessions shall tend to their great good...to bring them from their base condition to a farre better"; but "so many as obstinately refuse to unite themselves unto us, or shall maligne or disturb *our* plantation...shall be dealth [sic] with as enemies of the Commonwealth of *their* country." Emphasis added. Robert Johnson. (1609), *Nova Britannia* (London) f. C2^r; in Parker (1979), 253.

[7] A particularly interesting example of this appropriation and abjection occurs when Hale takes June down to meet his Bluegrass relatives: "Rumour had gone ahead of June. Hale had found her rushing about the mountains on the back of a wild bull...She was as beautiful as Europa" (231). Here, Fox recalls the girl of whom he was told in the late 1880s (Titus, 1971: 24) and who became the inspiration of his first Appalachian story, "A Mountain Europa." This is a central image, therefore, in Fox's relation to Appalachia; indeed, it is the germ of his literary career. But the girl in the anecdote and in Fox's story was calmly riding the bull along a path on the way to market—a practice sometimes actually followed in the absence of other draft animals. She is, in short, a mistress, or rather master, of the bull's male force (the word *bull* is cognate to *phallus*). But to call her "Europa" is to identify her with a *helpless victim* of the bull of All-Father Zeus in an act of *bride-capture*. (One is reminded of the observation of Levi-Strauss that kinship is a language in which women function as words and their exchange as communication.) Thus, this metaphor reduces June to a functional sign in the semiotic exchange between Appalachian and American cultures—and in Fox's communicative exchange with the reader. Serres observes that all logocentric discourse occurs over a third party, a muted and abjected Other; here that party is June/Appalachia reduced to feminine passivity in a dialogue between the two parts of Jack/America—a dialogue constantly pulling toward monologue.

[8] In an earlier chapter, the "railroad that had been creeping for many years toward the Gap" is seen by Hale as a "worm" whose "head...was just protruding from the Natural Tunnel twenty miles away" (126). Despite this sinister phallic imagery, though, the railroad at this point is described in positive terms. Its

passage was made by "the Almighty," who had "stored" the resources of the mountains and "driven this passage himself to help puny man to reach them" (126). Thus, the phallicism is redeemed by attributing it to a Father-God made in Man's/Hale's image, endorsing and reinforcing man's own 'puny' phallicism and, indeed, creating the female by that force. Yet in the threatening unpleasantness of the image, there is an undertone of doubt about Hale's male impulses and those of his civilization. (Hale's name means "healthy," but when June first hears it she spells it "Hail" [208, 356], the name of a phenomenon sent from Heaven but dreaded by rural people.)

[9] Fox explicitly labels as "lawlessness" some things that are simply face-to-face, human-scaled, oral-cultural means of social control: "[E]llections were held *viva voce* under the beeches.... Here...the people had come together during half a century for sport and horse-trading and to talk politics" (141). This is part of a long passage in which violence is mentioned as sometimes incidental to these processes, but is implied to be the essential feature of them. One of the first ordinances passed by the outside 'civilizers' is to ban shouting in the streets (142), and "the lawlessness of the town itself" is attributed to "its close environment" (142)—evidently a prejudicial name for face-to-face interaction. One moonshiner is "dubbed Caliban" (143)—shades of D.O. Mannoni and other colonial-discourse critics of *The Tempest*.

[10] The feudist Devil Judd Tolliver is based on Devil John Wright, a notorious opportunist "who had supposedly fought on both sides of the Civil War.... When Fox knew him, he was serving as a Kentucky peace officer and helping the Consolidation Coal Company buy up land in Letcher and Pike County, Kentucky" (Titus, 1971: 96). Fox himself presents Devil Judd as an entrepreneur, a non-'traditional' person, while simultaneously making him a symbol of 'barbarism': "It was not often that he found a mountaineer who knew what a parting in a coal seam was" (25).

[11] Even earlier, he has deprived them, in her eyes, of agency in the conduct of their own lives: "They were not to blame—her people, they but did as their fathers had done before them" (362). She sees their actions as only passively following the groove set down by their discourse. But, here again, as with Sam Budd's dismissal of the reasons for the strike, the real master-discourse is 'civilization's' and Fox's—and, here, Hale's as June has fallen into that groove.

[12] I am indebted for this insight to Linda Gill, my student in Appalachian Literature at Sue Bennett College.

[13] And, indeed, industrial waste is to this day poured on Appalachia because Appalachia is itself the semiotic residue of America. Thus do the 'symbolic' and the 'imaginary' redound upon the 'real.'

Rodger Cunningham, a native of West Virginia, teaches English and Appalachian studies at Sue Bennett College in London, Kentucky. He is the author of *Apples on the Flood: The Southern Mountain Experience*.

Household Composition and Early Industrial Transformation: Eastern Kentucky 1880 to 1910[1]

Thomas A. Arcury

This paper describes household composition in Appalachian Kentucky in 1880 and in 1910, and analyzes change in household composition during this period. There is general agreement that the family and household have great importance in Appalachian society today, and that the importance of the family and the household have historical depth (Brown and Schwarzweller, 1971; Titon, 1988). While their importance in the region is acknowledged, empirically little is known about the composition and functioning of households and families in the 19th century or the first third of the 20th century. The lack of materials for these earlier periods means there is currently no way of understanding the changes in household and family which have occurred in the region.

The earliest description of Appalachian household and family composition was completed by Brown (1952a, 1952b, 1988). Brown used ethnographic and survey data, collected in the "Beechcreek" neighborhood of Eastern Kentucky in the early 1940s, to describe household and family structure, their developmental cycles, and their variation. Brown's work, however, was conducted in a single neighborhood; generalizations to the contemporary population (1940s), or the historic Appalachian or Eastern Kentucky populations must be tempered.

No surveys predating Brown's work provide data on household and family composition. Nor were any ethnographies completed before Brown which contain information on household and family structure. The available "ethnographic novels," particularly those of Arnow (1936, 1949), give an understanding of familial bonds, roles and behavior for a period somewhat earlier than that of Brown's research, but these novels cannot give the data needed to analyze early composition.

Several surveys were conducted in the 1940s in Eastern Kentucky which include information on household and family. These are analyzed by Boyd (1948). Since 1960, there have been analyses of households and families in Appalachia using survey and ethnographic data (e.g., Bryant, 1981; Beaver, 1986; Schwarzweller, et al 1971; Ford, et al, 1985). Other research has examined family roles and values in different segments of the Appalachian population (e.g., Lewis, 1970). These materials provide information to help interpret earlier structural characteristics, and something to which earlier materials can be compared to measure change, but they do not provide basic information on the household composition for earlier periods.

Some efforts toward the empirical analysis of Appalachian household composition during the 19th and early 20th centuries have begun. These include the paper by Arcury and Porter (1985) for 1900 Eastern Kentucky comparing household composition in Pike County to that in Ashland. Titon (1988) analyzes household economy in Page County, Virginia, from settlement to the present to establish the continuity in the value for household based production. Billings and Blee (1989) have begun publishing their historical work on the Beech Creek neighborhood of Kentucky studied by Brown in the 1940s. Waller's (1988) analysis of the Hatfield-McCoy feud also includes an examination of the socioeconomic circumstances influencing changes in family relationships at the turn of the century in Pike County, Kentucky, and Mingo and Logan Counties, West Virginia. Each of these studies, however, is based on one or two counties and do not have regional data available for comparison.

While there is little detail about the structure of Appalachian households and families before 1940, there is a growing literature on the economy of the region from 1880 to date. The 1880 to 1910 period was the beginning of industrialization in Eastern Kentucky. During this period the regional economy changed from one more geared to subsistence production to one more geared to commercial production (Eller,

1982; Moore, 1984). In this period large scale commercial coal mining and timbering began. These economic changes were not evenly distributed throughout Eastern Kentucky. In 1910, 7 of the 31 counties did not have a railroad. In this same year, coal was being commercially mined in only 13 of the 31 counties. Arcury (1988) shows that there was wide variation in agricultural production throughout the 1880 to 1910 period.

The theoretical framework which guides this research is that of cultural ecology. From this perspective, in addition to its psychoemotional and symbolic functions, the household is the basic unit for the economic activities of production, distribution and consumption (Wilk and Netting, 1984). The household is a means by which individuals organize and adapt themselves economically. As changes occur in the economy of the communities of which the households are a part, or in the subsistence pursuits of the household residents, the composition of the households should reflect these changes. The expectation is that the closer the economic base of the community or household(s), is to a subsistence type, the greater is the tendency for households to be large and structurally complex. The closer the economic base of the community or household to a more cash or commercial type, the greater is the tendency for households to be small and structurally simple (Arcury, 1984).

Methods

This research focuses on 31 Eastern Kentucky counties commonly included in the Appalachian Region (Ford, 1962). See Figure 1. Data on household and family are taken from the 1880 and 1910 U.S. census manuscripts. Three samples were selected.

(1) A stratified random sample of 600 households from the 1880 census;
(2) A stratified random sample of 600 households from the 1910 census; and
(3) A random sample of 260 households from the 1910 census in which the household heads were employed by a coal mine company.

The 1880 and 1910 samples were stratified to insure the inclusion of (1) households located in enumeration districts containing towns as well as those which were totally rural, and (2) households located in counties in which commercial coal mining was present by 1910 as well as in those counties in which there was no commercial coal mining. For this analysis these samples are weighted.[2]

Operationally, households include all individuals listed as being part of a household in the manuscript census. Household type in this analysis is based on the Hammel and Laslett (1974) typology. Five types are used.

(1) A *nuclear family household* includes the nuclear family of the household head, but no other relatives.
(2) An *extended family household* includes the nuclear family of the household head, and any other relatives who are not part of a nuclear family; or an individual household head and a related nuclear family.
(3) A *multiple family household* includes the nuclear family of the household head, as well as any nuclear family related to the household head. It may also include any other relatives who are not part of a nuclear family.
(4) A *solitary household* includes no relatives of the household head.
(5) An *other household* contains relatives of the household head, but no nuclear family which includes the household head or any relative of the household head.

Each of these types may contain any number of individuals or families not related to the household head.

Household size is the total number of persons living in the household. Generations spanned is the maximum number of generations related to the household head in a household. A household including a grandparent and a grandchild would span three generations whether or not members of the parental generation are present. A household including a head with no other relatives present would span only one generation even if it included three generation family of resident employees.

The components of household type are the presence of nuclear families and individuals. A *nuclear family* is a conjugal pair (husband and wife) with or without children; or a conjugal stem, a parent with at least one coresident child. In addition to a *primary nuclear family* (a nuclear family in which the family head is the household head), there are *subfamilies* (a nuclear family in which the family head is not the household head, but members of the family are related to the household head through kinship), and *secondary families* (a nuclear family in which the family head is not the household head, nor are members of the family related to the household head).

Individuals are household residents who are not part of a nuclear family. There are two major type of individuals: *primary individuals* are those who head households, and *secondary individuals* are those who do not head households. Secondary individuals are further divided into those related to the household head and those not related to the household head.

In describing Eastern Kentucky household composition, general structure and size are presented for each sample. To examine the developmental aspects of household composition, structure and size are then examined by age of head. Four household head age groups are used: (1) *young adult* household heads aged 15 to 29; (2) *middle aged* household heads aged 30 to 49; (3) *older* household heads aged 50-59; and (4) *elderly* households aged 60 and older.

The analysis of household developmental cycle is limited to those households with male heads; few households in any of the samples have female heads. The small number of female headed households does not lend itself to more specific analysis. The distributions of size and type for households with female heads differ from those with male heads. It would distort the analysis to combine households with female and male heads.

1880 Household Composition

The majority of 1880 households have a nuclear family structure (79%), and are large, with an average size of 5.8 persons (Table 1, Panel A). The majority of all households have male heads. Households with male and female heads differ in composition. Female headed households are a person smaller. Fewer female headed households are nuclear family and extended family, while more are multiple family, solitary and other.

When the age of the male household head is controlled, the influence of the developmental cycle on variation in household composition is apparent (Table 2). With the increasing age of head, there is a tendency for households to become complex. Over 80% of the households with heads under age 50 were nuclear family in structure, 76% of those with heads aged 50-59 are nuclear, and only 55% of those with heads aged 60 and older are nuclear. Extended family households increase from 8.5% of those with young adult heads, to 13.3% of those with older heads, and 29.0% of those with elderly heads. Multiple family households increase from 1.1% of those with young adult heads to 11.8% of those with elderly heads.

TABLE 1: HOUSEHOLD STRUCTURE AND MEAN SIZE, TOTAL SAMPLES AND BY GENDER OF HOUSEHOLD HEAD — 1880 GENERAL SAMPLE, 1910 GENERAL SAMPLE, AND 1910 COAL MINE EMPLOYEE SAMPLE.

	A 1880 General Sample		B TOTAL SAMPLE 1910 General Sample		C 1910 Mine Sample	
	N	%	N	%	N	%
Household Structure						
Nuclear Family	476	79.3	473	78.6	217	83.5
Extended Family	70	11.7	75	12.5	31	11.9
Multiple Family	26	4.3	30	4.8	3	1.2
Solitary	14	2.4	12	2.0	3	1.2
Other	14	2.3	12	2.0	6	2.3
Mean Household Size	5.8		5.3		4.8	
Unweighted N	600.0		600.0		260.0	

	MALE HEADED HOUSEHOLDS					
	1880 General Sample		1910 General Sample		1910 Mine Sample	
	N	%	N	%	N	%
Household Structure*						
Nuclear Family	445	80.2	448	80.1	217	83.8
Extended Family	68	12.3	71	12.8	31	12.0
Multiple Family	22	4.0	26	4.6	3	1.2
Solitary	10	1.7	7	1.2	3	1.2
Other	10	1.8	7	1.3	5	1.9
Mean Household Size #	5.8		5.4		4.8	
Unweighted N	555.0		560.0		259.0	

	FEMALE HEADED HOUSEHOLDS					
	1880 General Sample		1910 General Sample		1910 Mine Sample	
	N	%	N	%	N	%
Household Structure*						
Nuclear Family	31	68.5	24	58.2	0	.0
Extended Family	2	4.4	4	9.6	0	.0
Multiple Family	4	8.0	3	7.8	0	.0
Solitary	4	10.0	5	12.5	0	.0
Other	4	9.1	5	11.0	1	100.0
Mean Household Size	4.9		4.4		4.0	
Unweighted N	45.0		40.0		1.0	

*Chi Square of household structure by gender of head for 1880 and 1910 general samples significant at .05 level.
#T-test of household size by gender of head for 1880 and 1910 general samples significant at .05 level.

Other components of household composition reflect the tendency for greater complexity. Households with any secondary individuals increase from 15.5% of those with young adult heads, to about 20% of those with heads aged 30 to 59, and to 44% of those with elderly heads. Households with related secondary individuals increase from 9% to 31% with the increasing age of the household head.

Households with subfamilies increase from 1.1% of those with young adult heads to 11.8% of those with elderly heads. Households with secondary families, while fewer than those with subfamilies, also reflect the trend for complexity with age of household head. Households with secondary families increase from 1.3% of those with young adult heads, to 2.5% of those with middle aged heads, to about 3.5% of those with heads aged 50 and older.

Over 80% of households with heads under age 60 span two generations, but only 52.9% of those with heads aged 60 and older span only two generations. Households spanning three generations increase from 3.3% of those with young adult heads to 9.3% of those with older heads, and then jump to 35.4% of those with elderly heads. Fifteen percent of households with young adult heads span only one generation. This relatively high percentage probably results from the formation of new households. Single generation households decline to about 7% of those with heads aged 30 to 59, and then increases to 12.2% of those with elderly heads. This increase in single generation households among the oldest household heads results from the departure of marrying children.

Household size and the number of head's children in the household have a curvilinear rather than a direct relationship to head's age. The mean number of persons increases from 4.2 for households with young adult heads, to its peak of 6.9 for households with middle aged heads. Average size then decreases to 6.6 persons for households with older heads, and to 5.2 persons for those with elderly heads.

Households with children of the head present increase from 84.4% of households with young adult heads, to 92.6% of those with middle aged heads, and then decline to 91.3% of those with older heads, and to 80.5% of those with elderly heads. The average number of head's children in the household increases from 1.8 for those with young adult heads, to over four children for those with heads aged 30 to 59, and then declines to 2.3 for those with elderly heads.

TABLE 2: HOUSEHOLD COMPOSITION BY AGE OF MALE HOUSEHOLD HEAD, 1880 GENERAL SAMPLE.

	Age of Household Head			
	15-29 Young Adult	30-49 Middle Aged	50-59 Older	60+ Elderly
Household Structure				
Nuclear Family	87.2	81.6	75.9	55.3*
Extended Family	8.5	11.3	13.3	29.0
Multiple Family	1.1	3.5	7.0	11.8
Solitary	2.7	1.1	1.3	2.0
Other	.4	2.5	2.4	2.0
Secondary Individuals				
Any	15.5	22.9	20.4	44.1*
Related	9.0	12.7	14.7	30.9*
Unrelated	6.6	13.8	7.0	15.0
Subfamilies	1.1	3.9	7.0	11.8*
Secondary Families	1.3	2.4	3.8	3.5
Number of Generations Spanned				
One	15.0	6.6	7.0	12.2*
Two	81.7	86.8	83.7	52.9
Three or More	3.3	6.6	9.3	35.4
Mean Number of Person	4.2	6.9	6.6	5.2#
Children of the Household Head Present				
Any				
One or more	84.4	92.6	91.3	80.5*
Mean	1.8	4.4	4.1	2.3#
Under Age 18				
One or more	84.4	90.4	83.7	49.0*
Mean	1.8	4.0	3.0	1.1#
Age 18 and Older				
One or more	1.4	23.3	58.6	60.8*
Mean	.0	.4	1.1	1.2#
Nonrelatives				
Employees	4.3	8.2	9.4	13.5
Boarders	3.0	5.6	2.4	5.2
Unweighted N	174	259	73	50

*Chi Square by age of household head significant at .05 level.
#F-test by age of household head significant at .05 level.

1910 Household Composition—The General Population Sample

The majority of the 1910 general population households have a nuclear family structure (79%), and are large, with an average size of 5.3 persons (Table 1, Panel B). The majority of all households also have male heads. Size and type differ between households with male and female heads. Female headed households are on average a person smaller. Fewer female headed households have a nuclear family or extended family structure. More female headed households are multiple family, solitary or other.

There is a moderate tendency for household complexity to increase relative to the age of the household head (Table 3). There is also, however, a limited tendency for household complexity to have a curvilinear relationship to age of household head; for some characteristics which indicate complexity, the highest percentage of households is among those with heads aged 50-59, and this percentage decreases among those with heads age 60 and older.

Households with a nuclear family structure decrease from 86.9% of those with young adult heads, to 67.5% of those with elderly heads. Households with an extended family structure increase from 9.1% of those with young adult heads to 22.0% of those with elderly heads. For the multiple family type the highest percentage, 9.3%, is among those households with heads aged 50-59.

Households with any secondary individuals increase from 13.6% of those with young adult heads, to 29.0% of those with older heads, before declining to 24.5% of those with elderly heads. Households with unrelated secondary individuals increase from 3.3% of those with young adult heads to 10.0% of those with older heads, and then decline to 5.6% of those with elderly heads. Households with related secondary individuals increase from 10.3% of those with young adult heads to 21.5% of those with older heads, and again to 23.2% of those with elderly heads.

TABLE 3: HOUSEHOLD COMPOSITION BY AGE OF MALE HOUSEHOLD HEAD, 1910 GENERAL SAMPLE.

	Age of Household Head			
	15-29 Young Adult	30-49 Middle Aged	50-59 Older	60+ Elderly
Household Structure				
Nuclear Family	86.9	83.0	70.8	67.5*
Extended Family	9.1	11.5	15.8	22.0
Multiple Family	3.4	3.5	9.3	4.5
Solitary	.0	.7	3.2	2.9
Other	.6	1.4	.9	3.2
Secondary Individual				
Any	13.6	16.9	29.0	24.5*
Related	10.3	12.3	21.5	23.2*
Unrelated	3.3	5.8	10.0	5.6
Subfamilies	3.4	3.5	10.2	6.1
Secondary Families	1.2	2.4	.9	1.6
Number of Generations Spanned				
One	17.1	5.1	14.3	25.1*
Two	80.0	86.9	69.1	55.8
Three or More	2.9	8.0	16.6	19.1
Mean Number of Persons	3.9	6.5	5.5	4.4#
Children of the Household Head Present				
Any				
One or more	82.3	92.9	81.8	61.9*
Mean	1.6	3.9	3.1	2.0#
Under Age 18				
One or more	82.3	92.2	71.5	43.3*
Mean	1.6	3.7	2.0	1.2#
Age 18 and Older				
One or more	.0	17.4	58.8	38.8*
Mean	.0	.2	1.0	.8#
Nonrelatives				
Employees	2.7	4.8	1.7	4.3
Boarders	1.1	4.5	4.8	1.3
Unweighted N	150.0	247.0	108.0	60.0

*Chi Square by age of household head significant at .05 level.
#F-test by age of household head significant at .05 level.

About 3.5 percent of the households with heads aged under 50 include subfamilies. While 10.2% of those with heads aged 50-59, but only 6.1% of those with heads aged 60 and older have subfamilies.

Households spanning two generations generally decrease with the aging of the household head. After increasing from 80.0% of households with young adult heads to 86.9% of those with middle aged heads, two generation households decrease to 55.8% of those with elderly heads. Three generation households increase from 2.9% of those with young adult heads to 19.1% of those with elderly heads. However, the increase in one generation households is even greater; 25.1% of households with elderly heads span only one generation.

Household size and the number of head's children in the household have a curvilinear relationship to head's age. Average household size by age of head increases from 3.9 to 6.5 persons, and then declines to 5.5 and 4.4 persons. The average number of children similarly increases from 1.6 to 3.9, and then declines to 3.1 and 2.0. Households with children relative to head's age increase from 82.3% to 92.9%, and then decrease to 81.8% and 61.9%.

1910 Household Composition—The Coal Mine Employee Sample

The dominant household type in the 1910 coal mine employee sample is the nuclear family (Table 1, Panel C). In addition to nuclear family households (84%), only extended family households represent a substantial part of the sample (12%). Average household size in the mine sample is 4.8 persons. Only one of the households in this sample has a female head.

There is little developmental change in household composition among the coal mine employee households (Table 4). The analysis of the developmental cycle for this sample is made difficult by the small number of households with older and elderly heads; 19 households have heads aged 50 to 59, and only two have heads aged 60 and older. Measures of significance were calculated for variation in household characteristics by age of head for all of the age groups, excluding the two households with heads aged 60 and older. There was no difference in results.

TABLE 4: HOUSEHOLD COMPOSITION BY AGE OF MALE HOUSEHOLD HEAD, 1910 COAL MINE EMPLOYEE SAMPLE.

	Age of Household Head			
	15-29 Young Adult	30-49 Middle Aged	50-59 Older	60+ Elderly
Household Structure				
Nuclear Family	84.0	82.4	89.5	100.0
Extended Family	11.8	13.4	5.3	.0
Multiple Family	.0	1.7	5.3	.0
Solitary	2.5	.0	.0	.0
Other	1.7	2.5	.0	.0
Secondary Individual				
Any	26.1	26.9	15.8	.0
Related	11.8	14.3	10.5	.0
Unrelated	16.0	13.5	5.3	.0
Subfamilies	.0	1.7	5.3	.0
Secondary Families	.8	2.5	.0	.0
Number of Generations Spanned				
One	26.1	8.4	31.6	50.0*
Two	71.4	86.6	57.9	50.0
Three or More	2.5	5.0	10.5	.0
Mean Number of Persons	3.9	5.7	5.2	4.0#
Children of the Household Head Present				
Any				
One or more	69.7	90.8	68.4	50.0*
Mean	1.5	3.3	2.9	2.0#
Under Age 18				
One or more	69.7	89.1	63.2	50.0*
Mean	1.5	3.1	2.0	2.0#
Age 18 and Older				
One or more	.0	12.6	47.4	.0*
Mean	.0	.2	.9	.0#
Nonrelatives				
Employees	4.2	5.9	.0	.0
Boarders	8.4	10.9	5.3	.0
Unweighted N	119.0	119.0	19.0	2.0

*Chi Square by age of household head significant at .05 level.
#F-test by age of household head significant at .05 level.

Over 80% of the households have a nuclear family structure no matter the age of the head, and this percentage increases from 84.0% of those with young adult heads, to 89.5% of those with older heads. Extended family households decline from 11.8% of those with young adult heads, to 5.3% of those with older heads.

The other components of household composition also indicate limited variation relative to the age of the head. Households with any secondary individuals decrease from about 26% of those with young adult and middle aged heads, to 15.8% of those with older heads. Households with unrelated secondary individuals decrease from 16.0% of those with young adult heads, to 13.5% with middle aged heads, and to 5.3% of those with older heads. There is almost no change in the presence of related secondary individuals.

The number of generations spanned in these households generally decreases with the increased age of the head. Among those with young adult heads, 26.1% span one generation and 71.4% span two generations. Two generation households increase to 86.6% of those with middle aged heads; those with one generation decline to 8.4%. Among households with older heads only 58% are two generation and 31.6% are one generation. Households spanning three generations do increase with the age of the head, but this is from 2.5% of those with young adult heads, to 10.5% of those with older heads.

Household size increases relative to age of head from 3.9 to 5.7 persons, and then declines to 5.2 persons. Almost 70% of households with young adult heads have a child present, and the mean number of children is 1.5. For households with middle aged heads, 90.8% have children and the average number of these is 3.3. Among households with older heads, only 68.4% have a child present, and the average number of children is 2.9.

Continuity and Change in Household Composition, 1880 and 1910

The comparison of the 1880 and 1910 data indicate how households changed during this period. Comparison of data for the 1910 coal mine employee households indicates the features they share with the 1910 general population.

Households in Appalachian Kentucky in 1880 were large. During most of the development cycle most of the these households had a simple, nuclear family structure. Household structure became more complex through the developmental cycle, particularly among households with heads aged 60 and older. These characteristics seem reasonable given the agrarian base of the Eastern Kentucky economy at that time and the large average size of the farms (Arcury, 1988). Waller's (1988) analysis of the resources of elder household heads at this time in Southeastern Kentucky supports this interpretation.

In 1880, as well as in the 1910 general and coal mine employee populations, household size had a curvilinear relationship to age of head. For each population this was largely the result of the common developmental pattern of growth, with the addition of children followed by decline with the loss of these children.

In 1880, however, as household size and the number of children in the household began to decline relative to age of head, household structure was becoming much more complex. As most children were leaving their natal homes, they were replaced in some cases with the families of procreation of one or more of the head's children or with other of the head's relatives. This would result in a smaller size but a more complex, extended or multiple family household structure.

For 1880, while there is a decline in the presence of children in households with elderly heads, the large number of all households with children present must be emphasized. Even among households with elderly heads, 80% still have a child residing with them; the mean number of children is over 2. Among households with the oldest heads, 49% have minor (under age 18) children in their homes, and 60.8% have a least one adult child present. Why this large number of children? The resources controlled by these older household heads are sufficient both to support these remaining children and to require a large workforce.

Greater household complexity with the increased age of head resulting from greater resource control is further supported by the number and roles of unrelated secondary individuals. Unlike related secondary individuals, unrelated secondary individuals do not influence household type. Nonrelatives who are household employees increase from 4.3% of those households with young adult heads, to around 9% for those with heads aged 30 to 59, and then to 13.5% of those with elderly heads.

There is general continuity when 1880 and 1910 households are compared (Tables 1 and 5). There is only 30 years difference between these years. Many of those who were householders in 1880 were still householders in 1910. While a great deal of economic change occurred in the region, the majority of the population made its living by farming in 1910 as well as in 1880.

TABLE 5: HOUSEHOLD COMPOSITION BY AGE OF MALE HOUSEHOLD HEAD, 1880 GENERAL SAMPLE AND 1910 GENERAL SAMPLE COMPARED.

	1880 General Sample Age of Household Head				1910 General Sample Age of Household Head			
	15-29	30-49	50-59	60+	15-29	30-49	50-59	60+
Household Structure								
Nuclear Family	87.2	81.6	75.9	55.3	86.9	83.0	70.8	67.5
Extended Family	8.5	11.3	13.3	29.0	9.1	11.5	15.8	22.0
Multiple Family	1.1	3.5	7.0	11.8	3.4	3.5	9.3	4.5
Solitary	2.7	1.1	1.3	2.0	.0	.7	3.2	2.9
Other	.4	2.5	2.4	2.0	.6	1.4	.9	3.2
Secondary Individuals								
Any	15.5	22.9	20.4	44.1	13.6	16.9	29.9	24.5*
Related	9.0	12.7	14.7	30.9	10.3	12.3	21.5	23.2
Unrelated	6.6	13.8	7.0	15.0	3.3	5.8*	10.0	5.6
Subfamilies	1.1	3.9	7.0	11.8	3.4	3.5	10.2	6.1
Secondary Families	1.3	2.4	3.8	3.5	1.2	2.4	.9	1.6
Number of Generations Spanned								
One	15.0	6.6	7.0	12.2	17.1	5.1	14.3	25.1*
Two	81.7	86.8	83.7	52.9	80.0	86.9	69.1	55.8
Three or More	3.3	6.6	9.3	35.4	2.9	8.0	16.6	19.1
Mean Number of Persons	4.2	6.9	6.6	5.2	3.9	6.5	5.5#	4.4
Children of the Household Head Present								
Any								
One or more	84.4	92.6	91.3	80.5	82.3	92.9	81.8	61.9*
Mean	1.8	4.4	4.1	2.3	1.6	3.9#	3.1#	2.0
Under Age 18								
One or more	84.4	90.4	83.7	49.0	82.3	92.2	71.5	43.3
Mean	1.8	4.0	3.0	1.1	1.6	3.7	2.0#	1.2
Age 18 and Older								
One or more	1.4	23.2	58.6	60.8	.0	17.4	58.8	38.8*
Mean	.0	.4	1.1	1.2	.0	.2#	1.0	.8
Nonrelatives								
Employees	4.3	8.2	9.4	13.5	2.7	4.8	1.7*	4.3
Boarders	3.0	5.6	2.4	5.2	1.1	4.5	4.8	1.3
Unweighted N	174.0	259.0	73.0	50.0	150.0	247.0	103.0	60.0

*Chi Square significant at .05 level for comparison of 1880 and 1910 variables for each age group of household heads.

#T-Test significant at .05 level for comparison of 1880 and 1910 variables for each age group of household heads.

Households in both 1880 and 1910 are large. In both populations most heads are male. The differences between male and female headed households in 1880 are similar to those 1910. In both years male headed households are one person larger and have a greater tendency to have a nuclear family only structure. Female headed households tend to be more variable in composition, including large proportions of each of the five types. The developmental cycle for both 1880 and 1910 male headed households is for households to become more complex.

There is also evidence of change from 1880 to 1910. The largest differences are among households with older and elderly heads (aged 50 and older). These indicate a change in developmental cycle; from 1880 to 1910 there is a decline in complexity with increasing age of the household head. In 1880, there is a strong tendency for households to become complex with the aging of the head; in 1910, this tendency is weaker.

Households are smaller in 1910, with a decline of half a person. The largest size differences are between households with older and elderly heads; these 1910 households include one fewer person. In 1880 and 1910, structure is very similar among households with male heads aged 15 through 59. Among households with elderly heads, there are more pronounced differences in structure: for example, 55.3% of the households with elderly heads are nuclear family in 1880, versus 67.5% for 1910; 11.8% are multiple family in 1880, versus 4.5% in 1910.

Similar proportions of households with heads up to age 59 have secondary individuals for 1880 and 1910. However, among those with elderly heads 20% fewer have secondary individuals in 1910 than in 1880. This difference holds true for related secondary individuals (30.9% in 1880, 23.2% in 1910), and unrelated secondary individuals (15.0% in 1880, 5.6% in 1910). Households with household employees increase from 4.3% to 13.5% in 1880, but only from 2.7% to 4.3% in 1910.

There are also fewer households with subfamilies and secondary families. Households with subfamilies increase to 11.8% for those with elderly heads in 1880, but to only 6.1% in 1910. Of 1880 households with elderly heads, 3.5% include a secondary family; only 1.6% of their 1910 counterparts do.

In 1880 and 1910, similar percentages of households with young adult and middle aged heads have children present. The average number of children is lower in the 1910 households. Fewer households with older and elderly heads in 1910 have any children of the head present. The number of children present for these 1910 households with older and elderly heads is also smaller. In particular, in 1880, 60.8% of households with elderly heads included children aged 18 or older; for 1910, only 38.8% of these households contain adult children.

The 1910 coal mine employee households differ substantially from those of the 1910 general population (Tables 1 and 6). The 1910 coal mine employee households have essentially no female heads, or male heads aged 60 and older. Even with no female or elderly headed households, the coal mine employee households are relatively small with an average size of 4.8 persons. More of the coal mine employee households are nuclear family in structure. In the 1910 general population, there is a trend toward complexity with the aging of the household head. Among the coal employee households there is very little structural change relative to the age of the household head.

The differences between the 1910 general population and coal mine employee households are even more pronounced when household composition is examined by age of head. Among coal mine employees there is a smaller increase in three generation households with age of head than among the 1910 general population. There is a larger increase among coal mine employee households in one generation and a smaller decrease in two generation households with the increasing age of the head.

Variation in household size relative to the age of the head in the 1910 coal mine employee sample results from the common developmental pattern of growth and decline with the addition and loss of children. Size among the coal mine employee households is also influenced by the number with unrelated secondary individuals, particularly boarders. More 1910 coal mine employee households with young adult and middle aged heads have secondary individuals. Fewer 1910 coal mine employee households with older heads include secondary individuals. As the coal mine employee household heads have more children, these children replace non-relatives. These unrelated individuals were largely boarders rather than employees (as in 1880), and their departure results from their beds being needed by the heads' children.

Finally, there are fewer households with any children, under age 18 children, or age 18 and older children, in the 1910 coal mine employee households. The average numbers of children, however, do not differ that much between the 1910 coal mine employee and 1910 general population households. This indicates that if the coal mine employee households have children present, they have more of them. This follows Haines' (1979) analysis of miners' fertility.

TABLE 6: HOUSEHOLD COMPOSITION BY AGE OF MALE HOUSEHOLD HEAD, 1910 GENERAL SAMPLE AND 1910 COAL MINE EMPLOYEE SAMPLE COMPARED.

	1910 General Sample Age of Household Head				1900 Mine Sample Age of Household Head			
	15-29	30-49	50-59	60+	15-29	30-49	50-59	60+
Household Structure								
Nuclear Family	86.9	83.0	70.8	67.5	84.0	82.4	89.5	100.0
Extended Family	9.1	11.5	15.8	22.0	11.8	13.4	5.3	.0
Multiple Family	3.4	3.5	9.3	4.5	.0	1.7	5.3	.0
Solitary	.0	.7	3.2	2.9	2.5	.0	.0	.0
Other	.6	1.4	.9	3.2	1.7	2.5	.0	.0
Secondary Individual								
Any	13.6	16.9	29.0	24.5	26.1*	26.9*	15.8	.0
Related	10.3	12.3	21.5	23.2	11.8	14.3	10.5	.0
Unrelated	3.3	5.8	10.0	5.6	16.0*	13.5*	5.3	.0
Subfamilies	3.4	3.5	10.2	6.1	.0*	1.7	5.3	.0
Secondary Families	1.2	2.4	.9	1.6	.8	2.5	.0	.0
Number of Generations Spanned								
One	17.1	5.1	14.3	25.1	26.1	8.4	31.6	50.0
Two	80.0	86.9	69.1	55.8	71.4	86.6	57.9	50.0
Three or more	2.9	8.0	16.6	19.1	2.5	5.0	10.5	.0
Mean Number of Persons	3.9	6.5	5.5	4.4	3.9	5.7#	5.2	4.0
Children of the Household Head Present								
Any								
One or more	82.3	92.9	81.8	61.9	69.7*	90.8	68.4	50.0
Mean	1.6	3.9	3.1	2.0	1.5	3.3#	2.9	2.0
Under Age 18								
One or more	82.3	92.2	71.5	43.3	69.7*	89.1	63.2	50.0
Mean	1.6	3.7	2.0	1.2	1.5	3.1#	2.0	2.0
Age 18 and Older								
One or more	.0	17.4	58.8	38.8	.0	12.6	47.4	.0
Mean	.0	.2	1.0	.8	.0	.2	.9	.0
Nonrelatives								
Employees	2.7	4.8	1.7	4.3	4.2	5.9	.0	.0
Boarders	1.1	4.5	4.8	1.3	8.4*	10.9*	5.3	.0
Unweighted N	150.0	247.0	103.0	60.0	119.0	119.0	19.0	2.0

*Chi Square significant at .05 level for comparison of 1910 general and 1910 mine employee variables for each age group of household heads.

#T-Test significant at .05 level for comparison of 1910 general and 1910 mine employee variables for each age group of household heads.

Economic Change and Household Variation: Interpretation

Is the economic process of industrialization reflected in household composition changes from 1880 to 1910? Average household size did decline during this period. The most important structural change can be summarized as a modification in the household developmental cycle that resulted in a decrease in household complexity among households with heads aged 60 and older.

Did any of these changes in household structure and size between 1880 and 1910 actually result from industrialization and consequent changes in the regional economy from a subsistence to cash orientation? It is not possible to directly observe causation with the data presented. The household composition changes which occurred between 1880 and 1910 could have resulted from other factors. For example, the majority of the household heads in both samples were farmers. Elsewhere, analysis has shown that average farm size for the counties of Appalachian Kentucky declined greatly between 1880 and 1910 (Arcury 1988). This decline in farm size might account for the changes in household composition, without industrialization or the commercialization of the local economy either occurring or, if occurring, influencing household composition.

Differences between household composition in the 1910 general sample and the 1910 coal mine employee sample, are more easily attributed to differences in economic lifestyle. The requirements of being a coal mine employee, generally being young and male, would lead us to expect the households of coal mine employees to be different from the households of the general population. Even when the attributes which make coal mine employee households distinctive, having younger and only male household heads, are controlled, the characteristics of the households of the coal mine employees differ non-trivially from the household characteristics of the general population.

The households of those employed by coal mines are smaller. In the 1910 general population, households tend to become more complex with the increased age of the head; in the 1910 coal mine employee sample, household structure changes very little relative to the age of the head.

This analysis provides some support for the general relationship between changes in economy and household composition. The next step for this research is to conduct a more indepth analysis of variation in household and family composition for 1880 and 1910. For example, the influence of changes in agriculture must be examined by comparing the household composition of farmers in 1880 to the household composition of 1910 farmers, and the nonfarm households of 1880 to the nonfarm households of 1910.

This research must examine more specific issues. For example, what was the influence of greater participation in a money economy on the cooperation between families and households? Analysis of another rural U.S. population (van Willigen, 1989) indicates that these economic changes led to less cooperation. What are the effects of city versus small town versus rural residence on household and family composition? Residence in cities and towns would indicate an even greater participation in a commercial rather than a subsistence economy, there then should be even greater variation in household and family composition. Finally, what are the effects of ethnic and migrant status on household composition?

Finally, the 1880 and 1910 data for Eastern Kentucky should be compared to data for the national U.S. population and other local and regional populations for these years. These comparisons will indicate the uniqueness of Appalachian social organization during this period. The 1880 and 1910 data should also be compared to data for more recent populations of the Appalachian region. Comparable data exist for Eastern Kentucky in the 1940s (Boyd, 1948), and for the larger central Appalachian region in 1950s and the 1970s (Ford et al, 1983, 1985).

Notes

1. This material is based upon work supported by the National Science Foundation under Grant No. BNS 8519633. The map for this paper was prepared by the University of Kentucky Cartography Lab.
2. A description of the sampling and weighting procedures is available from the author upon request.

Works Cited

Arcury, Thomas A. 1984. "Household Composition and Economic Change in a Rural Community, 1900 to 1980: Testing Two Models." *American Ethnologist* 11: 677-698.

Arcury, Thomas A. 1988. "Agricultural Diversity and Change in Industrializing Appalachia: An Ecological Analysis of Eastern Kentucky, 1880 to 1910," *CDC Development Paper* 23. Lexington: University of Kentucky, Center for Developmental Change.

Arcury, Thomas A. and Julia D. Porter. 1985. "Household Composition in Appalachian Kentucky in 1900." *Journal of Family History* 10: 183-195.

Arnow, Harriette S. 1936. *Mountain Path.* Lexington: University Press of Kentucky.

Arnow, Harriette S. 1949. *Hunter's Horn.* Lexington: University Press of Kentucky.

Beaver, Patricia Duane. 1986. *Rural Community in the Appalachian South.* Lexington: University Press of Kentucky.

Billings, Dwight B. and Kathleen M. Blee. 1989. "Family Strategies in a Subsistence Economy: Beech Creek, Kentucky, 1850-1942." Lexington: University of Kentucky, Department of Sociology.

Boyd, Virlyn A. 1948. "Household and Family Composition in Selected Rural Areas of Eleven Kentucky Counties. Lexington: University of Kentucky, Department of Sociology, M.A. thesis.

Brown, James S. 1952a. *The Farm Family in a Kentucky Mountain Neighborhood.* Kentucky Agricultural Experiment Station, Bulletin 587. Lexington: University of Kentucky.

Brown, James S. 1952b. *The Family Group in a Kentucky Mountain Farming Community.* Kentucky Agricultural Experiment Station, Bulletin 588. Lexington: University of Kentucky.

Brown, James S. 1988. *Beech Creek: A Study of a Kentucky Mountain Neighborhood.* Berea, KY: Berea College Press.

Brown, James S. and Harry K. Schwarzweller. 1971. "The Appalachian Family." In *Change in Rural Appalachia: Implications for Action.* eds. John D. Photiadis and Harry K. Schwarzweller. Philadelphia: University of Pennsylvania Press, 85-97.

Bryant, F. Carlene. 1981. *We're All Kin: A Cultural Study of a Mountain Neighborhood.* Knoxville: University of Tennessee Press.

Eller, Ronald D. 1982. *Miners, Millhands, and Mountaineers: Industrialization of the Appalachian South, 1880-1930.* Knoxville: University of Tennessee Press.

Ford, Thomas R., ed. 1962. *The Southern Appalachian Region: A Survey.* Lexington: University of Kentucky Press.

Ford, Thomas R., Thomas A. Arcury, and Julia D. Porter. 1983. "Changes in the Structure of Central Appalachian Mountain Families and Households, 1958-1976." *CDC Development Paper 19.* Lexington: University of Kentucky, Center for Developmental Change.

Ford, Thomas R., Thomas A. Arcury, and Julia D. Porter. 1985. "The Impact of Economic Change on Central Appalachian Households and Families." *Sociological Focus* 18: 289-299.

Haines, Michael. 1979. *Fertility and Occupation: Population Patterns in Industrialization*. New York: Academic Press.

Hammel, Eugene A., and Peter Laslett. 1974. "Comparing Household Structure Over Time and Between Cultures." *Comparative Studies in Society and History* 16: 1, 73-109.

Lewis, Helen Matthews. 1970. "Occupational Roles and Family Roles: A Study of Coal Mining Families in the Southern Appalachians." Lexington: University of Kentucky, Department of Sociology. Unpublished Ph.D. dissertation.

Moore, Tyrel G., Jr. 1984. "An Historical Geography of Economic Development in Appalachian Kentucky, 1800-1930." Knoxville: University of Tennessee, Department of Geography. Unpublished Ph.D. dissertation.

Schwarzweller, Harry K., James S. Brown and J.J. Mangalam. 1971. *Mountain Families in Transition: A Case Study of Appalachian Migration*. University Park: Pennsylvania University Press.

Titon, Jeff Todd. 1988. *Powerhouse for God: Speech, Chant, and Song in an Appalachian Baptist Church*. Austin: University of Texas Press.

Van Willigen, John. 1989. *Gettin' Some Age on Me: Social Organization of Older People in a Rural American Community*. Lexington: University Press of Kentucky.

Waller, Altina L. 1988. *Feud: Hatfields, McCoys, and Social Change in Appalachia, 1860-1900*. Chapel Hill: University of North Carolina Press.

Wilk, Richard R. and Robert McC. Netting. 1984. "Households: Changing Forms and Functions." In *Households: Comparative and Historical Studies of the Domestic Group*. eds. Netting, Robert McC., Richard R. Wilk, and Eric J. Arnould. Berkeley: University of California Press, 1-28.

Thomas A. Arcury is research coordinator in the Center for Developmental Change, adjunct assistant professor of anthropology, and an associate of the Appalachian Center at the University of Kentucky. His research interests include household and family composition, aging, and environmental issues in rural America, particularly Appalachia.

Bringing Modern Notions of Childhood and Motherhood to Preindustrial Appalachia: Katherine Pettit and May Stone, 1899-1901

When asked how old a dirty but bright looking baby was, the mother said,
"Waal people, I don't know how old hit is."

excerpt from Katherine Pettit's account of Camp Sassafras 1901

Rhonda George England

In the summer of 1899, Katherine Pettit and May Stone, along with other teacher/volunteers from the Bluegrass section of Kentucky, established the first social settlement in the Kentucky mountains. In Chautauqua-like-fashion, the women pitched tents in and around the vicinity of Knott County, Kentucky, for three consecutive summers. In an attempt to accommodate the settlement to the region, Pettit and Stone established the first rural settlement school in 1902, and in 1915, the town of Hindman incorporated the school, providing it with the permanent title of Hindman Settlement School.

Since the primary purposes of the social settlement were social justice and community uplift, one can assume that Pettit and Stone's work in Appalachia was motivated in part by a belief that the mountaineer had been neglected. While the women found many of the older, more traditional aspects of Appalachian culture preferable to the changing values in the more industrialized areas of the country, they also found many elements in the culture that were backward, especially in the areas of health and education. In order to help the mountaineer to help himself, the women believed they should "teach the mountaineers to make the best use of the material they had" (author unknown, 1899).

In *All That Is Native and Fine* (1983), David Whisnant examines "the politics of culture" at Hindman Settlement School. Whisnant's argument focuses on two major points: (1) the women professed a reverence for mountain culture and hoped to offset the dire effects of impending industrialization, but inadvertently they themselves became powerful instigators of cultural change; and (2) the women, like clergymen of the time, took a very cautious approach to social issues.

Whisnant's argument places him in a paradoxical situation similar to the one he assigns to Pettit and Stone. On the one hand, he argues that the women brought some of the very changes they hoped to forestall (modernity). On the other hand, he argues that the women were too conservative in their approach; in other words, they did not effect enough change. Perhaps part of Whisnant's dilemma stems from his point of view: he addresses only one side of the issue, the cultural losses incurred by modernization through schooling.

Cultural conflict, or the losses and gains incurred through schooling, has long been a major concern in educational historiography. Because schooling as a socializing agent has had the double agenda of preservation and assimilation, the outcomes of schooling have always appeared to be contradictory. So, in order to strengthen their point of view, many scholars focus primarily on one side of the loss/gain issue. However, Lawrence Cremin reminds us that the loss is inherent in the gain, and the combination is a continuum of what he refers to as "generic polarity." That is, schooling like education in general, "never liberates without at the same time limiting. It never empowers without at the same time constraining. It never frees without at the same time socializing" (1976). Therefore, Cremin says, the important question to be addressed is not whether the losses and gains are occurring in isolation, but what the balance is, and to what end, and in light of what alternatives.

We are indebted to Whisnant for revealing the cultural losses the mountaineer incurred through the process of schooling, a process that began in the summer settlements when the teachers began to plaster on modern notions by teaching Appalachian boys and girls such things as "how to make a cake with chocolate icing, dress a chicken properly, cook beans without lard, and sing songs to the accompaniment of a portable reed organ" (Whisnant, 1983). This paper, however, hopes to extend and balance Whisnant's work by looking at the cultural gains that Pettit's and Stone's modern notions of childhood and women's role brought to Appalachia at the turn of the century.

The concepts of childhood and adolescence are social constructs. Therefore, we must remember that Pettit's and Stone's notions of childhood and adolescence were part of an evolving process. Although educators and youth workers between the years 1900 and 1920 worked under the assumption that childhood and adolescence would soon become a universal experience, variations in regional and class lifestyles of the nation delayed both the attitudes and the institutions; the concepts did not become a universal in this country until the 1950s (Kett, 1977). For that reason, it is difficult to label Pettit's and Stone's views or approaches to social issues in Appalachia as conservative or progressive during that time period.

For example, although Pettit and Stone were probably involved in the child labor laws problem in the Bluegrass, child labor in itself was not an issue in their early reports of Appalachia. An explanation for this is found in the 1919 report of the *Child Labor Committee*. The report cites the popular conception of child labor as employment for wages in factories, mines, and stores; farm work was not considered since the farm was usually viewed as an ideal place for children (Bush, 1919).

Therefore, when Pettit and Stone comment on the children working, it is not the work alone that is the primary issue, but the lack of good educational facilities and the mountaineers' attitude toward schooling as something irrelevant in their lives that receives the emphasis:

> The play life of the child is cramped. They go early into the fields and from there to the school room about the middle of July. The schools have to begin in summer and close before cold weather, because the buildings are not warm enough and the children cannot walk over the mountains and down the swollen streams in winter. Mr. Combs, although one of the best teachers in the County, does not realize the responsibility of his calling. For the last four weeks he has had no school, he gave two weeks for foddering and the other time he has been away hunting criminals (Pettit, 1901).

Pettit and Stone probably realized the need for children to work in the self-sufficient farm economy, but they were concerned about the lack of opportunity for the mental and spiritual development of the children. The settlement teachers' emphasis on the importance of "play life" for the children was, perhaps, one of the strangest notions that the women brought to pre-industrial Appalachia: In most cases, mountain parents expected the children to act like adults. May Stone describes the parents' lack of knowledge concerning the play life or imagination in the child:

> The mother told me that Tilda, who is the older of the two girls, of five and six, is known all over the community as "the worst child that ever wuz," that she would slip and put on long dresses and walk around and say she was

somebody else and fool that way all day. I tried to explain to them that this imagination was a good thing if well directed, but she said 'hit was pure meanness and she ought to be killed for 'hit (Stone, 1901).

It is apparent from these excerpts that Pettit and Stone viewed the child as one who needed to be nurtured, or, as Susan Blow described it, "nudged" into being. For that reason, the concept of childhood represented by the kindergarten program at the settlements was probably one of the most modern notions that the settlement teachers brought to the region. The similarities in the goals of the kindergarten and the social settlement were so similar that Nina Vandewalker said "the settlement has often been referred to as a kindergarten for adults" (Vandewalker, 1908).

Both the kindergarten movement and the social settlement movement resulted from a spiritual enlightenment that had its origin in Europe. They both proclaimed a kind of "new gospel"— that of man as a creative being, and both saw education as a process of development. Therefore, Pettit's and Stone's emphasis on the importance of the "play life" of the child was not a trivial notion; it was the crucial first step in the philosophy of Friedrich Froebel, who saw "education as a continuation of the world's unceasing evolution on the level of consciousness, with the child's play being the first signs of life's urge toward purposeful activity" (Froebel, 1887).

Not only were flights of fantasy forbidden to mountain children, but the presence of toys was a very unusual thing. Although the Presbyterian Sunday School had distributed some dolls in the region prior to the settlement of 1899, Pettit says "the dolls were never in the arms of the children." In one home where there was a large family of girls, Pettit says they counted six dolls disposed on the wall "cruelly out of reach of the children." "The dolls were objects of beauty only, not living, breathing, loving babies, to be carefully dressed and cared for and punished" (Pettit, 1901).

However, securing the mountain child with a play life was only a step in Pettit's and Stone's attempts to foster some kind of spiritual activity for the children. For not only were children expected to behave like adults, in many cases they were allowed the same privileges that are usually confined to the adult world.

In Appalachia, the children "were allowed the use of tobacco as soon as they could walk and talk" (author unknown, 1899), and their indulgences in alcoholic beverages often had devastating consequences. Pettit says one young boy, about twelve years old, came to borrow a book from the circulation library. "He had a lame hand, with the bullet showing plainly in his wrist where he had shot himself while he was drunk"

(Pettit, 1901). While the settlement teachers used temperance pledges and/or the "love of God" to encourage the children to relinquish these negative habits, their work with the mothers was also an essential part of the process.

In "Let Us Live with Our Children: Kindergarten Movements in Germany and the United States, 1840-1911," Ann Taylor Allen says one of the reasons that the kindergarten flourished more in the United States during its early years than it did in Froebel's native Germany, was the difference in the conservative and liberal political traditions of the two countries. Allen uses German sociologist Ralf Dahrendorf's work to substantiate her findings. Darhendorf relates public/private boundaries to conservative and liberal political traditions. He lists Germany as one the conservative societies because it promoted the private or inward-turning virtues, such as piety, profundity, and a strict maintenance of public and private boundaries. The United States is included in the liberal list of countries because it promotes the public virtues of sociability, good citizenship, and political responsibility. Because cultural definitions of the private sphere during the nineteenth-century were assigned to women and children, the kindergarten movement, which was an attempt to join the private with the public, was much too liberal for Germany during that time period. Allen says, "the kindergarten movement, which in both Germany and America was often led by women, exemplified a major theme of nineteenth-century feminism: an attempt to redefine public/private boundaries that, as interpreted by patriarchal culture, condemned both women and children to confinement and subjection (Allen).

Even though Pettit and Stone came from the Bluegrass section of Kentucky, there is little doubt that the society they came from was male dominated. Coming from the upper/middle class, however, provided them with freedoms that did not exist for many women during that time. In Appalachia, they found a patriarchal culture that was in many ways distinct from their own. As Pettit writes:

> It is the deplorable condition of the women that appeals so strongly to me. Their condition is truly wretched. The domestic life of the mountaineer is crude. They know absolutely nothing of decent living. How can they when the women who should be fitted for housekeepers and homemakers are doing the work of men, who think their duty consists in hunting, fishing, and sitting on the fence talking politics. While the women hurriedly cook their meals and spend the rest of the time in cultivating crops, building fences, milking cows.... Many of the country women marry, have real large families and die without ever having the diversion of a visit to the little

village of their county. The poor unfortunates who have not even this one opportunity must spend their lives, as Miss Henderson down on Laurel Fork told us, "jest bummin' around among their folks" (Pettit, 1899).

When the mountain women brought their children to the kindergarten classes at the settlement, it was a policy of the settlement to involve them in classes also. Teaching the women home improvement through sewing, cooking, weaving or grooming was the way of the settlement to supplement rather than to supplant the family's role and to further integrate the individual into society. Realizing the rigid restraints of their gender and their "fotched-on" (or outsiders') role in Appalachia, one has to appreciate Pettit and Stone's rather daring attempts to uplift the role of both women and children in Appalachia. In the following passage, Pettit describes one of the daily ways that the settlement women attempted to uplift the woman's role:

> The people were unusually kind to us. Mr. Sam Kilgore, one of the lawyers, sent a cow for us to use. Monroe Maggard, our hired boy, said that he could not milk, that boys and men did not milk in the mountains. But we did not intend to set any such example to the women, so, we told Monroe that he must learn and then undertook to teach him. At first the cow refused to let the boy milk her, but we all gathered around her and kept her in place, while Monroe learned. One had to keep the flies from her head, one hold the bucket, while the boy milked. In a short while, he could milk alone, but he never was a success and whenever we wanted an extra supply of milk, Arminta, the hired girl, would help him. Many people from the country would look on in amazement to see a boy milk and were much more surprised when we told them that the men did the milking in the level country and that women did not work in the field. (We finally had to put a skirt on the boy to fool the cow.) (Pettit, 1900.)

So, while David Whisnant has revealed some of the cultural losses that the mountaineer incurred through the process of schooling, one can see by these brief examples that Whisnant's work does not tell the whole story. The work that Katherine Pettit and May Stone carried on with the women and children in Appalachia should certainly be recognized as cultural gains. Whisnant appears to hold a rather mixed kind of view; for in one sense, he sees the culture as something static, and, at the same time, he dreams of change. *All That is Native and Fine* may be limited because it is written from a male's point of view: a view that looks for the "big happenings" or "great events," and underestimates the amazing transformations that a group of women can make with the subtleties of a pen or needle.

Works Cited

Allen, Ann Taylor. 1988. "Let Us Live With Our Children: Kindergarten Movement in Germany and the United States, 1840-1911." *History of Education Quarterly:* Spring 1988, 24.

Author Unknown. "Camp Cedar Grove Summer 1899." Hindman Settlement School Archives. Hindman, Kentucky, 6.

Bush, Mrs. Lorain B. 1919. "Child Labor." *Child Welfare in Kentucky.* New York: The National Child Labor Committee, 200.

Cremin, Lawrence A. 1976. *Traditions of American Education.* New York: Basic Books, 36-37.

Froebel, Friedrich. 1887. *The Education of Man.* Trans. W.N. Hailmann. New York: D. Appleton, 35.

Kett, Joseph. 1977. *Rites of Passage.* New York: Basic Books, 245.

Pettit, Katherine. 1900. "Camp Sassafras." 1900 Hindman Settlement School Archives. Hindman, Kentucky, 20, 54.

Pettit, Katherine. 1901. "Camp Sassafras." 1901 Hindman Settlement School Archives. Hindman, Kentucky, 11, 25.

Stone, May. 1901. "Camp Sassafras." 1901 Hindman Settlement School Archives. Hindman, Kentucky, 76.

Vandewalker, Nina C. 1908. *The Kindergarten in American Education.* New York: MacMillian, 38.

Whisnant, David E. 1983. *All That is Native and Fine: The Politics of Culture in an American Region.* Chapel Hill: The University of North Carolina Press, 15, 48.

Rhonda England is adjunct professor at Eastern (Central) University, Richmond, Kentucky, and part-time English faculty at Lexington Community College. She is a doctoral candidate at the University of Kentucky, writing a dissertation on Katherine Pettit, May Stone and Elizabeth Watts at Hindman Settlement School, 1899-1956.

Four Perspectives on Appalachian Culture and Poverty

Roger A. Lohmann

Poverty in The Appalachian Context

Poverty is as closely associated with the Appalachian region as coal mining and the hammer dulcimer. Appalachian poverty has seldom been portrayed simply as poverty, but as the expression and symbol of something larger. Images of poverty—poorly dressed, sooty, emaciated, barefooted, mostly white, rural children and adults beside cabin porches—are as closely associated with Appalachia as cowboy hats with the West or moss-covered trees and white-columned mansions with the Old South.

Buried deeply beneath the images and stereotypes, the realities of poverty in the Appalachian region have changed greatly in the past 25 years. Yet our views of poverty have remained remarkably stagnant during that period. Such a situation might be tolerable if there were evidence of the continuing decline—and eventual disappearance of poverty as a major fact of life in the region. Current data suggest a quite different picture, however. Poverty rates in Central Appalachia remain nearly twice the national average (Tickamyer and Tickamyer, 1987). The collapse of employment in the steel industry has been added to the earlier decline of mining employment to make the problem of structual unemployment a region-wide phenomenon. Further, recent indications are that the situation for poor children in Appalachia may have gotten significantly worse during the 1980s, after nearly two decades of gradual improvement (West Virginia Human Resources Assn., 1988).

An electronic media wag on one of the all-news channels suggested (in 1988) that nobody believed theories of poverty anymore—not even the theorists who had developed them. This statement may represent a slight exaggeration—academic theorists are generally quite reluctant to give up on their favorite theories. It does not, however, adequately convey the present overall lack of enthusiasm with theories and explanations of poverty.

While we have recently been subjected to a number of laser-like penetrating insights into contemporary poverty, summed up by terms such as "new poor," "near poor," "feminization," "urban underclass," "rural ghetto" and "deindustrialization," nothing like the sustained interest of two decades ago in theorizing about (or, even thinking about) poverty appears to be evident at present. And no single theoretical approach or perspective seems capable of provoking much reaction. Even the seemingly heretical view that federal programs are the ultimate causes of poverty draws largely a yawn from most of the academic community.

Such lack of interest is particularly true with respect to poverty in Appalachia. With the notable exception of poverty among the elderly, most of the poverty-related problems which attracted significant attention in the 1960s are more or less as serious in the 1980s, while some new forms of poverty have emerged alongside the older forms. Yet, nothing like the sustained interest of that earlier time can be found today. Two decades of energy crisis, federal deficits, social program cutbacks, accountability, and privatization has had remarkably little impact on the remaining poverty problems in Appalachia. Mine and factory closings have made problems worse; inadequate public benefits, occasional new industries, and outmigration have, each in its own way, acted to lessen the severity of problems without ever offering a realistic hope to completely eliminate them.

One of the things which is most needed, at present, is renewed discussion and debate over the nature and circumstances of poverty in Appalachia. First and foremost, researchers and scholars with interests in the Appalachian region need to recognize the continued existence of poverty as an important economic, political, and social fact of life. One way to begin refocusing our attention on the phenomenon of poverty in the region, is to begin where we left off: to reexamine some of the thrusts and foci of previous research and writing on Appalachian poverty.

In the most general terms, there are probably four identifiable positions on poverty in Appalachia which have impacted most directly upon issues of public policy and community life in the region. These four positions, outlined in Table 1, can be termed: Bureaucratic Realism, Appalachian Culturalism, Predatory Capitalism, and Domestic Colonialism. It is possible to begin with any of these four dramatically different world-views on Appalachia and to reach startlingly different conclusions regarding the problem of poverty in the region. Like the television commentator cited above, however, each of these perspectives rings somewhat hollow in the world of the 1990s.

We shall briefly examine each of them in turn:

Bureaucratic Realism

This is a view of the Appalachian region shared by most federal and state public agencies, including the Appalachian Regional Commission and the state government departments which administer the categorical aid programs for the eligible poor. From this vantage point, the Appalachian Region is a congressionally defined, 12 state, multi-jurisdictional, administrative district characterized chiefly by a number of inter-related social and economic problems, the solutions of which are important objects of public policy concern. The region as a whole is the administrative domain of a federal agency, the Appalachian Regional Commission, which has ultimate responsibility for the problems of the region.

The lack of employment opportunities for residents of the region is a high priority consideration in any list of such problems (Zeller and Miller, 1968). Economic development, heavily concentrated upon capture of new industries for the jobs and tax revenues they bring, is perhaps the most important proximate objective of recent public policy in the Appalachian region. In bureaucratic realism, the problem of poverty has dissolved into the more general problem of economic underdevelopment.

The sources of this dissolution are not hard to trace. Shortly after its creation in 1965, the Appalachian Regional Commission embarked upon its imaginative, but controversial, regional development strategy, which stressed highway construction and health care facilities as the key elements in the improvement of the economic infrastructure of the region. This strategy still tends to enrage many in the region who see it as a strategy of bringing a distinctive cultural minority into the homogenized middle-class mass, or who feared that "highways in are also highways out" and will contribute further to the depopulation of the region.

To administrative realists, poor people are fairly normal people—clients of public assistance, perhaps distinguishable by their eligibility or "ineligibility." Poverty is an economic condition whose principal characteristic is lack of money. Work is what people must do in order to enjoy a satisfactory quality of life. Unemployment, or underemployment therefore, are the principal proximate causes of poverty.

Above all else, stress upon national public policy and economic development tends to discount most of the unique or distinguishing characteristics of poverty in Appalachia. Poverty is defined in largely statistical terms following standard methods. Orshansky (1966, 1968), Perry (1979), and Tickamyer and Tickamyer (1987) are among the many statistical studies of poverty in the region. Poverty may exist in the region in greater numbers and proportions, but the essential characteristics of Appalachian poverty are not seen as fundamentally different from poverty elsewhere.

Traditionally, bureaucratic realism has been built for the past two decades upon a two-fold strategy against poverty in the region: On the one hand, reliance upon the same programs and services found elsewhere in the U.S., and, on the other hand, the Appalachian Regional Commission "growth centers" strategy in which health and other services are concentrated in areas with high growth potential while highway development provide egress to these areas from more isolated pockets of poverty. (U.S. News and World Report, September 27, 1965; WVGOECD, 1980; WVGOECD, 1983). Largely because of this continuing Appalachian Regional Commission strategy, community-level economic development remains as the preferred anti-poverty strategy of bureaucratic realism in the 1970s and 1980s. (Whitman, 1986; Trent, Weigand and Smith, 1985; Blair, 1973; McNeill and Miller, 1971). Grave doubts continue, however, about the efficacy of bureaucratic realism as an anti-poverty strategy.

Appalachian Culturalism

One of the sources of those doubts is a view of poverty which is grounded in a social outlook on the region which can be termed "Appalachian Culturalism," and which tends to stress the uniqueness of beliefs, attitudes, and folkways in the region as important factors in understanding poverty. At least since the time of the local colort writers of the 19th Century, and probably well before, there has been a conception of the Appalachian region as a place apart in which ways of life unique and distinct from those known by most Americans existed. Whether in the form of pop-culture stereotypes like Lil Abner and Snuffy Smith, or in serious scholarly studies of Appalachian values, or Appalachian arts and crafts, the sense of a unique and cherished cultural heritage has been encouraged and promoted. One of the defining characteristics of this strange place is the acceptance of subsistence life styles and high levels of poverty as normal or characteristic.

From this vantage point, Appalachia as a cultural unity is not in any fundamental sense the large region associated with the federal administrative district served by Appalachian Regional Commission, but a much smaller area composed of parts of western North and South Carolina, eastern Tennessee and Kentucky and most of southern West Virginia. (Approximately this same area is known in the Appalachian Regional Commission argot as "Central Appalachia.")

Weller (1965) identified a long list of traits which he says define Appalachian culture. Probably the most important for an understanding of the Appalachian poor is the sense of resignation and fatalism. Irelan (1966) summarized studies of social attitudes, family patterns, education levels, health, and consumer practices among the poor in Appalachia and other "subcultures." Dial (undated) has discussed the uniqueness of Appalachian language, and Coles (1971) has discussed distinctive Appalachian child-rearing practices.

In its more romantic strains, Appalachian culturalism is prone to view work as passé in the world of the hollows, where people survive by hunting, fishing, gardening, and collecting welfare. As with other cases of romantic poverty in distant, remote and picturesque places, poverty may not be viewed as quite so negative because it is part of a traditional way of life.

As one source puts it:

> Thus, the mountaineer appears to be at variance with the standardized image of the American in everyday life. Consequently, he is accused of possessing negative attitudes, of being a defeatist, of having an inferiority complex, and of lacking appreciation for education. His lack of social skills in modern social situations is dubbed by some as having a "backwoods flavor." His inability to follow expected behavior patterns in group situations is assigned to what some call "rural values." (Zeller and Miller, 1968.)

Appalachia, it is often said, was a region settled by rugged individualists, more interested in "their own private little worlds" than in any large-scale plans for society or the state (Zeller and Miller, 1968).

This view of Appalachian uniqueness as an indigenous cultural product has not been entirely unchallenged. While others have viewed the region as a distinct subculture within contemporary American life, Shapiro (1980) views "the myth of Appalachia" as largely a fabrication of journalists and intellectuals which began in the colonial era, when the region was the "wild west." It was substantially supplemented by the missionaries and local color writers, who among other things, fostered the arts and crafts movement in the region—thus originating mountain music, quilting, and clogging—some of the more colorful cultural artifacts found in the region.

This view has often been associated with other culture of poverty arguments, for obvious reasons. It is even quite likely that such culture of poverty explanations have been largely discounted as general explanations of poverty in Appalachia. For example, Billings (1974) casts doubt upon the theories of Ford, Weller, Photiadis, et al, that traditional Appalachian culture is a cause of continuing poverty in the region, and suggested that fuller understanding of the causes of poverty in the region would "require a comprehensive social history." It seems likely that Appalachia might better be viewed as a culture of subsistence than a culture of poverty. It is also reasonable that poverty is not an individual, but a family and community concern. Everywhere in the region, localism prevails, with relative indifference to the outside world.

Appalachian culturalism accounts for a large portion of the total research output on poverty-related phenomena in the region. Rebow, Berkman and Kessler (1983) isolated "learned helplessness" as a component of the culture of poverty in Appalachia. Lowndes (1972) examined the impact of mass communications on modernization among the Appalachian poor. Ball (1968) examined Southern Appalachians in what he termed an "analgesic subculture." Peterson, Stivers, and Peters (1986) studied the role of family members and others in the career decisions of low-income Appalachian youth.

Gender is one of the most examined issues in this literature. Thus, Philliber (1982) examines the phenomenon of working wives in relation to low-income status of low-income Appalachian migrants. Kenkel (1980) examines the occupational and marriage plans of low-income high school girls in Appalachia and the Southeast. Hennon and Photiadis (1979) investigated the changing role of rural Appalachian males in low-income family structures.

Predatory Capitalism

Bureaucratic realism and Appalachian culturalism generally fail to capture the sense of frustration and anger among the Appalachian poor and those who speak for them. Others have sought in various ways to get at these questions.

One of these views is the "social control" thesis which posits that the function of public assistance in capitalist society is to regulate the poor and keep them underemployed for the benefit of corporate profits. The most extensive general statement of this view of poverty is by Richard Cloward and Frances Fox Piven in the book *Regulating the Poor* (1971), and a paper presented by them at a conference on public welfare held at West Virginia University in 1971.

Although the paper discusses the Anglo-American public welfare tradition, and makes numerous references to contemporary national issues, it contains no unique or distinct references to the Appalachian region. Piven and Cloward (1972), and Walls (1976), however, applied a similar perspective to the region.

From the vantage point of predatory capitalism, poverty is a necessary precondition of the effective functioning of labor markets in capitalist economies. Succinctly stated, in Appalachia, profits of outside corporations are dependent upon a large, enduring class of workers who are kept unemployed and/or underemployed. Walls (1976), for example, speaks of this as "cultural hegemony and capitalist domination."

Two issues have been particularly important to an understanding of poverty from the viewpoint of predatory capitalism: The declining importance of mining (and more recently, manufacturing) as a source of employment in the region, has resulted in a growing "surplus population" of workers. In addition, ownership of a large percentage of the land in Appalachia is by outside interests (Miller, 1972; Gaventa and Horton, 1982). One of the most persistently heard criticisms of the Appalachian Regional Commission development strategy from this perspective is the view that the principal effect of economic development will be for the natives to become the servants of middle-class retirees and vacationing second-home owners (Whisnant, 1974).

In large measure, predatory capitalism has served the historic mission of giving voice to the alienation and sense of powerlessness often shared by poor and nonpoor alike in the region. At the same time, from this perspective poverty is often reduced to a mere background or preamble concept serving only to introduce other questions. Alas, the essentially sound insight that an understanding of poverty also requires an understanding of the wealthy and powerful, has proven to be the pretext for a generalized loss of interest in the problem of poverty in the region.

Domestic Colonialism

A fourth model is based on an implicit comparison of Appalachia with "underdeveloped" regions in Africa and Asia formerly colonized by European nations. Although this view overlaps to some degree with that of predatory capitalism (e.g., Walls, 1976), the primary emphasis here is generally more political than economic.

In one of the earliest statements of the domestic colonialism view, Friedmann (1966) suggests that comparisons of characteristics common to poor regions and poor nations suggest the existence of a syndrome of collective poverty, but do not support a hypothesis of structural similarities. Kahn (1970) blends aspects of the culturalism and colonialism views in his comparison of rural Appalachian and urban poverty.

Appalachia, he says, is an economic colony, drained of important resources by absentee ownership and political control. Parsons (1969) raised questions about the appropriateness of the comparison with underdeveloped countries as a basis for issues of public policy. Lewis (1978) brings together a variety of perspectives on this issues.

The colonialism model appears to be largely an outgrowth of the experiences of local community organizers in the War on Poverty. Much literature from that period is approached from that standpoint. For example, Bould (1977) argues that rural poverty is a political, as well as an economic, problem.

The domestic colonialism perspective often shares much of the anger and stridency of poverty in the context of an unbroken history of Anglo-American class domination; adherents of this view tend to set issues within a unique regional history of exploitation.

The basic view of domestic colonialism is that Appalachia represents a domestic colony within the United States—with a largely surplus population stockpiled for national emergency purposes, and rich mineral resources exported by outside sources with maximum cost and minimum gain to the state. Unlike any of the other three positions, the domestic colonial view typically links public welfare issues directly with environmental issues (strip mining, air, and water pollution), land ownership, housing, and other issues.

The following excerpt summarizes important aspects of this view:

> Appalachia is America's Third World. The absolute control the coal companies had over people's lives in the old company towns is no more, but the power of absentee corporate owners to affect the economic future of local communities is still massive. The situation is most severe in the coal counties, where half the land surface is corporately owned and 72 percent is absentee-owned. In Logan County, West Virginia, 11 corporations own nearly everything... (*Southern Exposure*, Jan-Feb, 1982, 41).

One of the most basic issues raised by the domestic colonialism model is a definitional one: What exactly is that that is being referred to as poor? The region itself, or a portion of the population within it? Simon, for example, focuses on the region in his contrast of domestic colonialism with what he calls the "uneven development" model (1981). The question, then, which is begged by domestic colonialism is one very comparable to that raised by Appalachian cultures: Is the experience of poor persons in Appalachia in any way different than that of being poor elsewhere in American society?

Universes of Discourse and Poverty

The essential differences between these four perspectives are less a matter of rival hypotheses about the nature and causes of poverty than a matter of the different universes of discourse with which they are anchored. Without remarking at all on the truth or values of the statements produced in these perspectives, we can make some observations about each perspective solely as a system of terms. For example, the language of bureaucratic realism is primarily the language of policy analysis, with heavy accents of political and economic utilitarianism and individualism. In general, the language of bureaucratic realism tends to rationalize poverty into a series of negative strategic choices that tend to infuriate Appalachian culturalists in particular. "Unemployed? Then move where the jobs are!" and so forth. Statements of Appalachian culturalism are often spoken in local dialects of the region, with heavy reliance upon metaphorical or archaic localisms. Appalachian culturalism often tends to romanticize Appalachian poverty into a developmental experience, moral challenge, or personal and family struggle. The words "poor but happy" come easily in this language. Predatory capitalism, and to a lesser extent, domestic colonialism tend to be built on a substructure of Marxian sociology and critical theory, relying heavily on terms like "alienation," "class," and "exploitation." Such language seems, to many, particularly apt to describe aspects of the localism, Jacksonian populist politics, and tradition of exploitive business practices of the region. At the present time, speakers of these dialects are finding it easy to adopt the term "underclass" as a suitable descriptor of the Appalachian poor.

It is almost as though we were faced with theoretical statements about poverty in English, Swahili, Farsi and Korean. So long as the purpose of statements in these various languages is (as it often may be) to support the general world views of their respective communities, one need feel little discomfort with this state of affairs.

If the problem is defined as one of constructing a coherent general theory of poverty in Appalachia, however, quite a different problem arises. Before we can possibly compare or evaluate these four perspectives on Appalachian poverty in any great depth, it would be desirable to translate them into a single language. Except that, in this case, there is no apparently neutral fifth language into which to translate statements about Appalachian poverty. Thus, the challenge of furthering general understanding of Appalachian poverty at present may well boil down to translation of the key insights of each perspective into the theoretical languages of the other perspectives. Some of this translation happens already on a more or less ad hoc basis. One commonly hears references to "empowerment" scattered among statements of bureaucratic realism and Appalachian culturalism, for example. And, at least for a time, the term "underclass" may well permeate all four perspectives.

Conclusions

What is needed at the present time is yet another "rediscovery" of poverty in Appalachia. A contemporary rediscovery of Appalachian poverty has not one, but four, rich traditions of research and inquiry with which to work. Each of these perspectives has its strengths and weaknesses. These perspectives are, however, as a group somewhat dated and out of touch with the realities of poverty in the region in the late 1980s. The simplistic division of the region into Northern, Central, and Southern Appalachia by the bureaucratic realists of Appalachian Regional Commission, for example, fails to deal adequately with the essential social, economic, and political boundaries within the region. However, the tendency of the Appalachian culturalists to deal only with the Central subregion as *the* real Appalachia is similarly limited. Both might well benefit from the much more refined subregions offered by the Economic Research Service Population Section in the U.S. Department of Agriculture which divides the counties of Appalachia into at least five separate subregions.

The rediscovery of poverty in Appalachia should seek a more balanced view of the continuing political, economic, and social phenomena of poverty in the region and in the nation than that offered by any of the four past perspectives. Future studies of Appalachian poverty should take into account such factors as regional urbanization and deindustrialization, and the impact of recent national trends such as rural poverty, deinstitutionalization, growing homelessness, and the feminization and racialization of poverty. Such approaches are likely, of necessity, to touch upon many of the themes most central to each of the four perspectives.

One of the most important themes for contemporary research on poverty is likely to be the convergence of the Appalachian poor into the mainstreams of poverty in the U.S. In the past twenty years, the Appalachian Regional Commission growth centers strategy appears to have brought a clustering of populations—poor and nonpoor alike—into the cities of the region. As a result, it is quite likely that both the urban Appalachian poor and the rural poor left behind are much more like urban and rural poor of the rest of the country than they were twenty years ago. In this context, family breakup may be as important a factor in Appalachian poverty as in mainstream America (Pierce, 1978). Similarly, deinstitutionalization, deindustrialization, urbanization, and an increasingly ancient housing stock have all contributed to the phenomenon of homelessness in the region as they have elsewhere.

This convergence thesis is likely to be closely associated with the perspectives of bureaucratic realism. Acceptance of such convergence arguments should not necessarily be equated with rejection of culture of poverty explanations of the causes of poverty. There is still a role for studies of the family structure and other subcultural characteristics of the Appalachian poor. Such foci need not dwell exclusively on the poor, however. There is probably still merit in Weller's (1967) question asked in the title of an article in Volume 1 of *Appalachian Review*: "Who is the Target Group?" (of research and intervention)? His recommendation in that article was to concentrate upon studying wealthy industrialists and economically secure residents of the region to gain a more complete picture of the problem of poverty in Appalachia. In many cases, studies of small town businessmen, politicians, social welfare professionals and other "middlemen" would prove equally rewarding.

Nor should one ignore or reject the insights possible with the Predatory Capitalist and Domestic Colonial approaches. The Appalachian land ownership study (Gaventa and Horton, 1982), as well as recent indictments of local officials in a southern West Virginia county, shows that there is still merit in such approaches in a region where economic exploitation and political corruption remain important realities bearing upon the condition of the poor.

The cleavages in ideology, politics, and world views which are behind the four viewpoints on Appalachian poverty identified in this paper, remain strong within the region and the scholarly community today. Thus, it is probably naive to argue for any theoretical or research convergence among them. It is not naive, however, to suggest that each of these perspectives is a bit dated and showing signs of age due to the general neglect of any research interest in Appalachian poverty in recent years. Yet, each points to important research questions which have gone uninvestigated and to hypotheses which have gone untested. At the same time, none deals adequately with the "new poverty" which has arisen in the region and the nation. All things considered, therefore, the time has come to reopen serious study of Appalachian poverty.

Table 1
Four Perspectives on Appalachian Culture and Poverty

APPALACHIAN PEOPLE ARE

	Typically American	Culturally Unique
The Poor Are:		
Disadvantaged	Administrative Realism	Appalachian Culturalism
Oppressed/ Exploited	Predatory Capitalism	Domestic Colonialism

Works Cited

Austin, Richard C. 1967. "A Search for Appalachian People." In *Parish Studies*. San Francisco, Ca.: San Francisco Theological Seminary.

Ball, Richard A. 1968. "A Poverty Case: The Analgesic Subculture of the Southern Appalachians." *American Sociological Review* 33: 6, 884-894.

Bassett, Jeffrey E. 1973. *Regional Delineation of Poverty Levels in Appalachia*. Thesis. Lexington, Ky: University of Kentucky.

Billings, Dwight. 1974. "Culture and Poverty in Appalachia: A Theoretical Discussion and Empirical Analysis." *Social Forces* 53: 2, 315-232.

Blair, John P. 1973. "A Review of the Filtering Down Theory." *Urban Affairs Quarterly* 8: 3, 303-316.

Bould, Sally. 1977. "Rural Poverty and Economic Development: Lessons from the War on Poverty." *Journal of Applied Behavioral Science* 13: 471-488.

Clarkson, Ray B. 1964. *Tumult on the Mountains—Lumbering in West Virginia, 1770-1920*. Parsons, WV: McClain Publishing Co.

Coles, Robert. 1971. *Migrants, Sharecroppers and Mountaineers*. Boston: Little, Brown & Co.

Cloward, Richard and Frances Fox Piven. 1971. *Regulating the Poor*. New York: Free Press.

Dial, Wylene. "Appalachian Culture" (mimeo)

Eller, Robert D. 1982. *Miners, Millhands and Mountaineers: Industrialization of the Appalachian South, 1880-1930*. Knoxville: University of Tennessee Press.

Fenton, John H. 1957. *Politics in the Borders States*. New Orleans: Hauser Publishing.

Friedmann, John R. 1966. "Poor Regions and Poor Nations: Perspectives on the Problem of Appalachia." *Southern Economic Journal* 32: 465-477.

Gaventa, John. 1980. *Power and Powerlessness: Quiescence and Rebellion in an Appalachian Valley*. Hagerstown MD: University of Illinois Press.

Gaventa, John and Bill Horton. 1982. "Who Owns Appalachia? Digging the Facts." *Southern Exposure*. January-February, 34-35.

Harrington, Michael. 1984. *The New American Poverty*. New York: Macmillan.

Hennon, Charles B. and John Photiadis. 1979. "The Rural Appalachian Low-Income Male: Changing Role in a Changing Family." *The Family Coordinator* 28: 4, 608-615.

Irelan, Lola M. 1966. Low Income Life Styles. Washington: U.S. Welfare Administration. Washington D.C.

Kahn, Si. 1970. "New Strategies for Appalachia." *New South* 25: Summer, 57-64.

Kenkel, William F. 1980. "Occupational Saliency and Age at Marriage Plans of Low Income High School Girls." *Sociological Forum* 3: Fall, 62-74.

Lewis, Helen. 1978. *Colonialism in Modern America: The Appalachian Case*. Boone, N.C.: Appalachian Consortium Press.

Miernyk, William. 1982. "The West Virginia Economy." Prepared for the West Virginia Legislative Tax Study Commission (mimeo).

Miller, Tom D. 1982. "Who Owns West Virginia?" Huntington, WV: series of newspaper articles (paperbound, undated).

Orshansky, Mollie. 1968. "Shape of Poverty in 1966." Washington: *Social Security Bulletin* 31: March 1968, 3-32.

Parsons, Kenneth H. 1969 "Poverty as an Issue in Development Policy: A Comparison of United States and Underdeveloped Countries." *Land Economics* 45: February, 52-65.

Perry Charles, S. 1979. "Income and Poverty in Kentucky, 1959-1976: A Comparative County-Level Analysis." Paper presented to the Rural Sociological Society, Lexington, KY.

Peterson, Gary W., Mary E. Stivers and David F. Peters. 1986. "Family Verses Nonfamily Significant Others for the Careet Decisions of Low-Income Youth." *Family Relations* 35: 3, 417-424.

Philliber, William W. 1982. "Wife's Absence from the Labor Force and Low Income Among Appalachian Migrants." *Rural Sociolgy* 47: 4, 705-710.

Photiadis, John D. 1970. "The Economy and Attitudes Toward Government in Appalachia." John Photiadis and Harry Schwartzweller, eds. *Change in Rural Appalachia: Implications for Action Programs.* Philadelphia: University of Pennsylvania Press, 115-127.

Piven, Frances Fox and Richard Cloward. 1972. "Enforcing Low Wage Work: Administrative Methods." *Public Welfare...Right or Privilege: System Under Attack.* Wil J. Smith and Frederick, eds. Morgantown, W.Va: West Virginia University, Office of Research and Development, 24-54.

Pierce, Diana. 1978. "The Feminization of Poverty: Women, Work and Welfare." *Urban and Social Change Review* 11: 28-36.

Pierce, Neil. 1975. "West Virginia: The Saddest State." *The Border South States.* New York: W.W. Norton.

Rabow, Jerome, Sherry L. Berkman and Ronald Kessler. 1983. "The Culture of Poverty and Learned Helplessness: A Social Psychological Perspective." *Sociological Inquiry* 53: 4, 419-434.

Rosenberg, Bernard and Joseph Bensman. 1968. "Sexual Patterns in Three Ethnic Subcultures of an American Underclass." *Annals of the American Academy of Political and Social Science* 376: 61-75.

Shapiro, Henry O. 1978. *Appalachia On Our Mind: The Southern Mountains and Mountaineers in the American Conciousness: 1870-1920.* Chapel Hill, N.C.: University of North Carolina Press.

Simon, Richard. 1981. "Uneven Development and the Case of West Viriginia: Going Beyond the Colonialism Model." *Appalachian Journal* 8: 3, 165-186.

Smith, Wil J., ed. 1971. *Critical Issues in Public Finance in an Underdeveloped Region.* Morgantown, W.Va.: West Virginia University, Office of Research and Development.

Stephens, L.F. 1972. "Media Exposure and Modernization among the Appalachian Poor." *Journalism Quarterly* 49: 2, 247-257.

Tickamyer, Ann R. and Cecil Tickamyer. 1987. *Poverty in Apppalachia*. Appalachian Data Bank Report #5. Lexington, Ky: University of Kentucky, Appalachian Center.

Trent, Roger B., Nancy S. Weigand and Dennis K. Smith. 1985. "Attitudes Toward Development in Three Appalachian Counties." *Rural Sociological Society*.

U.S. News and World Report. 1965. "New Way to Beat Poverty—the Plan for Appalachia." 59: 27 September 1965, 68-70.

U.S. National Advisory Commission on Rural Poverty. 1967. The People Left Behind. *A Report*. Washington D.C.: U.S. Gov. Print. Off.

Walls, David. S. 1976. "Central Appalachia: A Peripheral Region within an Advanced Capitalist Society." *Journal of Sociology and Social Welfare* 4: 2, 232-247.

Weller, Jack. 1967. "Who Is the Target Group?" *Appalachian Review* 1: Winter, 15-20.

Weller, Jack. 1965. *Yesterday's People: Life in Contemporary Appalachia*. Lexington, Ky: Kentucky University Press.

West Virginia Governor's Office of Economic and Community Development. 1980. *State Development Plan*. Charleston, W.Va.

West Virginia Governor's Office of Economic and Community Development. 1983. *State Plan Update*. Charleston, W.Va.

West Virginia Human Resources Association, Inc. 1988. *Children In Crises, State at Risk*. Charleston: HRA.

Whisnant, David E. 1974. "Growing Old by Being Poor: Some Cautionary Notes About Generalizing from a Class Phenomenon." *Soundings* 57: Spring,101-112.

White, David B. 1987. "A Social Epidemiological Model of Central Appalachia." *Arete* 2: 1, 47-66.

White, Theodore. 1960. "The Art of the Primary: Wisconsin and West Virginia." *The Making of the President-1960*. New York: Atheneum Press, 93-138.

Whitman, Gloria. 1968. "Economic Development." *Trends in Human Services*. Kevin Meeghan, Roger Lohmann and Barry Locke, eds. Morgantown, W.Va: West Virginia University School of Social Work.

Wilensky, Harold and Charles LeBeaux. 1965. *Industrial Society and Social Welfare*. New York: Free Press.

Zeller, Fred and Robert Miller. 1969. *Manpower Development in West Virginia*. Morgantown, W.Va: West Virginia University.

Roger A. Lohmann is professor of social work at West Virginia University. He has long had an interest in rural poverty.

Organized Medicine and the U.M.W.A. Welfare and Retirement Fund: An Appalachian Perspective on a National Conflict

Richard P. Mulcahy

Introduction

Recently, the *New England Journal of Medicine* editorialized that if health care in the United States was to remain accessible for most Americans, some sort of national health insurance scheme had to be created. The significance of such a statement being printed in such a respected medical journal cannot be underestimated. Although publications like the *New England Journal of Medicine, The Journal of the American Medical Association,* and *The Journal of the American College of Surgeons* are noted for their contributions to advancing medical science, they have also served as forums for writers interested in medical politics. In their turn, each of these publications, in addition to those sponsored by state and county medical societies, have continuously published articles which opposed socialized medicine, closed panel practice, third party medicine, and have promoted free choice of physician, and fee-for-service payment.

The terms listed here comprise the basic working vocabulary used in discussing medical policy, and have served as rallying cries for people concerned about the issue. In general, free choice of physician and fee-for-service payment has been the method of operation for most physicians in the U. S. It means that any licensed physician is regarded as competent to practice medicine in all of its branches, unless proven otherwise by his peers, and that a patient is free to choose among various physicians available for any treatment needed. A medical third party refers to any group or individual who pays the patient's medical bills, and thereby acts as a third party between a doctor and the patient. Closed panel practice refers to an organizational method used by some medical third parties that limits participation in the program to a group of selected doctors. Designed to restrict a program's medical costs, it automatically limits the patient's free choice of physician.

According to its critics, closed panel organization reduces the quality of care a patient receives, since the participating physicians do not face the pressure of free competition to maintain high standards of professional competence. This same reasoning also serves as the principle rationalization for opposition to socialized medicine by the medical profession. Proponents of closed panel argue, conversely, that restriction of care does not significantly reduce a patient's free choice. Under closed panel, a patient can choose from a group of physicians who have been proven to be honest and highly competent.

During the 1950s, this argument became *the* central point of a struggle between organized medicine, the American Medical Association and its various state and county medical societies, and the United Mine Workers of American Welfare and Retirement Fund. Because of its experience as a medical third party, the Fund adopted closed panel organization, which earned it the A.M.A.'s formal condemnation in 1958. Nevertheless, a large minority movement within the A.M.A. opposed the policies of the Association and believed that the actions of the Fund were justified. Because the A.M.A. was basically the sum total of its parts, much of the controversy is fought out on the state level. The central question of this paper was whether organized medicine in Appalachia behaved in a manner which was appreciably different from the A.M.A. and other state societies outside of the region.

From its inception the Fund has been surrounded by controversy. John L. Lewis began demanding the creation of a miners' health and welfare program in 1938, after the larger questions of union recognition, wages, and hours had been settled. It must be remembered that in addition to his duties as President of the United Mine Workers of America, Lewis was serving as Chairman of the Congress of Industrial Organizations, which he had founded. At the time, the C.I.O. had just won important organizing victories in such basic industries as rubber, steel, automobile, and electrical manufacturing, all of which had successfully resisted unionization in the past. Confident of the U.M.W.A.'s position within the coal industry, Lewis now decided that the time was right to demand the creation of a fund.

The plan Lewis envisioned was to be administered by the U.M.W.A. and was to be financed through a tonnage royalty assessed on all coal mined for sale or use, without any deductions from the earnings of union miners (Dubofsky and VanTine, 1977). Lewis's demand was radical for two reasons. First, all other union health plans had been based, at least in part, on contributions from the membership. Second, all hospitalization and medical schemes in existence in the coal industry at the time were controlled by the mine operators.

These plans fell into two categories: hospitalization and office care, and were funded through wage deductions known as "check-offs." Taken as a whole, these plans were thoroughly inadequate to meet miner health needs. In general, the hospitalization plans did not cover treatment for tuberculosis, a common disease among miners, obstetrical services, nor treatment for venereal disease (Wysang and Williams, 1981). Office care plans were little better. Usually office care was provided by a single physician who served as the "company doctor." His practice consisted of the miners and their families only, and he was paid through the check-off. The treatment limitations listed above for the hospitalization plans generally applied to treatment given by the company doctor as well, and the treatment tended to be low quality. The causes for this problem varied. Although some physicians were underqualified to perform all of the treatment their patients needed, there was a consistent problem of check-off practices being filled by individuals who suffered from alcohol or drug abuse (Kerr, 1988).[1]

The creation of a welfare fund administered through the U.M.W.A. meant the end of these check-off arrangements, and the loss of one area of control which the operators had over their employees. Because of this fact, and the costs involved in financing such a program through a tonnage royalty they would have to pay, coal operators vehemently opposed the idea, and managed to delay its creation until after the end of World War II. In 1946, however, Lewis managed to force the Fund's creation by calling the union's membership out of the mines just at the time when the U.S. government was reconverting to a peace-time economy. Because coal stockpiles were low, the strike threatened to derail the reconversion plans. Unable to break the strike, the Truman administration invoked the War Labor Disputes Act, seized the mines from the operators, and negotiated directly with Lewis. Acting for the operators, Secretary of the Interior Julius A. Krug agreed to Lewis's demand for a fund's creation, and provision for it was made in the national contract Lewis and Krug signed on May 26, 1946.[2]

Although the Fund was a reality, it did not begin full operations as a medical care program until January, 1948. Part of the problem was that the overall performance of the Fund was hampered by a struggle for its control between Lewis and the coal operators. Lewis eventually won the conflict, but not until 1950. Another source of delay concerned the man who Lewis originally appointed as the medical director of the Fund, Dr.

Royd R. Sayers. For most of his professional life, Sayers had worked within the medical section of the U.S. Bureau of Mines, and eventually became the director of the Bureau. Noted for his pro-union sentiments, Sayers had done extensive research on ventilation and carbon monoxide poisoning, which later formed the design basis for the air circulation system in the Holland Tunnel (U.M.W. Journal, 1947). Despite Sayers' qualifications, he became unacceptable to members of the Fund's staff, in particular Josephine Roche.

At the time when Sayers was appointed in 1947, Roche was serving as the assistant director of the Fund. From there, she would eventually rise to the directorship and become a member of the Board of Trustees. The reason for Roche's rapid promotion was her close relationship with John L. Lewis. This connection began when Roche inherited the Rocky Mountain Fuel Company from her father in 1927. Because of her liberal sentiments, Roche signed a contract with the U.M.W.A. a year later, and was the first major coal operator west of the Mississippi to do so.[3] From that year forward, Roche established a close working relationship with Lewis, and served as his principle advisor in all matters.

Roche's objection to Sayers centered upon Sayers' original plan on how to implement the health care program of the Fund. Instead of developing an integrated system, Sayers wished to establish separate health care plans for each district of the union.[4] The plan envisioned the Fund acting as a health services payer, while allowing county and state level medical societies affiliated with the A.M.A. to set prices, treatment standards, and participation rules. Roche claimed that the plan was too expensive and would prevent the Fund from establishing its pension system. From Roche's point of view, Sayers conceded too much authority to organized medicine, which she regarded with suspicion as overly conservative.[5]

Roche's opinions concerning the A.M.A. probably arose out of her experience as an Assistant Secretary of the Treasury during the New Deal. While serving in this position, Roche oversaw the operation of the United States Public Health Service (Current Biog., 1941). As a rule, organized medicine was antagonistic to the U.S.P.H.S. and to health insurance systems such as Blue Cross/Blue Shield. Referred to as "Medical Third Parties" by physicians, doctors resented the systems as intruders into the private relationship between physician and patient. In addition, physicians feared that the use of third party payers distributed accepted health care arrangements and could eventually lead to socialized medicine. For most doctors, the only acceptable method of health care delivery was free choice of physician by the patient and payment on a fee-for-service basis. Any deviation from these methods was to be condemned.

Due to Roche's dissatisfaction with Sayers' plan, Sayers was eventually moved out as the chief medical officer of the Fund, and eventually off the medical staff itself (Kerr, 1988). To replace Sayers, the Fund hired Dr. Warren F. Draper. For most of his career, Draper had worked in public medicine. During the New Deal he served the U.S.P.H.S.'s chief medical officer, and had worked with Roche. With the outbreak of the Second World War, Draper was promoted to Deputy Surgeon General of the U.S. Army, where he was assigned to work at Supreme Headquarters Allied Expeditionary Forces under Eisenhower (Kerr, 1988; Ploss, 1981). Regardless of Draper's qualifications, members of the staff were uneasy at first about his appointment, since Draper appeared to be very conservative. Draper not only was a ranking member of the ruling body of the A.M.A., the House of Delegates, but he also accepted the belief of the Association in free choice of physician and fee-for-service payment as the best method of providing health care (Kerr, 1988). Despite these facts, Draper's career showed that he regarded medicine as a public service instead of a private business, and was flexible in his views. Aside from working for the U.S.P.H.S. for most of his professional life, Draper had been a co-founder and charter member of the A.M.A. Council on Health Care for Industrial Workers, which was established in 1938.[6] Previously, the A.M.A. did not have any sort of official body to address issues concerning industrial health.

Upon becoming the Executive Medical Officer of the Fund in the spring of 1948, Draper devised an integrated health care system to enable the Fund to pursue its work. Under Draper's direction, ten regional medical offices were established in strategic cities in the bituminous coal fields. These cities were Pittsburgh and Johnstown, Pennsylvania; Morgantown, Charleston, and Beckley, West Virginia; Knoxville, Tennessee; Birmingham, Alabama; Louisville, Kentucky; St. Louis, Missouri; and Denver, Colorado. Each office was headed by a physician who served as the Area Medical Administrator, and each had the responsibility of overseeing the medical program of the Fund in each of the respective districts. Through this system, general policies on health care were established at the headquarters of the Fund in Washington D.C. The Area Medical Administrators were, however, allowed wide discretion on how best to fulfill these policies within the local context[7] (Ploss, 1981: 131-135).

By the end of the 1948, the new system was in place and the Fund began its work. Originally, the Fund placed no restriction on what sort of health care it covered, nor on who could participate. In fact, the Fund invited all licensed doctors, including general practitioners, to participate (Wysang and Williams, 1981:8). The only limit placed on the program was a demand that all obstetrical and minor surgical work be done in the hospital instead of the patient's home or doctor's office.[8]

Aside from offering an all-out and unrestricted program, Draper worked to foster good relations between the Fund and organized medicine on both the national and local levels. As a gesture of goodwill, Draper managed to persuade John L. Lewis to discontinue U.M.W.A. support for the establishment of a government supported national health insurance system (Mulcahy, 1988). In addition, Draper appointed Dr. Carl M. Peterson to the Advisory Board of the Fund. At the time, Peterson was Secretary of the A.M.A. Council on Industrial Health, and while concerned about health care needs in basic industry, Peterson was no friend of "state medicine."[9] As a final measure, Draper sponsored the creation of county and state level liaison committees whose members represented the Fund and organized medicine. The purpose of these committees was to ensure cooperation by providing a forum where mutual concerns and conflicts could be discussed and solved. Implicit in Draper's policies was a belief that the medical profession would effectively police itself, and so prevent and discourage any abuse of the Fund.

By the end of 1951, however, it became clear to Draper that the Fund needed to exercise greater control over its program. Although situations and cases varied, the difficulties of the Fund centered around two general categories: overcharging for services, and the rendering of poor treatment by both physicians and hospitals. In the case of individual physicians, the Fund discovered that many doctors were charging inflated fees for common procedures or were giving excessive office care. On the average, a given patient in the early 1950s visited his or her physician three times a year. The Fund's records showed that some beneficiaries were seeing their doctors four times above the yearly average.[10] In addition, some doctors, especially general practitioners, were resorting to surgery far more often than necessary.

Prior to April 1954, 65% of all surgery covered by the Fund was performed by general practitioners at a rate of 76 operations per 1000 beneficiaries.[11] Even more disturbing was the fact the Fund was having problems with poor treatment of workmen's compensation cases, indifference toward beneficiaries by company doctors, and poor hospital care.[12]

Although no one section of the bituminous coal fields had a monopoly on physician fraud or poor practice, the records of the Fund showed that southern Appalachia demonstrated a consistent pattern in this regard. Most of the physicians in those areas were general practitioners, usually in their late fifties, and had been trained in medical schools which had disbanded.[13]

As far as poor hospital care was concerned, southern Appalachia again was the single largest problem area. The cause was that most of the hospitals in the southern section of the region were small, containing 100 beds or less, and worked on a for-profit basis. Usually owned by a single physician, these proprietary hospitals maximized profits by offering low-quality care at an inflated rate[14] (Wysang and Williams, 1981:16). Also, these institutions were generally lacking in terms of staff, modern equipment, sanitation, housekeeping, and specialized facilities.[15]

Similar deficiencies were noted first in a survey which studied medical and living conditions in the bituminous coal fields that had been sponsored by the U.S. Department of the Interior in 1946, when the Fund was established. The project had been overseen by Rear-Admiral Joel T. Boone, surgeon-general of the U.S. Navy, who had been appalled by the findings of the Boone Report.[16] A second survey, directed primarily at viewing hospital conditions in southern Appalachia, was sponsored six years later, in 1952, by the A.M.A. itself. Done in response to allegations from the Fund about poor treatment given to its beneficiaries, the survey demonstrated that conditions had not improved since 1946, nor had the medical staff of the Fund been exaggerating its case. The A.M.A. survey team was so disturbed by what it had seen, and because their findings were so shocking, they wished to keep their report confidential.[17]

In response to the situation, Draper pursued a dual policy of restructuring the program of the Fund while seeking to maintain and broaden the cooperation of organized medicine, especially in Appalachia. As a direct outgrowth of the A.M.A. hospital survey, the Fund sponsored a series of four medical conferences between 1952 and 1956; these included representatives of the Fund and the state level medical societies of the Appalachian region. The first meeting was held in Charleston, West Virginia. The main objectives were to secure a consensus on how to improve medical practice and conditions in the region, and to secure a clear commitment from the state societies that they would discipline unethical members. Unfortunately, no such consensus on either issue was ever formed.

As time progressed, participating state associations, especially Kentucky and Pennsylvania, used the meetings as a forum to air their grievances concerning the policies of the Fund. At the same time, however, some of the most constructive ideas offered at the meeting were made from the representatives from the Tennessee State Medical Association, which was usually represented by Dr. B. M. Overholt. During the first conference, Overholt suggested that organized medicine take an active role in improving the quality of health care in their areas by providing postgraduate training for practicing physicians. Under the scheme Overholt envisioned, the A.M.A. would periodically send instructors into the field to demonstrate new medical techniques to practitioners working in isolated rural areas.[18] Overholt's idea, however, was ignored.

Even more frustrating was that organized medicine on the national and state levels refused to take any decisive action to discipline unethical physicians. Time and again, when Draper raised the issue, the leaders of the medical profession responded that better liaison between the Fund and the profession was the answer to all problems. Yet, it became increasingly apparent to Draper that liaison was not working. Out of the several ethics cases the Fund brought to the A.M.A., only one resulted in disciplinary action, and then only by a letter of censure which was originally intended to remain confidential.[19]

Because of the situation, Draper came to rely solely upon restructuring the program of the Fund as a method to ensure quality and limit costs. Under normal circumstances, Draper would have been concerned about cost containment. But by the early 1950s, the financial position of the Fund demanded that all expenses be limited as far as possible. The cause of the problem had several interrelated sources.

First, between 1949 and 1953, income fell due to a decline in coal demand (National Coal Assoc., 1960: 80). As this happened, the pension program of the Fund was placed under a great strain. As coal demand declined, miners were losing their jobs and an ever-increasing number of the older men who were scheduled to be laid off were now taking early retirement.[20] Because these retirees were leaving the mines at an earlier age than before, their life span increased. Second, by the early 1950s the Fund had committed itself to building chain of hospitals that it planned to operate in south/central Appalachia. Owing to inflation, and the hidden expenses attendant with building a modern health care complex in a comparatively isolated area, the expense of the hospital project rose to twice as much as originally estimated.[21]

To meet the crisis, the Fund began an across-the-board policy of benefit restriction. In the area of health care, the Fund discontinued direct payment for general-practice office treatment and started to require prior approval for certain common surgical procedures, such as tonsillectomies (Kerr, 1988; Wysang and Williams, 1981: 7). Under the new policy, the Fund now covered all hospitalization costs, and all specialist treatment given to its beneficiaries in a hospital, clinic, or office (Kerr, 1988). Also, the Fund began developing usage of payment systems other than fee-for-service. While participating physicians could continue using fee-for-service if they wished, the Fund also began offering payment arrangements based on fee-for-time.

Essentially fee-for-time was a monthly retainer the Fund paid to a participating clinic or physician that based payment on how much work time of a given practice was taken up with treating Fund patients.[22] With this arrangement, the physician or clinic was provided with a guaranteed income, and relieved of the problems of billing the Fund for each individual service rendered. Also, since the payment was guaranteed, the physician or clinic was able to provide the patient with a more thorough form of treatment than what would have been possible under fee-for-service (Durmaskin, et al, 1982: 17). It also should be noted that the retainer system of the Fund was responsible for the establishment of a number of group practice clinics in areas which had been medically under-served in the past (Durmaskin, 1982: 7).

None of these actions were popular with organized medicine. Not only did the A.M.A. frown upon its retainers, but most of its members were disdainful of group practice. Although group practice was officially accepted by the A.M.A. as a legitimate method of offering health care, most of the members refused to accept it. The reason was that a group pooled its income and could offer lower fees. Not only was such behavior regarded as unfair competition, but its cooperative aspect resembled the mentality behind socialized medicine. It is for this reason that members of group practices were generally persecuted by their peers.[23]

Despite this disapproval, neither the early restrictions on the program of the Fund, nor retainers, nor the encouragement of group practice caused an open break between the Fund and organized medicine, either in Appalachia or on the national level. However, two events did eventually lead to just such a breach: the Fund's hospital project and Draper's decision to adopt closed panel organization.

The decision for the Fund to build its own set of hospitals stemmed back to the difficulties that had been reported about the proprietary hospitals in southern Appalachia. Although building a group of hospitals at a time of diminishing income may have appeared as extravagant, the reasoning behind the project was sound. First, when the decision to build the facilities was first made in 1951, the available statistics on coal production had not yet indicated that the industry had entered into a recession. By the time the trend was clearly recognizable, the building program was already in progress and could not be stopped.

Second, the hospitals appeared to be a good long-term investment from the perspectives of cost limitation and quality treatment. Although the Fund paid inflated prices to the physician/operators of the proprietary hospitals, Fund beneficiaries were not receiving quality care. Nor were the operators of these institutions upgrading the quality of their facilities in any meaningful way. According to Draper, continued use of these facilities meant that the Fund was subsidizing low-quality care.[24] Draper was also deeply concerned by the fact that these institutions were usually organized on closed staff basis, and denied visiting staff privileges to all outside practitioners.[25] In such a setting, the A.M.A rule concerning free choice of physician by the patient was effectively denied.

In reaction, Draper gave his support to the Fund building a chain of hospitals which stretched from Eastern Kentucky, through West

Virginia, into Virginia. With these institutions, the Fund could offer better hospital care than previously available, and could reduce its costs since it would no longer be paying the inflated fees charged in the past.

Completed and opened in 1956, the hospital chain worked as a centralized unit under its own distinct administration. Originally headed by Dr. Frederick Mott, the chain's chief administrator was Dr. John Newdorp, who had experience with other miner health needs due to his work in Harlan County, Kentucky, during the 1930s. In order to secure tax-free status for the chain, the hospitals were organized under a non-profit corporation, separate from the Fund, named the Miners Memorial Hospital Association. All of the M.M.H.A. doctors were hired directly by the corporation, were paid on a salary basis, and had been recruited from medical schools across the U.S.[26]

As it was, the M.M.H.A. was a cause of controversy within the Fund itself since some of Draper's area administrators either doubted the wisdom of using a salaried medical staff, or questioned whether or not the hospitals were just an expensive luxury. Another source of trouble within the Fund was the demand made by some of the area administrators that they have the right to review the care given in these hospitals as they did with other participating institutions. The M.M.H.A rejected the claim since it infringed upon the authority of its director. Draper was never able to reconcile this conflict to the satisfaction of either side.[27]

While such infighting hurt the project, the real problem was the unalterable hostility the hospitals encountered from organized medicine in Kentucky. The objections voiced by the various local medical societies in the counties where the hospitals were located, and from the Kentucky State Medical Association itself, ran as follows: The hospitals, with salaried staffs, engaged in unfair competition; salaried staffs restricted free choice of physician for the patient; and the use of the hospitals as teaching institutions placed local practitioners under the stress of having their work watched and criticized.

These claims ignored certain basic facts concerning hospitals and the state of medicine in Kentucky prior to the chain's establishment. The most glaring misstatement was that the hospitals denied physician free choice. In direct contrast to the proprietary hospitals with which the M.M.H.A. now competed, all ten M.M.H.A. hospitals were organized on an open staff basis.[28] Moreover, the ten new hospitals contained the more sophisticated diagnostic and treatment facilities that the proprietary institutions lacked. The K.S.M.A. ignored this fact, nor had it ever raised the free choice issue in relation to the proprietary hospitals. Thus, the complaints made by the branch of organized medicine in Kentucky did not have any standing in fact, and did not reflect a genuine concern for the welfare of the patient. Instead the K.S.M.A. on the state and county levels was behaving like a trade protection society, working for the best business interests of its current membership.

To fight the Fund, the K.S.M.A. county societies used the most potent weapon available to them, they barred the M.M.H.A. doctors from membership. Because the A.M.A. was the sum total of its parts, denial of membership in a county medical society meant that a physician was not a member of the state or national organization.[29] In addition, membership in the A.M.A. was a prerequisite to belonging to any specialist organization, as well as final certification to practice in some states. The M.M.H.A. attempted to fight this unfair practice through the K.S.M.A. appeal procedure, to no avail. Finally, certain M.M.H.A. hospitals retaliated by forming rival county societies in an attempt to force acceptance of M.M.H.A. doctors on the K.S.M.A.[30] According to the K.S.M.A. bylaws, whenever two rival county medical societies existed, it was the responsibility of the state society to bring the two groups together into one organization.[31] Although this solution was creative, the hospital chain did not have the opportunity to pursue it to a conclusion.

Because of a disastrous fall in coal demand which began in 1958, the Fund was forced to sell the chain in 1963. All ten hospitals were eventually purchased by the Board of National Missions of the Presbyterian Church USA. Renamed Appalachian Regional Hospitals, the hospital chain managed to retain most of its staff physicians, and the hospitals were reorganized upon a group practice basis.

While the difficulties of the Fund with the K.S.M.A. centered around the hospital chain, the conflict took place within the wider context of an open breach between the Fund and organized medicine which finally took place between 1955 and 1956. On all levels of the struggle, the general cry was that the Fund was denying its beneficiaries a free choice of physician because of Draper's decision to adopt closed panel practice.

By late 1954, it had become apparent to Draper that the initial restrictions which had been placed upon the medical program of the Fund were not enough to limit excessive costs arising from medical fraud, nor did they appreciably improve the quality of care provided. To deal with the situation in a more effective manner, Draper decided to make the following changes. He ordered that the Fund review all of its participation lists, and that authorization for service by physicians be limited to those areas of medicine in which they were fully qualified. Participation with the Fund now would be limited to those physicians willing to arrange for adequate diagnostic work on an office or outpatient basis. Hospitals were to be reviewed on the basis of quality of treatment, and detailed medical audits would now be required to determine if low quality or unnecessary surgery was being performed.[32]

The results of the changes were encouraging. Prior to the new guidelines, 65% of all Fund covered surgery was performed by general practitioners. Under the new policy the figure declined to 25%, and the number of operations performed per 1,000 beneficiaries had been cut in half.[33] Convinced that he was moving in the right direction, Draper ordered in March, 1955, that the Pittsburgh, Johnston, and Morgantown offices require all doctors to seek specialist consultations prior to hospitalizing Fund beneficiaries.[34] Draper's previous orders had been resented; however, this final decision was too much to be accepted, and the A.M.A. House of Delegates passed a resolution condemning the order in June of the same year. Faced with this opposition, Draper withdrew the order. However, during the June meeting of the House, Draper was approached by representatives of the Medical Society of the State of Pennsylvania.

The M.S.S.P. had vehemently opposed Draper's actions, and had suspended all participation with the Fund.[35] Nevertheless, the M.S.S.P. leadership was anxious to come to an arrangement with Fund, and initiated negotiations for a formal agreement. These discussions were successfully completed in November, 1955. Under the terms of the "Pennsylvania Agreement" the M.S.S.P. agreed to weed out unethical physicians within its ranks, while not conceding that the Fund had the right to judge the quality of a physician's work. The agreement called for all hospitals to form medical audit committees, and endorsed a uniform policy of granting visiting staff privileges to any doctor who sought them. The Fund retained the right to remove any unethical physician from its list, and the agreement even covered how participating practitioners were to be paid. Using a system similar to fee-for-time, the agreement created a "block fee-for-service" based on what percentage of a physician's practice consisted of Fund beneficiaries.

The agreement was hailed as a major achievement, and was published in the May 12, 1956 edition of the *Journal of the American Medical Association.*[36] While avoiding an argument over closed panel, the agreement did commit the M.S.S.P. to actively police its membership. Because of the goodwill the agreement created, other state medical societies were interested in using it as a model to govern their relations with the Fund. Tragically, this goodwill was lost when the M.S.S.P. House of Delegates abruptly voted to abrogate the agreement in October, 1956. The pretext for the action was that the M.S.S.P. Committee on Medical Economics had negotiated the accord without the knowledge of the general membership and had overstepped its authority.

In the midst of the acrimony, Dr. Elmer Hess, the M.S.S.P. president, spoke to the delegates. He told them the agreement had been made in good faith, and that there was no just cause to terminate it. Going further, Hess warned that this action would leave Draper with no other recourse than to adopt closed panel organization. The delegates responded to Hess's pleas by booing him, and then voted to terminate the agreement immediately thereafter.[37]

With the Pennsylvania Agreement ruined, Draper was finally forced to move in the direction that Dr. Hess predicted. This action not only worsened relations with organized medicine in Pennsylvania and Kentucky, but with other state organizations across the U.S., as well as the A.M.A. national office, and culminated with its formal condemnation of the Fund in 1958.

Judging from the record, the response of organized medicine in Pennsylvania and Kentucky was not distinctive. Although these groups were vehement in their opposition to Draper's policies, this behavior did not differ from the reaction of other state medical societies outside of Appalachia, and reflected the majority opinion of the A.M.A. House of Delegates. Conversely, the Tennessee State Medical Association continued to maintain good relations with the Fund throughout the crisis, as did the West Virginia State Medical Association. In this respect, these two groups were representative of a minority within the A.M.A. national organization which did not wish to condemn the Fund, nor break relations with it. While not agreeing with everything Draper did, the members of this minority insisted that Draper's actions arose out of the failure of the medical profession to police itself. Just how much sway the minority view held is seen by the fact that the vote tally on the 1958 resolution to condemn was 110 in favor to 72 opposed.[38]

Ironically, both the A.M.A. and its more combative state branches were soon forced to drop their stand against the Fund. By 1958, the number of men working in the mines had declined considerably due to the overall drop in coal demand and the greater level of mechanization in the industry. Also, before the end of the year, it became apparent that liberal members of the U.S. Congress intended to push for direct federal involvement in providing health care for the elderly. Frightened by this prospect, organized medicine discontinued its conflict with the Fund to prevent the creation of what ultimately became Medicare.

Conclusions

Over the past thirty years, an entire genre of literature has appeared about Appalachia which views the region from the point of view of poverty and degradation. In this vein, writers have presented medicine in Appalachia as being based on superstition and home remedy. Obviously this view is false. However, there is no question that the quality of medical care in the region was poor. This fact was proven by both Admiral Boone's report and the A.M.A. hospital survey mentioned in this essay. Essentially, the Fund, through its work as a medical third party, strived to improve medical standards. The success of the Fund here is attested to by its creation of what became Appalachian Regional Hospitals, and the growth of a system of primary care clinics, which were either created by the U.M.W.A., the Fund, or other groups, and which received financial support from the Fund.

In essence, this process of improvement was *the* distinctive aspect of the Fund's experience as a health care agency in Appalachia, and not its struggle with some branches of organized medicine in the region. While the behavior of the K.S.M.A. and the M.S.S.P. demonstrated hypocrisy and mean-spiritedness, other state-level medical societies outside the region, as well as the A.M.A. national office, behaved in a similar manner. In fact, what was unique about the relationship of the Fund with organized medicine in the region was the attitude of the Tennessee State Medical Association. Far from combative, the T.S.M.A. always cooperated with the Fund, and was one of the few groups in the A.M.A. which offered constructive suggestions on how the Fund and organized medicine could work together to improve the quality of health care. Thus, the attitude of the Kentucky and Pennsylvania branches of the A.M.A. demonstrated that physicians across the nation were motivated to action by a similar set of concerns, and used the same arguments to protect their interests.

Works Cited

Bituminous Coal Facts, 1960. Washington, D.C.: National Coal Association.

Current Biography. 1941, 725.

Dubofsky, Melvyn and Warren Van Tine. 1977. *John L. Lewis: A Biography.* New York: Quadrangle/The New York Times Book Co: 376.

Durmaskin, Bettina, Ronald C. Althouse, William Wyant, and Edward Bosnar. 1982. *The Impact of Changes in Health Care Coverage Provides by the United Mine Workers of America Health & Retirement Funds in West Virginia Primary Care Clinics and Multi-Specialty Clinics having Extensive Miner Case Loads.* West Virginia University: Department of Community Medicine, Office of Health Services Research. Unpublished Report.

Kerr, Lorin, M.D., M.P.H. Interview taped at Dr. Kerr's home in Washington, D.C., 30 May 1988.

Mulcahy, Richard. 1988. "To Serve A Union: The United Mine Workers of America Welfare and Retirement Fund, 1946-1978." Morgantown: West Virginia University. Unpublished Ph.D. Dissertation, 240.

Ploss, Janet. 1981. "A History of the Health Care Program of the United Mine Workers of America Welfare Retirement Fund." Baltimore: Johns Hopkins University. Unpublished M.S. Thesis, 53.

United Mine Workers Journal. 1 April 1947; *United Mine Workers Journal.* 1 August 1947.

Wysang, Jere A. and Sherman R. Williams. 1981. *Health Services for Miners: Development and Evolution of the United States Mine Workers of America Health Care Program.* Washington D.C: National Center for Health Services Research, U.S. Department of Health and Human Services, Office of Health Research, Statistics and Technology, 3.

Wysang and Williams, 1981: 8.

Footnotes

[1] Kerr, Dr. Lorin, M.D., M.P.H. Interview taped at Dr. Kerr's home in Washington D.C., 30 May 1988. Most of Dr. Kerr's career had been spent in either working for the Fund or the U.M.W.A. Dr. Kerr joined the Fund's staff in 1947 and served as medical administrator for Morgantown, WV until 1952. In 1952, Dr. Kerr came to Washington and worked directly under Dr. Draper. In 1968, Dr. Kerr left the Fund to work for the U.M.W.A. An expert on Coal Workers' Pneumoconiosis, Dr. Kerr organized and headed the Union's office on occupational health and safety. Currently in retirement, Dr. Kerr maintains both his connections with the Union, the Fund, and his interest in occupational health issues. The author wishes to thank Dr. Kerr for his invaluable help on this research project.

[2] Thurmond Diary, 22 March 1946, 1 April 1946, F.F. *Goodykoontz vs. Shatle,* 1918, A&M Series 4, Goody County Box 5, West Virginia Collection, West Virginia University, Morgantown, West Virginia; Press statement of John L. Lewis on Retirement Fund, dated 14 May 1946, F.F. 10, Box 1 of 3, 1946 Fund Files, Series II, Office of the Director Records, United Mine Workers of America Health and Retirement Funds, A&M 2769, West Virginia Collection; Thurmond Diary, 14 May 1946; Seltzer, Curtis. 1985. *Fire in the Hole: Miners and Managers in the American Coal Industry.* Lexington: University Press of Kentucky, 58.

[3] Biographical data on Josephine Roche, Box 3 of 3, 1946 Fund Files, Series II, Office of the Director Records, United Mine Workers of America Health and Retirement Funds; "Josephine Roche Dead at 89, Treasury and U.M.W. Official." *The New York Times Biographical Service,* July 1976.

[4] Memos from Josephine Roche to John L. Lewis, dated 29 March 1948; F.F. J.L.L. Medical and Hospital; Dr. Sayers' Memorandums, Box 6 of 11, United Mine Workers of America Correspondence, 1946-1972, Series II, Office of the Director Records, United Mine Workers of America Health and Retirement Funds.

[5] Memos from Josephine Roche to John L. Lewis dated 18 May 1948, and 30 May 1948, Ibid.

[6] Memo from Dr. Draper to Josephine Roche, dated 1 November 1948, F.F. A.M.A. Council on Industrial Health, 1948 & 1949, Box 6 of 52, Subject Files, Series III, Executive Medical Officer, United Mine Workers of America Health and Retirement Funds.

[7] Daniels, Mr. Henry C. 14 June 1988. Taped Interview. Like Dr. Kerr, Mr. Daniels began his association with the Fund in 1947. Although not an M.D., Mr. Daniels worked in the Fund's hospitalization section, and was involved in monitoring the quality of care Fund beneficiaries received in various participating institutions.
[8] Letter from Dr. Lorin Kerr to Dr. Draper, dated 19 August 1949; Letter from Dr. William Dorsey to Dr. Draper, dated 11 August 1949, F.F. Office of the Director Records, M.M.H.S. Correspondence, 1947 Fund Area Reports, Box 1 of 4, Medical, Hospital, and Health Services Correspondence, Series II, Office of the Director Records, United Mine Workers of America Health and Retirement Funds.
[9] Clipping of article entitled "Should Industry Back Compulsory Federal Health Insurance?" F.F. A.M.A. Council on Industrial Health, Box 6 of 52, Subject Files, Series III, Executive Medical Officer, United Mine Workers of America Health and Retirement Funds.
[10] Dr. Draper. 1950. Annual Conference on Medical Health Services, Palmer House, Chicago: 5 Feb. 1950.
[11] Letter from Dr. Draper to All Area Administrators, 30 December 1954, F.F. American Medical Association, General 1952-1955. Ibid.
[12] Letters from Dr. Draper to Dr. Carl M. Peterson. 5 January 1951 & 12 February 1951. F.F. A.M.A. Dr. Draper (Correspondence), Box 39 of 52.
[13] Third party Medicine in Kentucky," presented by Dr. Asa Barnes, M.D., Before the Jefferson County Medical Society, Jefferson County, Kentucky, 19 October 1959, 4-5, F.F. A-II-6, Relations with Medical Societies, Box 6 of 16, Subject Files, Series IV, Miners Memorial Hospital Association, Ibid.
[14] Remarks given by Dr. Warren Draper at the groundbreaking ceremonies at Man Memorial Hospital, Man, West Virginia, 31 October 1953, F.F. M.M.H.A. Publicity - Publications, Box 2 of 5, Construction/Administration, Series IV, Miners Memorial Hospital Association, United Mine Workers of America Health and Retirement Funds.
[15] *A Medical Survey of the Bituminous Coal Industry, Report of the Coal Mines Administrator* (The Boone Report), Department of the Interior (Washington, D.C.: United States Government Printing Office, 1947), 171-187, Box 1 of 1, Bibliography—U.M.W.A. Health and Retirement Funds, United Mine Workers Health and Retirement Funds.
[16] Ibid., 1-2 & 59.
[17] "Medical Hospitals in the Bituminous Coal Mining Areas of Kentucky — Tennessee—West Virginia, Preliminary Study to Survey Extent of Problems," 5-6, 8-12, F.F. Council on Medical Service U.M.W. Survey Report, Box 7 of 52, Subject files, Series III, Executive Medical Officer, Ibid.
[18] *Conference on Medical Care in Bituminous Coal Mining Areas*, Charleston, West Virginia, 6-7 Sept. 1952,.3-4, F.F. American Medical Association, Committee on Health Care for Industrial Workers, Box 17 of 52, Ibid.
[19] " Report of Survey Team to the Committee on Medical Care for Industrial Workers of the Councils on Medical Service and Industrial Health," American Medical Association, 15-16 April 1952, 2-5, 10-12; Telegram to Dr. Carl M.

Peterson, dated 10 April 1953, F.F. American Medical Association, Council on Industrial Health.

[20] *Statistical Abstract, Welfare, and Retirement Fund, United Mine Workers of America.* 10 January 1949, 29-30, *Statistical Abstract, Welfare, and Retirement Fund, United Mine Workers of America*, 11 December 1951, 11; *Statistical Abstract, Welfare and Retirement Fund, United Mine Workers of America*, 10 December 1952, 11-12; F.F. Statistical Abstract Series, 1947 Fund, 1 July 1948 through June 1950, Box 1 of 7, Statistical Reports, 1952-1974, Series V, Office of Research and Statistics, Ibid.

[21] Excerpts from the Minutes of the 12th Meeting of the Board of Trustees of the United Mine Workers of America Welfare and Retirement Fund of 1950, 32-40; F.F. Minutes of Welfare and Retirement Trustee Meetings with Respect to the Miners' Memorial Hospital Association, Box 2 of 7, Legal and Contracts, Series IV, Miners' Memorial Hospital Association.

[22] Koplin, Allen M., M.D., M.P.H. "Retainer Payment for Physician Services," 4-6, Box Addendum 1981, July 8, Annual Reports, 1952-1979 and Misc. Staff Publications, Gift Yale University Library, United Mine Workers of America Health and Retirement Funds.

[23] " Report of A Survey of the Group Practice Medical Centers Serving Beneficiaries of the United Mine Workers of America Welfare and Retirement Fund in the Pittsburgh Area," 12-17 October 1957, F.F. A-II-3, Box 6 of 16, Subject Files, Series IV, Miners Memorial Hospital Association, United Mine Workers of America Health and Retirement Funds.

[24] Remarks given by Dr. Warren Draper at the ground-breaking ceremonies at Man Memorial Hospital, Man, West Virginia, 31 October 1953, F.F. M.M.H.A. Publicity-Publications, Box 2 of 5, Construction/Administration, Ibid.

[25] Ibid.

[26] Letter from Dr. Asa Barnes to Dr. Draper, dated 8 August 1956, F.F. A-II-2, Relationship between Fund medical service and the M.M.H.A., Box 6 of 16, Subject Files; Letters from Dr. Frederick Mott to Dr. Draper dated 7 December 1956 and 22 January 1957, F.F. Integrations of M.M.H.A. and the Medical Service of the Fund, Box 5 of 12, Clinical Operations, Ibid.

[27] Memo from Dr. Draper to Medical Services and Hospital Service, Miner's Memorial Hospital Association, dated 5 December 1956; Letters from Dr. Frederick Mott to Dr. Draper, dated 7 December 1956 and 22 January 1957, F.F. Integration of M.M.H.A. and the Medical Service of the Fund, Box 5 of 12, Clinical Operations, Ibid.

[28] Letter from Dr. Asa Barnes to Dr. Draper, dated 8 August 1956; Letter to Dr. Asa Barnes from Dr. Francis Hodges, dated 2 May 1956, F.F. A-II-6, Relations with Medical Societies, Box 6 of 16, Subject Files, Ibid.

[29] Memo to Dr. Draper from Dr. John Newdorp, dated 28 October 1959, Ibid.

[30] Memo from Dr. Gordon Meade to File, dated 21 October 1959; Letters to Drs. Clark, Judd, Wishman, and Owens, dated 28 November 1959, F.F. A-II-6, Relations with Medical Societies, Draft Letter to Chairman of the Board of Trustees of the American Medical Association, F.F. A-II-7, The Society of Medicine of Pike County, Ibid.

[1] Memo from Dr. John Newdorp to Dr. Draper, dated 28 October 1959, F.F. A-II-3, Relations with Medical Societies, Ibid.
[12] Letter from Dr. Draper to Area medical Administrators, dated 6 April 1954, F.F. American Medical Associations, General, 1952-1955, Box 6 of 52, Subject Files, Series III Executive Medical Officer, Ibid.
[13] Letter from Dr. Draper to All Area Medical Administrators, dated 30 December 1954, Ibid.
[14] Letter to Dr. Draper from Dr. William A. Sawyer, dated 26 April 1955, Resolutions of the Pennsylvania and West Virginia Delegations to the House of Delegates of the American Medical Association, June 1955 meeting held in Atlantic City, New Jersey, Ibid.
[35] Resolution of the Pennsylvania delegates to the House of Delegates of the American Medical Association, June 1955 meeting held in Atlantic City, New Jersey, Ibid.
[36] "Problems of the United Mine Workers of America Welfare and Retirement Fund in Providing Medical Care to its Beneficiaries," by Warren F. Draper, M.D., P. 5. F.F. American Medical Association, Meetings in 1957, Box 12 of 52, Ibid.
[37] Report of the Meeting of the House of Delegates of the American Medical Association, San Francisco, California, 23-26 June 1958, F.F. A.M.A. General, Box 5 of 52, Subject Files, Ibid.
[38] Ibid.

Richard P. Mulcahy is in the department of history at the University of Pittsburgh, Titusville, Pennsylvania.

The Roving Picket Movement and the Appalachian Committee for Full Employment, 1959-1965: A Narrative

Kate Black

In Eastern Kentucky in the 1950s coalfield life was not easy for mining families. With each passing year in that decade, mine work was increasingly difficult to find, the United Mine Workers of America (UMWA) grew more antagonistic towards the rank-and-file, and the mines that were operating became even less safe, more economically marginal, and eventually, non-union. It was the decade when thousands left the area in search of jobs. No one "discovered" Eastern Kentucky; no major surveys were conducted; and no massive federal aid programs were implemented. No one outside the area paid attention to Eastern Kentucky. Yet, in the midst of this silence, disquieting activities occurred in the boardrooms of coal corporations and the UMWA International. Plans were made that, by the end of the 1950s, whirled Eastern Kentucky into the national limelight and ultimately forced mining families to organize and agitate to an extent not witnessed since the 1930s.

After World War II, the coal industry, notorious for its boom-and-bust cycle, headed into a slump. (Caudill, 1963; Hume, 1971; and Seltzer, 1985, provided the following information.) Because coal had a bad reputation—fluctuating prices in the marketplace and so-called unstable labor in the workplace—corporate America was anxious to find alternative energy sources. The home-heating market converted from coal to fuel oil and natural gas, and the railroads turned to diesel fuel. Even the thermo-electric market became highly competitive as steam generated power plants developed the capacity to convert from one fuel to another, depending on what was cheapest. In addition, the coal industry, known for its well-defined worker/management conflicts, was anxious to control its labor force. Historically, miners had been defiant and militant when faced with standard industry fare: low wages, deathly working conditions, virulent anti-union tactics, and job instability. The other "major enemy coal suppliers faced was themselves. They were too numerous, too divided, and too anarchistic to discipline their affairs" (Seltzer, 1985: 62). Increasingly the large coal operators and John L. Lewis, the autocratic President of the UMWA, recognized that they needed each other to insure mutual survival. They decided to end the old antagonisms; labor-management collaboration and collective bargaining would, they believed, stabilize the coal industry. Thus, by 1950, the newly formed organization, the Bituminous Coal Operators' Association (BCOA) began unprecedented **industry-wide** collective bargaining with the UMWA.

Headed by George Love of Pittsburgh-Consolidation Coal, the BCOA members represented companies producing half the coal mined in the United States. In keeping with the tenets of corporate capitalism, the number of votes each BCOA member could cast was proportionate to the tonnage their mines produced: the higher the tonnage rate, the more power they had in decision making (Seltzer, 1985: 63). From the beginning, then, the northern commercial operators and captive mine owners, both of whom produced far more coal than the southern commercial operators, clearly had the upper-hand; moreover, the group of smaller southern companies with UMWA contracts, the Southern Coal Producer's Association, were forced to enter national contract negotiations along side corporations having unbelievable capital advantage. The die was cast.

In 1950, the BCOA and UMWA negotiated a new contract swiftly and without a strike. In exchange for controlling labor costs industry-wide, the BCOA made three demands: a contract which could not be cancelled prior to its expiration date, a no-strike clause, and stipulations that only employees of companies signatory to the contract should receive benefits from the UMWA Health and Retirement Funds.[1] An essential ingredient of this agreement was mechanization. The new alliance saw automation, not as a choice to make, but as a fact to face:

> The logic that wedded [the UMWA and BCOA] was economic. To survive the competition of other fuels, coal had to remain cheap and free from the threat of strikes. Mechanization would raise productivity and keep coal

competitive with oil and gas... Those who could mechanize fastest would be able to get the best contracts and make the most money... [S]maller companies with UMWA contracts could not afford both to invest in mechanization and meet the new BCOA wage-and-benefit standards. [They] hoped that mechanization would lower the production costs of union-mined coal below what the small non-union suppliers could achieve by cutting wages. Machines, they hoped, would eventually suppress competition (Seltzer, 1985: 67).

The squeeze tightened in 1952, when the BCOA and UMWA negotiated a $1.90 per shift wage increase and a $.10 per ton increase for royalties to the Health and Retirement Funds and, in 1955, UMWA miners received a raise of $2.00 per shift. The collaboration was cemented when the UMWA secretly loaned money from their own bank, The National Bank of Washington, to some of the larger companies to capitalize their mechanization efforts.[2] Smaller mines, unable to compete with an industry-wide contract and mechanization, increasingly went bankrupt or non-union.

In Eastern Kentucky, however, the results of the BCOA-UMWA partnership were particularly dramatic and not according to plan. Instead of the smaller mines going out of business, they proliferated. Many were "dog-hole" mines—truck mines which "came into existence during World War II, when the demand for coal increased sharply and the big mines gave up operations that did not yield to mechanization" (Linton, 1959: 472). Truck mines were usually economically marginal businesses; they were labor intensive and even more unsafe than the larger operations. Coal from these mines was trucked to a preparation plant, or to a ramp located on a railroad. The ramp owner often owned or leased these truck mines to the operators. Actually "operator" is somewhat of a misnomer because many of these truck mines were "gang-worked" by small groups of miners who could no longer find work in larger, union mines. Usually the miners at the truck mines thought they were working for signatory companies because the ramp operators were signatory and, therefore, paying the royalties on the tonnage (purchased from the truck mines) to the UMWA Health and Retirement Funds. In many cases, however, the UMWA formed sweetheart contracts with the ramp owners, ostensibly to keep Eastern Kentucky unionized.[3] But by 1958, the UMWA clearly was interested in coal production which generated royalties, rather than in the rank-and-file.

The 1958 contract included a clause which later caused the coalfields, especially in Eastern Kentucky, to explode. The Protective Wage Clause forbade the signatory operators to do any business—mine, prepare, transport, or sell—with non-union companies:

It was *not* intended to protect the wages of UMWA miners (except perhaps in the most remote sense), since BCOA operators did not want to break their union contracts. [It] was a device to concentrate economic power within the boundaries of the UMWA-BCOA sphere [Emphasis original] (Seltzer, 1977: 446).

In Eastern Kentucky, where truck mines were not the exception but the rule, the stipulations of the clause were felt strongly. A ramp operator who remained competitive in the spot sales market by determining what the truck miners got for their coal could no longer use that leverage if everyone was actually paying union scale and the 40 cents-a-ton royalty. No longer could the truck mines have any economic edge over the large rail mines (i.e. BCOA members). This exceedingly complex situation led to a long, very violent strike in 1959, which has often been described as John L. Lewis' "last ditch effort to organize Eastern Kentucky" (Seltzer, 1985: 81; Maggard and Horne interviews, 1987).

Many of the smaller independent companies refused to sign the 1958 contract either because they actually could not afford to meet its demands or because they refused to be coerced by a BCOA-UMWA conspiracy.[4] So, when the miners came out on strike it was, in effect, an organizing tactic, not a contract strike. In fact, Lewis used, once again, his ultimate authority over the rank-and-file as a method of squeezing out yet more non-BCOA companies which, in his mind, would further stabilize the coal industry. It was a tactic that failed miserably. While many smaller rail and truck mines did go out of business, new ones popped up as non-union mines. Competition for jobs was fierce and UMWA miners were forced to work in non-union mines. By 1960, those who were lucky enough to be employed worked for even lower wages in more dangerous conditions than in the 1950s. The marginal economic system in which the Eastern Kentucky mining family lived narrowed.

In the meantime, throughout the 1950s the UMWA Health and Retirement Funds disenfranchised large numbers of disabled miners and prospective pensioners with ever-changing and arbitrary eligibility rules. A set of interconnected reasons caused these changes. Because the income to the Funds was tied to production — 40 cents-per-ton — its financial status was directly linked to the well-being of the coal industry. The perspective of the Funds became: people who do not produce tonnage (disabled and retired miners) do not produce royalties. In addition, the health care system, which featured a chain of hospitals and pre-paid services had to keep up with inflation but, since 1952, the royalty had not been increased. And, to make matters more sinister, the assets of the Funds, kept in the UMWA-owned Bank of Washington, "were loaned interest free to coal operators and its cash reserves were used to purchase coal company and utility stocks" (Seltzer, 1977a: 25). Finally, the

Funds, like the union, were under the iron fist of Lewis, whose quest for power had long surpassed his consideration of the miners' welfare. Participation by the rank and file in union politics and decision-making had been systematically, and even militantly, closed. The failure of the Funds to serve the mining communities—everyone, not just the miners—was the result of the mismanagement and corruption inside the UMWA itself.

In 1960, the Funds cancelled medical coverage for all miners who had been unemployed for more than a year, and for all those working in a non-union mine, even if all prior service had been in a union mine. The final blow came in 1962, when the Funds closed its ten hospitals located throughout the coalfields and revoked the medical cards held by miners working for companies not paying royalties. Thus, thousands of miners, who worked for below-scale wages because their employer had a sweetheart contract with the UMWA, were double-crossed. Retired miner, Robert McDonald, explained that the operators "may not have paid the wages [up to scale] but they did pay royalties, as I understand." Another miner, when asked how the men felt about sweetheart contracts, answered, "You never did hear them talk about it. Operators would say they had everything took care of" (McDonald, Hensley interviews, 1987). Miners who believed if they stuck with the union through the hard times their loyalty would be rewarded were wrong. Initially, it was hard to know who to blame.

Miners who had worked for years at below union wages had done so believing that at least they and their families could receive medical care at no additional cost—a considerable benefit. The surprise announcements by the UMWA Health and Retirement Funds in the fall of 1962 burst the dam. In Eastern Kentucky, especially Letcher, Knott, and Perry Counties, hundreds of effected miners came out on strike. Soon their ranks were joined by other unemployed miners and their families, as well as by those the Health and Retirement Funds had disenfranchised throughout the 1950s. Spontaneously, they began driving caravans from one mine to another, trying to close down operations that were non-union and those that were not paying their 40-cents-per-ton royalty. The press dubbed them the "Roving Pickets." When asked what the nature of the Roving Picket movement was, miners who were pickets explained:

> [We were] protesting the coal operators making sweetheart contracts with the [UMWA] field [representatives].
>
> They started trying to get rid of the union. These big mines did. [The operators] just shut the mines and hired new men to take their places for less wages. [The Roving Pickets] tried to organize [those mines].

[We were trying to] save our jobs and save our hospitalization (Campbell, Sexton, Horne interviews, 1987).

The Roving Pickets focused on several different, but not necessarily unrelated, circumstances. In some areas the pickets attempted to close mines and ramps whose owners failed to sign the 1958 contract and were therefore handling non-union coal. Others targeted mines holding sweetheart contracts with the UMWA; those operators had not paid their royalties to the Funds. The miners working at these operations were those who lost their hospital cards in the fall of 1962. The Roving Pickets also demonstrated at mines which closed or simply let their contract expire, changed names but not ownership, and re-opened as non-union.[6]

These were obviously confusing times. Striking and picketing had always been the union miner's recourse for unfair labor practices. But eventually the miners had to face the facts: the UMWA publicly denounced the Roving Pickets. Joe Scopa, a retired miner and former Roving Picket said that initially "[W]e got the impression the district was 100% behind us," but he later learned differently when the District 19 president announced over the radio, "They are on their own." Buck Maggard, another picket said the UMWA "disowned the men. They wouldn't sanction the strikes" (Scopa, Maggard interviews, 1987).

People involved with the movement are divided in their analysis of the UMWA refusal to support the Roving Pickets. Some believed that the UMWA secretly subsidized the pickets and encouraged them to close down mines and even destroy mine property (Hatmaker, Horne, Turner interviews, 1987). The theory was that the union would be slapped with too many law suits if they overtly sanctioned the strikes. The other side claimed that the union betrayed the rank-and-file miners of Eastern Kentucky and simply pitted them against one another to strengthen the UMWA-BCOA alliance (Maggard, Campbell interviews, 1987). If the UMWA did covertly instigate the Roving Picket movement, they still used the miners to fight back at the same operators with which the union had formed sweetheart contracts. Naturally the operators would have been furious if the UMWA had publicly sanctioned the strikes. However, if the UMWA did not covertly sanction the pickets, they nevertheless sacrificed their own members—those that were already the most marginal—to the cause: destroy the competition faced by BCOA members, created by small mines flooding the markets with cheap coal. Or, if the miners actually forced all the small non-union mines to sign union contracts, those mines, while paying union wages and royalties, could not have survived the competition with large rail and captive producers. Either way, the miners lost.

The Roving Picket movement was particularly intense for approximately a year after the UMWA Health and Retirement Funds announcement in the fall of 1962. Activity centered in Perry County, where Berman Gibson emerged as the leader. In Perry, as well as surrounding counties, the pickets used similar strategies. In the early morning hours, groups ranging from approximately 50 to 300 people gathered—usually at one of the Miners' Memorial Hospitals or at the local union hall—and a decision was made about which mines would be picketed before the car caravan departed.[7] Once they arrived at their destination the pickets attempted to prevent the scabs from going to work or tried to persuade them into coming out. As the local power elite became more organized, the pickets increasingly faced state police, injunctions, restraining orders, and eventually arrests. In Perry and Letcher Counties, in particular, violence was a tactic used by the pickets when all else failed:

> At first we would [ask the men to come out.] We'd do it the sensible way. And then, if bad things come to worse, they wouldn't have no place to dump their coal or tip [i.e. tipple] it... [A] ramp, or tipple, or big bridge right nearby—someway it would fall in... (Maggard interview, 1987).

Many supporters of the Roving Pickets, however, claim they were often prevented from picketing at mines by "gun thugs" hired by the operators and by the ruthlessness of people like Charlie Combs, Sheriff of Perry County and a mine owner himself (Hensley, Turner interviews, 1987). At any rate, mine and railroad property was destroyed and several pickets were indicted and convicted of related charges.

Throughout 1963, the Roving Picket movement changed from a miners' resistance to an unemployed/poor people's movement. As the roving pickets were increasingly challenged by the local political structure, it became clear the movement was not accomplishing its original intentions: saving jobs and UMWA health cards.[8] This realization crystalized in November, 1963, during the campaign for circuit judge in Perry County—Courtney Wells, who was sympathetic to labor, was up for re-election:

> On the morning of the election the State Police and County Sheriffs promptly showed up with warrants for Berman Gibson and seven of his followers who were carted off to the Letcher County Jail and charged before a Justice of the Peace with assault with a deadly weapon which carried the maximum penalty of death. This maneuver served two purposes: first to remove them from the polling places to help defeat the friendly Judge and to destroy the movement of the roving pickets. The opposition defeated the Judge... (Tharp, 1965:1).

The election was final proof that the issue was not simply a standard labor-management battle (if it ever had been) but a broader political-economic one.

Because their analysis of the situation was changing, the pickets realized their strategies must also change. Their old-style labor agitation was no longer effective or comprehensive enough to deal with such a complex situation. To use UMWA tactics when the union was part of the problem was clearly not the answer. In January, 1964, a small group of unemployed miners chartered a bus to Washington to call attention to the situation in Eastern Kentucky and to seek Federal relief for the unemployed. Everette Tharp, who was in the delegation, described the trip:

> We visited Senators and Representatives throughout Appalachia and also various governmental department heads. We asked for an appointment with President Johnson and received an invitation to meet with his Aide, Mr. George Reedy. It was in this discussion that Mr. Reedy suggested that we come back home and organize so as to be in a better position to aid and assist the Government to carry out their War on Poverty Program (Tharp, 1956: 2).

Upon returning home the Appalachian Committee for Full Employment (ACFE) was formed. Its goals were broad-based and radical:

> To expose corruption in the framework of our government... To continue to organize the unemployed... To promote the more equal distribution of the Nation's wealth... To fight for the enactment of a tax structure, humane in administration, equal in the tax burden... To conduct a [voter] registration campaign of the people in poverty... To take a vow ourselves to be men of courage and vision, to scoff at no brother because of his ideas and to unite without regard to color or creed, the better to cope with our enemies (Tharp, 1965: 5).

The ACFE established community action committees which protested how local politicians were spending War on Poverty monies, challenged the school board over its administration of the Federal school lunch program, and organized against the $1.00 hourly wage paid to those in the unemployed father's program, calling it "legislated poverty" (Tharp, 1965: 2). Eventually, the ACFE was embroiled with the local power structure over how Office of Economic Opportunity (OEO) funds should be expended.[9]

Another group that became an important part of the Roving Picket era was formed in the summer of 1963 under the leadership of Hamish Sinclair.[10] The Committee for Miners (CFM) was organized in New York to raise money and carry on the legal defense of all pickets who had been arrested. But Sinclair admitted that:

> [W]e were getting involved with a movement which was already in existence and the price we had to pay for a ready made constituency was the problem of transferring its aims to those defined by *our* analysis.... There was often sharp conflict between the needs of a movement for jobs and the needs of the preparation for the trials. Money and staff time was frequently diverted to trial work at times when both were urgently needed for an organizing development. [Emphasis added] (Sinclair, 1965: 90).

Nevertheless, the Committee, ACFE, and the Students for a Democratic Society (SDS) co-sponsored the "Easter Conference" in March, 1964, in Hazard (Perry County). The purpose was to introduce SDS members to the area and to encourage their interest in returning for a summer of organizing work with ACFE. SDS, at that time, wanted to foster an alliance between unemployed blacks and whites and saw the opportunity to begin this work in Eastern Kenucky.[11] One year after the Easter Conference, however, the Committee for Miners was defunct, citing as its reasons: "(1) disagreements between CFM and ACFE as to policies and leadership; and (2) ACFE's decision to raise funds independently."[12]

Since Hazard became the center for the Roving Picket movement—both the CFM and ACFE offices were there—most of the national publicity about the miners focused on that area. In addition, Berman Gibson, charismatic and colorful leader of the Perry County pickets and later chair of the ACFE, probably attracted press because he was naturally a "good story." According to Hamish Sinclair of the CFM, Gibson was one of the reasons his organization chose Perry County for its field office.

> The...problem was that with little resources (myself as the one organizer in the area) we could not cover the geographical expanse of seven counties adequately. The men who had been active in the picket movement, now threatened with reprisals by the FBI, the local police and political structure in the area, were not willing to set up their own cadres of leadership in the other six counties. Gibson stood out alone as the one man who was prepared to go on. (Sinclair, 1965: 91).

Of course, the arrival of so many outsiders—press, students, organizers—did not go unnoticed in Hazard. This added another dramatic dimension to the Roving Picket movement: red-baiting. As early as February, 1963, *the Hazard-Herald* printed stories with headlines that read, "Communism Comes to the Mountains of East Kentucky" and "Cuba Broadcast Tells Mine Woes" (Hatmaker, 1987). Of course, it was true that members of the Communist Party press came to investigate and write stories on the Roving Pickets as did the Maoist Progressive Labor Party.[13] But the Hazard press and the local power elite red-baited the miners and all who associated with them in hopes of diffusing the movement. Everette Tharp, Recording Secretary and theoretician of the ACFE, analyzed the elite's actions in a piece called "Outsiders."

> The cry of 'outsiders' [is a] political weapon to be used against certain classes of individuals in order that a small minority may perpetuate their strangle-hold upon [our] economic, political, and social lives (Tharp, 1964: 4).

When Buck Maggard, a former picket, was asked whether the red-baiting hurt the movement, he said it did not and then wryly added, "Can't you just see the Communists taking over Hazard? What in the hell would they have done with it?" (Maggard interview, 1978).

The cry of "Outsiders" and "Communists" has always been used in the coalfields to point a finger or raise suspicion whenever working class people have organized themselves to resist or agitate. These accusations come especially when the local power structure is being scrutinized nationally. Louise Hatmaker, who wrote for the *Hazard-Herald*, strongly illustrates this reaction when she bitterly recalled how national publications "wrote great glowing things about these miners, these pickets ... it was as if we were ogres and they were completely down-trodden. But they were having a wonderful time, believe me" (Hatmaker interview, 1987).

The local power elite worked relentlessly to break the spirit of the Roving Picket movement and later the ACFE: From red-baiting to forming the Citizen's Committee for Law and Order; and, from insuring that Courtney Wells was not re-elected as the Circuit Court Judge to using the local paper for powerful media manipulation.[14] Long after the end of the Roving Picket movement and even after the demise of the ACFE in the mid-1960s, this basic struggle continued. In fact, the fight to control federal OEO dollars between poor people and local politicians and bureaucrats ultimately diluted intensity of the ACFE.

Concluding Questions and Remarks

More original research needs to be conducted on the Roving Picket movement as I indicated in several footnotes. I have many unanswered questions:

—The union's position should be documented by interviewing UMWA officials, especially district officers, of that era and by obtaining official records, if they exist and are accessible. What exactly was the UMWAs role, what part did the International play and what parts did the Districts play? Were Districts 19 and 30 in Eastern Kentucky historically different from other districts?

—Why was the Roving Picket Movement strongest in certain Eastern Kentucky counties? Why was it limited to the Eastern Kentucky coalfields? Why was there no similar movement in West Virginia? Were those Eastern Kentucky counties structurally different somehow? Was the development of those coalfields (economically and technologically) significantly different?

—What was the relationship between the pickets and the "outsiders"? When differences of ideology and strategy surfaced between the ACFE, CFM, and SDS, what were they? What was the power struggle about? How did the ACFE effect the students? Did any of them later become AVs (Appalachian Volunteers)? Can the Roving Picket Movement and ACFE be tied to the larger Civil Rights Movement during this period?

—Women were active in the Roving Picket movement and, in fact, a woman, Lola Moore, was later Financial Secretary of the ACFE. Not surprisingly, I have found no sources which discuss women in the movement, beyond the briefest mention. Interviews with these women should be conducted and analyzed.

—How and why did the local power structure hinder the movement? What relationship do they have to a national and international power structure? How did their Citizens Committee for Law and Order affect the media's interpretation of the movement? In what ways did they collaborate with state and federal law enforcement agencies against the pickets?

—Finally, how did the pickets, who shifted their focus from labor organizing to a broad-based poor people's coalition view this process? In what ways did they create the process; in what ways did the process change their lives? And, how did the Roving Picket Movement and ACFE prepare them for subsequent activism—such as the Miners for Democracy and Black Lung movements?

Why is it so important to even ask all these questions and continue to analyze a relatively short-lived, local, historical event? I can think of three good answers. The first is quick and simple: because no one has. In 1978, I did a bibliographic search on the Roving Picket movement. Now, ten years later, I could locate less than a half-dozen new secondary sources on the subject. From what I can gather, no substantive work has been done, except for the interviews conducted in 1987 and a video-in-progress by Appalshop.

Second, the Roving Picket movement is more than simply an interesting event in Eastern Kentucky history, or Appalachian history, or even coalfield history. It is about a process that moved a people from one period to another, from one way of being and perceiving to another. It is about a people who took stock of their situation, and as a group fought back at the coal companies, the UMWA, and their own elected officials. It is about a people whose resistance led them to organize themselves into a force which unnerved the status quo. And that force, of their own creation, carried them into the late 1960s and 1970s armed with their own empowerment. The battles begun by the Roving Picket movement and the ACFE later became demands for social and economic justice expressed in the social movements of the era: anti-stripmining, Black Lung Association, welfare rights, and Miners for Democracy.

Finally, the Roving Picket movement is a challenge to an established view of Appalachian history and culture. It is extremely important to continually expose the historical myths and explode the cultural stereotypes about the region because the "idea of Appalachia" unfortunately remains implanted in the memory of the nation. The story of the pickets and the Appalachian Committee for Full Employment is further evidence that the history of the region is not static or necessarily provincial; and that, like all people, Eastern Kentuckians want to control and shape their own destiny.

Interviews

Black, Kate (interview by). Lexington, Kentucky: University of Kentucky Oral History Archives. Tape is housed in Special Collections.

Maggard, Charles Buck. 6 July 1978

Cantrell, Doug (interviews by). Coal Miner's Oral History Project. Lexington, Kentucky: Appalachian Center University of Kentucky. Tapes are housed in Special Collections.

Campbell, Darrell. 31 July 1987
Grubbs, Robert. 25 June 1987
Hatmaker, Louise. 17 July 1987
Hensley, Bige. 26 June 1987
Horne, Buster. 24 August 1987
McDonald, Robert. 23 June 1987
Maggard, Hobart. 26 June 1987
Morton, Bill. 30 July 1987
Philpott, Chester. 7 July 1987
Scopa, Joe. 16 June 1987; and 16 July 1987
Sexton, Lee. 26 July1987
Turner, Clayton. 19 August 1987

Tharp, Everette collection, Lexington, Kentucky: University of Kentucky, Special collections.

Works Cited

Berney, Barbara. 1978. "The Rise and Fall of the UMWA Fund." *Southern Exposure* 6: 2, Summer, 95-102.

Bethell, Tom. 1968. "Southeast Coal Co. in a Battle for Life." *Appalachian Lookout* 1: December, 3-6.

Caldwell, Nat and Gene S. Graham. 1961. "The Strange Romance Between John L. Lewis and Cyrus Eaton." *Harper's Magazine*. December, 25-32.

Carawan, Guy and Candie. 1975. *Voices from the Mountain*. New York: Knopf.

Caudill, Harry M. 1963. *Night Comes to the Cumberlands*. Boston: Little, Brown.

Caudill, Harry M. 1964. "The Permanent Poor: The Lessons of Eastern Kentucky." *Atlantic* 213: June, 49-53.

Caudill, Harry, M. 1962. *The Watches of the Night*. Boston: Little, Brown.

Christenson, C.L. 1962. *Economic Redevelopment in Bituminous Coal: The Special Case of Technological Advance in United States Coal Mines, 1930-1960*. Cambridge: Harvard University Press.

"Coal Royalties—Small Mines Win." 1963. *U.S. News and World Report* 54: 29 April 1963, 93.

"Coal Strike: What is the Real Issue?" 1959. *Mountain Life and Work* 35: Fall 1959, 5-7.

"Coal: When Machines Took Over." 1963. *U.S. News and World Report* 5: 29 April 1963, 69-73.

Donoughue, Bernard. 1959. "Bloody Harlan." *New Statesman* 58:14 November 1959, 654-658.

Dubofsky, Melvyn and Warren Van Tine. 1977. *John L. Lewis: A Biography*. New York: Quadrangle/The New York Times Book Co.

Gervis, Stephanie. 1963. "Gray Spring in Hazard." *Commonweal* 78: 17 May 1963, 220-222.

"How a Big Union Handles Money." 1963. *U.S. News and World Report* 54: 6 May 1963, 94.

Hume, Brit. 1971. *Death and the Mines: Rebellion and Murder in the UMW*. New York: Grossman Publishers.

Inventory to the Committee for Miners' Papers. University of Wisconsin.

"Is is Boycott?" 1958. *Business Week*: 13 December 1958, 94,96.

Kahn, Kathy. *Hillbilly Women*. 1972. New York: Avon Books.

"Kentucky: The Facts of Life." 1962. *Time* 80: 28 December 1962, 17.

King, Lawrence T. 1959. "Idle Mines, Idle Men." *Commonweal* 70: 29 May 1959, 228-230.

Linton, Ron M. 1959. "Kentucky's Tragic Strike." *The Nation* 188: 23 May 1959, 471, 473.

Marsh, Don. 1963. "Chaos in the Coal Fields." *The Nation* 196: 26 January 1963, 69, 72.

"Mining: Hot Coal." 1962. *Time* 79: 16 April 1962, 90, 92.

Moore, Lola. 1965. "Why Mountain Folks Walked in Frankfort Freedom March." *The Appalachian South* 1: Summer, 41-42.

"More Machines, Fewer Men—A Union That's Happy About It." 1959. (Interview with John L. Lewis) *U.S. News and World Report* 47: 9 November 1959, 60-64.

Myers, Robert J. 1967. "Mine Workers' Welfare and Retirement Fund: Fifteen Years' Experience." *Industrial and Labor Relations Review* 20: 2, January 1967, 265-274.

"New Threat in 'Bloody Harlan'." 1959. *Business Week:* 14 March 1959, 124.

Nyden, Paul. 1972. *The Coal Miner's Struggle in Eastern Kentucky.* Huntington, West Virginia: Appalachian Movement Press.

Nyden, Paul. 1970. "Coal Miners, 'Their' Union, and Capital." *Science and Society* 34: 2, Summer, 194-223.

Pearce, John, ed. 1963. "The Superfluous People of Hazard, Kentucky." *Reporter:* 3 January 1963, 33-35.

Peg. 1973. "A Letter from Perry County, Kentucky." In Axelrod, Jim, ed. *Growin' Up Country.* Clintwood, Virginia: Council of the Southern Mountains, 26-46.

Peterson, Bill. 1972. *Coaltown Revisited: An Appalachian Notebook.* Chicago: Henry Regnery.

"A Private 'Welfare State' Runs Into Trouble." 1962. *U.S. News and World Report* 53: 3 December 1962, 55-58.

Raskin, A.H. 1963. "John L. Lewis and the Mine Workers." *Atlantic Monthly* 211: May, 53-58.

Seltzer, Curtis. 1985. *Fire in the Hole: Miners and Managers in the American Coal Industry.* Lexington: University Press of Kentucky.

Seltzer, Curtis. 1977b. "Health Care by the Ton: Crisis in the Mine Workers' Health and Welfare Programs." *Health/PAC Bulletin* 79: November/December, 1-8, 25-33.

Seltzer, Curtis. 1977. *The United Mine Workers of America and the Coal Operators: The Political Economy of Coal in Appalachia, 1950-1973.* Columbia University, Ph.D. diss.

Shackleford, Laurel and Bill Weinberg, ed. 1977. *Our Appalachia: An Oral History.* New York: Hill and Wang.

Sinclair, Hamish. 1965. "Hazard, Ky.: Committee for Miners." *Studies on the Left* 5: Summer, 87-107.

Sinclair, Hamish. 1968. "Hazard, Ky.: Document of the Struggle." *Radical America* 2: January-February, 1-24.

"Stalemate in the Coal Fields." 1959. *Business Week,* 19 September 1959, 53-54.

"A Strike That Spells Bullets and Dynamite." 1959. *U.S. News and World Report* 46: 25 May 1959, 104-105.

Students for a Democratic Society. 1964. "Plight of Jobless Miners."

Tharp, Everette. 1965. "Appalachian Committee for Full Employment: Background and Purpose." *The Appalachian South* 1: Summer, 44-46.

"UMW Feels Pressure for Change." 1960. *Business Week*: 15 October 1960, 165.

"UMW On the Griddle in Court and Coalfields." 1962. *Business Week:* 3 November 1962, 49-51.

"A Union Got Rich—Then....." 1961. *U.S. News and World Report* 50: 24 April 1961, 104-105.

"Violence Lingers in Kentucky." 1959. *Business Week*: 25 April 1959, 48? 50.

Wakefield, Dan. 1963. "In Hazard." *Commentary*, September, 209-217.

Walls, David S. and John B. Stephenson, ed. 1972. *Appalachia in the Sixties*. Lexington: The University Press of Kentucky.

Waters, Mary-Alice. 1969. "Adventure in Hazard, Ky." In *Maoism the U.S.: A Critical History of the Progressive Labor Party*. New York: Young Socialist Alliance, December, 5-6.

Welsh, David. 1965. "Death in Kentucky." *Ramparts* 4: December, 50-64.

Wiley, Peter. 1968. "Hazard: Socialism and Community Organizing." *Radical America* 2: January-February, 25-37.

Wolfert, Ira. 1960. "Monster in the Mine." *Nation* 190: 2 January 1960, 3-12.

Footnotes

[1] The Health and Retirement Funds, created in 1946, were financed by royalties paid on the tonnage produced by each signatory company.
[2] Seltzer contends that the UMWA also made sweetheart contracts with certain BCOA companies, allowing them to pay less royalties and use the difference to finance mechanization. He also states, "By holding the Southern companies to the full wage and benefit package, the UMWA made them less competitive." (See Seltzer, 1985: 73.) Seltzer does not document this claim. While the literature on this subject does not refute Seltzer's theory, it tends to discuss more often the sweetheart contracts made with smaller, usually Southern and, in particular, Eastern Kentuckian coal operators in an effort to keep them from going non-union: better to have some royalties coming into Health and Retirement Funds than none at all; better to have miners employed at below-contract wage scales than not at all.

[3] When I was a paralegal at an Eastern Kentucky legal services in the mid-70s, working on UMWA Health and Retirement Fund cases, I heard this scenario described dozens of times. See also interview with Clayton Turner.

[4] In fact, some companies like Southeast Coal (Letcher Co., Ky.) charged the UMWA and Consolidated Coal of conspiring to break them and, after years in the courts, won large settlements. See Thomas Bethel. 1971. *Conspiracy in Coal*. Huntington, WV: Appalachian Movement Press.

[5] This is an interesting and significant point for which I have no definite answer. All the news accounts and other documentation establish Eastern Kentucky, and, in particular, Letcher, Knott, and Perry, as the focal point of the Roving Picket Movement. Why weren't similar responses made in West Virginia, for example? Were as many miners in other states disenfranchised by the UMWA Funds as in Eastern Kentucky? If not, why? Were more sweetheart contracts made in Eastern Kentucky and were more miners unemployed? Had the mining operations in these counties always been more marginal? If so, was that due to fewer rail and captive mines locating there? Were the coal seams substantially different, less adaptable to mechanization, and does that mean that mining operations were less likely to be large UMWA-BCOA mines? These questions require more research and consideration.

[6] The Blue Diamond Mine at Leatherwood in Perry County was infamous for using this tactic. See also interviews with Chester Philpott, Charles "Buck" Maggard, Lee Sexton, and Joe Scopa.

[7] This was not the first time that miners had used this method of picketing. During the 1959 strike, Gerald Griffen, a reporter for the Louisville *Courier-Journal* noted the new style of picketing as a "motorized picket line." *Courier-Journal*: 10 March 1959, 1.

[8] In Perry County, Hazard businessman, Bill Morton, helped form the Citizens Committee for Law and Order. In an interview with Morton he stated that the coal business was being impeded by the pickets which was bad for all business. The Committee used their influence to get the state and federal law enforcement agencies involved and to generate publicity.

[9] Within ACFE a division occurred between those who thought the organization should emphasize electoral politics and the faction who urged mass organizing and agitation.

[10] I do not know much about Sinclair except that he originally went to Hazard to make a TV documentary about the unemployed miners. See his "Hazard, KY.: Committee for Miners," 1965. *Studies on the Left* 5: Summer, 87-107, for his analysis of the Roving Picket movement. See also the clippings file in the Everette Tharp Collection, where he is mentioned briefly in several articles. He needs to be located and interviewed, as does Arthur Gorson who directed the New York office of CFM.

[11] I need to do more research on and thinking about the students' involvement with ACFE. Little has been written about what influence the two groups had on each other, what exactly the students did in the summer of 1964, etc. It would be interesting to know if and AV's came out of this group. See Peter Wiley. 1968.

"Hazard: Socialism and Community Organizing." *Radical America* 2: January/February 1968, 25-37. Wiley, a student that 1964 summer in Perry County, donated the Committee for Miners' papers to the University of Wisconsin where they are available for use; I have not, however, researched in that collection.

[12] Inventory to the University of Wisconsin's Committee for Miners' Papers, 2. In my files.

[13] The Progressive Labor Party (PLP), which split off from SDS, is a whole other story. The January, 1963, issue of the Party's journal, *Progressive Labor*, was devoted to the Roving Picket movement. The PLP also raised money and sent food and clothing to the miners. While the PLP's intentions were good, their approach was opportunistic, which ultimately stirred the local elite into a frenzy. *The Hazard-Herald* even reprinted several of the articles from that January, 1963, issue of *Progressive Labor* and many related editorials followed.

[14] This whole topic warrants more attention. Do the middle-class act as agents for the corporate class in this way? Do they do their dirty work, so to speak? How much do/did their economic lives rely on the health of the coal business? Does/Did this class in the mountains of Eastern Kentucky have more power or have more at stake than its counterpart in other regions?

Kate Black is the curator of the Appalachian Collection at the University of Kentucky.

Community Mobilization: The Tug Hill Landfill Site

Beth Degutis

Modern lifestyles, and the technical advances that support those lifestyles, have caused a proliferation of trash that is all packed up with "no place to go." Every American produces an average of one ton of solid waste each year, and American businesses make a total of 250 million tons of hazardous waste during the same amount of time ("Garbology," 1988). Nearly half of the cities in our country will have filled up their underground dumps by 1990. Consequently, there is a rush to find new and acceptable places (at least on paper) to build solid waste disposal dumps—called landfills by their proponents.

It is not unusual for the agencies in charge to try to locate these landfills in unspoiled areas, where people are assumed to be less informed about the dangers they pose to drinking water and to the environment in general. In some areas, environmental protest groups have formed to try to force the proponents of landfills to listen to another side of the story. They do not want their water polluted, or their environment spoiled by toxic waste. Sometimes they simply do not want trash dumped in their backyards.

Further industrial growth in our country depends upon mass consumption. We have become a throw-away society. But, we live in a finite system that cannot continue indefinitely to absorb the results of this lifestyle. Trade-offs are constantly made between the different interest groups toward meeting their goals of increased profits or protecting the environment.

Communities are sometimes shocked by the realization that governments and agencies, supposedly designed for their benefit, have agendas quite different from their own. Economic and political considerations may make these agencies willing to pollute the environmental resources in return for high salaries and political free-wheeling over the short term. People living in the communities are forced to deal with the realization that things are not what they seemed. They may react by mobilizing grassroots environmental protest organizations, determined to expose the problem being forced upon them, and forcing perpetrators to rethink their positions.

When the residents of the rural area surrounding the Tug Hill plateau realized that New York State planned to build a large landfill in their midst, they formed Pure Water for Life. Their goal was to prevent the building of the landfill in order to protect their water supply from being polluted and the natural wildlife habitat from being destroyed. This paper will examine the organizational process used by Pure Water for Life from a resource mobilization perspective.

Analytical Framework

Since the Love Canal incident and the subsequent formation of The Citizens' Clearing House on Hazardous Wastes in 1981, the numbers of grassroots environmental protest groups have increased at a geometric rate. The Clearing House has worked with a total of more that 2700 groups in the United States, Canada, and Puerto Rico (Interview, 1988).

These groups can be analyzed from a social movements perspective using the resource mobilization model (see Oberschall, 1973; McCarthy and Zald, 1973 and 1977; Gamson, 1975). It is a multifactored model emphasizing the mobilization of resources, the strengths of organization, and the timeliness of political opportunity. The approach argues that groups of people can be mobilized in a crisis through their other memberships and made available to help with the work of organizing a movement. Resource mobilization theory emphasizes the significance of outside contributions and the cooptation of institutional resources (Jenkins, 1983).

Anti-technology movements tend to develop when the technology is new or when it is forced upon people without their consent (Mazur, 1985). The membership is often middle-aged or older and relatively well educated, with a history of previous involvement in public affairs. Members tend to have occupations that allow them to devote considerable amounts of time to the controversy. Retired men, housewives with grown children, writers, teachers, and scientists in fields related to the technology are likely to be involved with the movement.

The research design for studying the Rodman protest group involved the use of newspaper articles to establish the chronological order of developments. Video tapes of various meetings, obtained from the Pure Water for Life officers, provided insight into the positions taken by various stakeholders. Another video tape surveyed the topography of the land by foot and helicopter, explaining the location of the site and providing a glimpse of the beautiful countryside that may soon contain acres of garbage. "Tug Hill Tug of War," a documentary video tape done by graduate students from Syracuse University included personal stories told by residents of the Town of Rodman and interviews with DANC board member and editor of the local newspaper, John B. Johnson, Jr., and State University of New York hydro-geologist, Donald Coates, Ph.D. Telephone interviews with Pure Water for Life members added a social-psychological dimension to this resource mobilization analysis.

Case History of Pure Water for Life

The Tug Hill plateau is located in Jefferson County, about 60 miles north of Syracuse, New York, the closest major city. It is about 15 miles from Lake Ontario and about 40 miles from the Canadian border. Virgin forests starting here continue into the Adirondack State Park about 35 miles to the east. Winters are long and severe and the people have developed a hardiness that allows them to survive and enjoy the climate. Enthusiasm for outdoor sports, especially snowmobiling, cross country skiing, and hunting, abounds. The residents are proud of the natural beauty of their land and express an awareness that they have a personal "stake" in preserving it for themselves and future generations (L. M. Evans, personal communication, October 16, 1988).

Background of the Rodman Area

New York State is divided into counties, which are then divided into towns. Tug Hill plateau is in the Town of Rodman and people live in the village by the same name, in smaller settlements of a few homes each, or on farms. The Town covers an area of 27,264 acres. In this rural area town governments provide important services; e.g., road maintenance and winter snow removal. People identify with a town and build family roots accordingly.

During the 1940s and 1950s, the economy was based on farming, cheesemaking, and a variety of family-owned service businesses. Some individuals commuted ten miles to the nearest city, Watertown, and worked for the New York Air Brake or Black Clawson Company. Most women were housewives, but some worked as nurses, teachers, secretaries, sales clerks, or telephone operators. Family and community ties were very strong.

By about 1960 the small businesses had trouble competing with the conglomerates. Young people went away to college and found higher paying jobs in other areas. During the 1960s and 1970s, Rodman became primarily a community of older people living on fixed incomes.

They lived in the midst of an extraordinary, natural wildlife habitat. Many of them grew part of their own food, used the barter system for some of the goods and services they needed, and recycled or disposed of their own trash.

Progress would not wait, even in this rural area, and it made its presence felt in 1977. The village of Rodman's water system was outdated and in a bad state of disrepair. The water came from a natural spring and there were no pumping facilities. Pressure depended on gravity. Some of the pipes were made of wood. Local officials applied for a federal grant to update the system. It was given, with the stipulation that chlorine and flourine be added to the water. At the same time, a water tower was built to increase water pressure and the tradition of taking water directly from a natural spring was changed. The people of Rodman were very proud of their spring water, but they cooperated in the name of progress.

The 1980s brought more changes. Eight miles from Rodman, Dry Hill Air Force Station closed and the property was turned into a federal prison. Rodman was not consulted because Dry Hill is in the Town of Watertown. Rodman residents benefited, however, through employment and economic prosperity; for the first time in many years new houses were built.

In 1986, Fort Drum, an army post outside of Watertown that had been used by summer reservists, was developed into a full time major installation for winter warfare training. Large amounts of government money flowed into the area for the construction of housing, and for the development of an infrastructure capable of supporting the influx of army personnel and their families to the areas immediately surrounding the fort. Changes were needed in the numbers of school classrooms available, and in the capacity of water and sewage facilities. The population of Watertown was expected to double from 30,000 to 60,000 over the next few years. Fast food restaurants sprang up. Salmon Run opened, the first major shopping mall in a radius of about sixty miles. The media capitalized on the situation, arousing concern over these changes and the effects they would have on the lifestyles of long-time residents. Newspaper reporters and radio commentators urged local governments to examine their ordinances and rewrite them, if necessary, to prevent the establishment of pornographic and other undesirable businesses that might open up around the expanded army post.

New York State and the local governments of Jefferson and Lewis Counties created a special agency, the Developmental Authority of the North Country (DANC), to help with adjustments needed in the infrastructure to accommodate the increase in population. An Executive Director was appointed and given the responsibility for solving several immediate problems. He was asked to oversee the implementation of adequate water and sewage systems and to build a state of the art, area-wide landfill. The landfill would meet the solid waste disposal needs of Jefferson and Lewis Counties, the city of Watertown, and part of Fort Drum.

The DANC is governed by a board of directors with eight voting, and five non-voting, members. Board members have consistently been business leaders and politicians. Most of them are local residents, but one was an investment banker from New York City. He resigned on 1 November 1988 because of difficulties in traveling from New York City to Watertown.

Initial Organization

The residents of the Town of Rodman read newspaper accounts regarding the DANC plans to test a site on the Tug Hill plateau for a landfill and noticed the sudden appearance of strangers on their land. Based on the sketchy information that was available to them, residents were concerned about the environmental consequences of a landfill in the area and began to investigate the potential effects on their water supply.

The site is 1100 feet above sea level, the highest spot in Jefferson County. Average annual rainfalls of 46 inches and snowfalls of 120-140 inches mean that very large amounts of water run down all sides of the plateau to feed tributaries and major streams leading into Lake Ontario and Oneida Lake. The site chose for the landfill is nearly on top of a 55-mile long underground lake, or aquifer, that supplies water for the wells of rural residents, the village of Rodman, and the village of Adams. The village of Rodman's waterworks is located at a 752 foot elevation about two and a half miles from the site. Adams, a larger village about eight miles away in another Town, gets water for its 2700 people from the aquifer It is thought to be one of the few last naturally pure aquifers in New York State.

Residents of the area started to organize in October, 1986. They chose the name "Pure Water for Life" and worked toward building a mass of support. A geologist, a retired school principal, a retired lawyer, an accomplished artist, and men and women with a variety of other talents and educations joined forces to stop the landfill from becoming a reality. The DANC Executive Director remarked at the November meeting of the Town of Rodman Board of Trustees that the people of Rodman could fight the landfill if they wanted, but he would bankrupt the Town and it would be built (V.R. Brown, personal communication, 18 October 1988). This remark played an important role in setting the tone of relationships between the DANC and the residents.

A community meeting was planned by the residents for 14 January 1987, and the DANC officials were invited to share information and answer questions about the proposed landfill. The meeting was held in the Fire Hall with the Town Supervisor presiding. Residents attended in numbers sufficient to fill the building and spill over into the street.

The DANC Executive Director was introduced and he in turn introduced a variety of consulting experts. Each of them talked at length and indicated that the Tug Hill site had been chosen as the one most suitable for the landfill and, unless some unexpected evidence of unsuitability arose during testing, the landfill would be built there.

By the time the residents got to speak, three and a half hours into the meeting, frequent remarks were made by the DANC officials about the late hour, and a few of them dozed off. Despite this, the Rodman citizens voiced their objections, offered some alternatives, and expressed their considerable discomfort with the way the DANC claims seemed to be prefixed with "probably" or "possibly," but never with any kind of guarantee regarding the safety of their water supply. The director of research for the Temporary State Commission on Tug Hill, a state funded planning agency, spoke against the use of the site for a landfill. He suggested that it should be built closer to a suitable site for an incinerator, planned by the state to be in operation by 1995. Without coordination, the cost of transporting waste between the two locations would be exorbitant, and truck traffic on the highway between the two facilities would increase much more that the predicted twenty new tractor trailers per day. He concluded that the Tug Hill site was too far removed from any population center to be a practical place for a power generating incinerator.

When the DANC presentation was finally finished, and the Town Superintendent allowed questions, the DANC Executive Director brought out a kitchen timer and set it for two minutes as each questioner approached the microphone. A few expressed their annoyance; most simply ignored the buzzing until they had asked their question and received an answer. Many questions were referred to the County Superintendent from nearby Oswego County, who approached the podium frequently to assure the people that there were no problems with the Oswego landfill. Many comparisons were made between the proposed landfill for Rodman and the one in operation in Oswego because of their similar designs.

One questioner referred to a study that was completed in 1972 which concluded that Fort Drum had the most suitable land in the area for a landfill operation. Another asked the DANC to contact St. Lawrence County officials and offer to help them meet the expenses of the incinerator they were planning as a larger, cooperative effort. A college student from Cornell said that he planned to live in Rodman after graduation. When the DANC official scoffed that he would not find any employment in the area, the young man said that although there were few jobs, some things (hunting, fishing, and a beautiful countryside) were more important than money. The meeting continued for more than six hours, with residents repeatedly voicing their fears and lack of trust in the representatives of the state.

Even though the DANC Executive Director frequently reminded the residents that he lived in Jefferson County and had a personal interest in the general welfare of the area, they noted that he had avoided putting the landfill in his part of the county. They were resentful that a landfill could be imposed upon them and endanger their environment without their even having an opportunity to vote on it. They considered the DANC official's remarks to be arrogant and accepted the challenge of the DANC and of New York State.

A second meeting, held at the City-County Building in Watertown, was attended by about 50 Oswego County residents who did not see their landfill as the success the DANC suggested in the first meeting in Rodman. They chartered a bus to attend the meeting, hosted by the DANC, for further exchange of information. Anyone who wanted to ask questions at the meeting was assigned a place on the agenda. The Oswego residents were given a time so late that they had to leave before speaking. Their bus started its return trip at midnight.

Pure Water for Life hired an environmental lawyer who had a history of successes in helping grassroots organizations prevent the building of landfills in their areas. They incorporated in March, 1987, as a local not-for-profit organization devoted to preventing the use of the Tug Hill site for the landfill. Pure Water for Life was organized and led by middle aged and older men and women who rearranged their schedules to allow time for the work of organization and for self-education in the particular technology of landfills.

Surrounding towns and villages expressed support for Pure Water for Life. Fifteen sportsmen's groups and clubs drafted resolutions, wrote letters, and donated money. A variety of civic organizations became involved, including the Central New York Toxins Association and the Citizen's Clearing House for Hazardous Wastes. Support was offered by conservation groups such as the Sierra Club, the National Audubon Society, the Adirondack Conservation Council, the New York Conservation Council, the Adirondack Mountain Club, the New York State Fish and Wildlife Management Board, Regions 6, 7, and 8, and the New York State Fish and Wildlife Management Organization. The New York State Bureau of Environmental Conservation, Division of Fish and Wildlife, wrote a letter to the DANC stating that they felt cutting the softwood cover in the area of the proposed landfill site would significantly impact both food and travel lanes in the deer wintering yard. They added that they felt there could be no mitigation for this loss. After a series of aerial and ground checks of the 140 square mile deer yard, they completed a fact sheet estimating that 850 deer winter there. The New York State Department of Environment Conservation did a second fishery survey at the request of Pure Water for Life members, and demonstrated that Fish Creek, one and a half miles from the Tug Hill site, is a natural spawning trout brook.

The main concern of Pure Water for Life members was the protection of the Rodman water supply from landfill leachate, but they also identified and carefully defined four other important issues: protecting the deer wintering yard on Tug Hill which they believed provided food and shelter for approximately 1000 deer; preventing unsafe use of a winding, curvy highway and the narrow old bridges; informing the DANC about climate conditions that may lead to 14 or 15 foot snowdrifts and high winds during winter months; and the guarding against unnecessary uses of taxpayers' money to truck solid waste from more populous areas to the Rodman site.

During its first year, Pure Water for Life members provided leaflets at county fairs and entered floats in parades. They raised about $150,000 through individual donations, raffles and other activities. In the middle of their second year, they raised $6,000 in one evening by sponsoring a bowl-a-thon. Retired members have taken part-time jobs in order to help support the activities of Pure Water for Life. They hired a wildlife biologist and two hydro-geologists to help them prepare a case that would prove the site unsuitable for a landfill operation and prevent the issuance of a Department of Environmental Conservation (DEC) permit for its construction.

Attempts were made to limit the DANC access to the property by seeking court help in enforcing trespassing laws. The judiciary responded by issuing an order allowing the DANC to proceed with the testing. Pure Water for Life officers learned quickly that political like-mindedness and personal friendships between the DANC officials and other powerful individuals would inhibit their progress. John B. Johnson, Jr., editor and son of the owner of the *Watertown Daily Times*, is one of the non-voting members of the DANC's board.

The DANC has had some difficulties other than those imposed on it by the Pure Water for Life activists. A state Department of Transportation engineer and voting board member of the DANC resigned from the board early in September, 1988. He claimed the board was "fiscally out of control" and that DANC officials were more concerned with pay raises and job title changes than with the original goal of meeting the infrastructure needs of the 30 mile radius around Fort Drum (Foy, 1988a). An engineer for the city of Watertown warned city officials in early

December, 1988, that the regional landfill was too costly and environmentally "marginal" at best. He put his job on the line by preparing a statement to read at the hearings scheduled for 6 and 7 December (Foy, 1988b).

Emergence of an Environmental Ideology

A Pure Water for Life member and retired lawyer, Donald R. Ravenscroft, ran for the 26th Congressional District seat on the Democratic ticket in November, 1988. Rural northern New York state has traditionally been a Republican stronghold. When the residents realized that local and state officials were not interested in their plight, many of them changed party affiliations in order to run their own candidates on the less tightly controlled Democratic ticket. Ravenscroft campaigned on an environmental program, promising legislation that would phase out 90 per cent or more of the ocean dumping, landfilling, and incinerating by 1990, require products entering interstate commerce to be accompanied with instructions for recycling any waste that would result from their use, prohibit non-recyclable goods from being sold across state lines, and permit waste to be transported from one state to another only when in transit to a recycler. Ravenscroft lost the election by a three to one margin, but Pure Water for Life members were proud of their association with this candidate. He challenged an established powerful incumbent with a non-traditional program and got a remarkable number of votes.

Pure Water for Life drilled nine test wells on the Tug Hill site, so that it would not have to rely on the DANC for information. Members feel that they have proven beyond a reasonable doubt that the aquifer is very close to the Tug Hill plateau site. The DANC has continued to deny the aquifer's presence. The landfill proposal requires the purchase of a total of 1,173 acres. The landfill would occupy 340 acres and the rest of the land would be used as a buffer zone. All of the owners of the 19 parcels of property involved, except one who is a state employee, have returned payments sent to them by the DANC as reimbursement for damage done by trespassing and the drilling of test wells. They felt that accepting payment would imply consent.

A recycling center was organized as a cooperative effort between Pure Water for Life and the Town of Rodman. The Town provided legislation that makes recycling mandatory and supplied money to pay for the materials to construct a building. Pure Water for Life members provided education for the residents and staffed the center with volunteers for its first year. In the first year of operation, from 1987 to 1988, they were able to reduce the quantity of solid waste that needed to be disposed in dumps or landfills by 67.8 per cent volume and 45.2 per cent weight. Only about 10 per cent of the residents do not participate in recycling (Recycle Report, 1988).

The New York State Environmental Commission has included mandatory recycling in its new solid waste regulations. The regulations are designed to be in place by the beginning of 1989. Municipalities will have to meet recycling quotas in order to get landfill permits. The goal is to reduce solid waste 50 per cent by 1997. Changes have already taken place at the grassroots level and are finally being written into law.

A two volume draft environmental impact statement was completed for the DANC near the end of October, 1988. Of the 101 sites considered, the Rodman site was found to be the best suited for the landfill. An engineering estimate had put the cost of testing at $300,000; $2,000,000 was spent. The study determined that the Rodman water supply is derived from a groundwater source independent of the regional flow system and that the landfill would pose no threat to it. The environment impact statement also found that there is no direct connection between the landfill site and the Tug Hill aquifer. Their consultants concluded that the landfill will actually benefit the deer by providing more winter food with greater accessibility that has existed in the past.

Asked about the deer herd, the DANC officials said that when the landfill is completed it will be covered and seeded and make excellent grazing for them. This information seemed strange to the Rodmanites who knew that deer do not graze, they browse. And they especially like the cover offered by the threatened virgin hemlock forest on the Tug Hill plateau during the cold winter months.

The public and, especially, the members of Pure Water for Life, have a few weeks to read and respond to the document. They are continuing to use every means at their disposal to put pressure on the DANC to consider the serious consequences of proceeding with this project. Reports have been made of a new flurry of activity on Tug Hill as the DANC rushes to complete a new series of tests. Telephone chains have been set up to keep members of Pure Water for Life informed and focused on the importance of a large turn out at the public hearings scheduled for 6 and 7 December 1988. The hearings, presided over by a judge, offer the people an opportunity to respond to the draft environmental impact statement.

The Rodmanites, confronted with a threat to their water supply and environment, realize that the government's and the Department of Environmental Conservation's interests are not the same as theirs. Rodman has the kind of natural balance that governments and conservation groups talk about protecting, and, in this case, the supposed protectors are the enemy. It has been especially alarming to the property owners that state employees could work on their land with bulldozers and backhoes, and even drill wells, without their permission. When the property owners tried to get an injunction to keep the trespassers away, it was denied. In the words of one resident, "They don't care about the people. It's the guy who makes the buck" (Walker, Mrozek, Hoffman, 1987).

Pure Water for Life signs have been very visible. The farmer who owns the biggest tract that the DANC wants for the landfill has a sign in his front yard that reads, "This farm was my dream, now it may become a landfill nightmare" (Walker, Mrozek, Hoffman, 1987). Residents have been dismayed at the arrogance of the state officials and have remarked over and over again that it would not be as bad if they could at least vote on whether or not they want a landfill on the Tug Hill plateau.

The landfill offers no benefit to the local people. Its large size seems to indicate plans to import waste from places other than Jefferson and Lewis Counties, the City of Watertown, and part of Fort Drum in order for it to be cost effective. The members of Pure Water for Life have built a network with other environmental activist groups and have kept up their battle for nearly two years; they have not simply joined the "Not In My Backyard" (NIMBY) bandwagon. As rural landowners, they take care of their own trash and are not anxious to take responsibility for that of New York City or the military at Fort Drum. But, their major concern is protecting their water supply and the natural wildlife on the Tug Hill plateau. They have a stake in protecting the land for themselves and future generations.

Real progress in controlling pollution is not made by containing pollutants once they are in the environment. It comes from eliminating the source by stopping the production of the pollutant. While "the levels of most pollutants have declined only modestly, and others not at all, a few have been reduced sharply: lead, DDT, and similar chlorinated pesticides, mercury in surface waters, radioactive fallout from nuclear-bomb tests, and, in some rivers, phosphates" (Commoner, 1987). These successes, which began to fulfill the aim of the environmental movement, have been achieved by simply eliminating the pollutants. Pure Water for Life was organized to stop the pollution of the Tug Hill aquifer before it happens.

Analysis and Discussion

Most of the residents of Rodman have lived there for a long time. Everyone knows everyone. They are proud of the beautiful countryside and feel they have a "stake" in protecting it. One family allowed the DANC to park vehicles on their property and soon felt snubbed by other residents. Pure Water for Life offers its members the social benefits of camaraderie for busy schedules.

A considerable proportion of the residents are retired, work in businesses that allow some flexibility in time schedules, or are housewives. They support the volunteer fire department, either as firemen or auxiliary, and other established organizations. Because of their flexible schedules and experience in organizing activities, many residents were available to be mobilized for this new cause.

The residents had already experienced the disappointment of giving up their pure spring water in the name of progress and had seen the nearby Dry Hill Air Force Base turned into a federal prison. They had been alerted by the media to look for major threats to their rural lifestyle as Fort Drum expanded into a major army training center for winter warfare. Meetings and planning sessions had been held between the counties and they considered the Development Authority of the North Country to be their invention, not their master. The landfill proposal came at a time when the residents had reached both the level of government interference in their lives that they would tolerate and had developed social networks that could be transformed into sympathy for the protest movement.

Fundraising became an extension of the regular social life of the residents. The summer time work of organization was highlighted by providing leaflets at county fairs and entering floats in parades. During the winter months, they sponsored some very successful fund-raising activities including bowl-a-thons. Pure Water for Life organizers looked for creative ways to add fund-raising dimensions to activities that members enjoy or would participate in normally. Friends and neighbors worked together in planning the fund-raising and those who could not help in the preparation participated in the actual event in the same way they have always supported the fire department's activities.

Pure Water for Life members concentrated on building networks with other environmental groups across the country, taking advantage of opportunities to learn about landfill technology. Their community is only about 175 miles from Love Canal and they quickly sought help from The Citizens' Clearing House for Hazardous Wastes and a wide variety of other state and national organizations concerned with conservation and the environment. The residents were repulsed by what they learned, and looked for alternative means for disposing of solid waste. The Recycling center that they built in cooperation with the Town of Rodman had been extraordinarily successful.

They are shocked by the willingness of government officials to trade off essential natural resources, even people's drinking water, for a few high salaries over the short term. People who might have the power to make a difference seem to be connected in a sort of "good ol' boy" system with an agenda quite different from that of the people of Rodman. Some supporters of Pure Water for Life have changed their political party affiliation because the locally powerful Republican party has consistently refused to hear their case. Donald R. Ravenscroft, a member of the organization, ran for Congress on the Democratic ticket with an environmental program. He challenged a powerful incumbent and raised issues that had not been raised in previous campaigns.

Activists fighting a proposed landfill differ from those coping with a landfill that is already leaking. The residents of Rodman have been able to take a proactive approach as opposed to the reactionary one they would have been forced into if the pollution was already occurring. Their effort has been directed toward proving that the Tug Hill site is not suitable for a landfill operation and demonstrating the feasibility of recycling as a means of gaining some control over the quantities of waste that accumulate. Pure Water for Life members have invested a lot of time in self-education. Older people and those with flexible schedules are leading the movement. In situations where the focus is on stopping pollution that has already started, younger people and mothers of young children anxious to avoid future health problems are most often involved in environmental activism (Hamilton, 1985).

The DANC spent $2,000,000 of taxpayers' money in testing the Tug Hill site. When the danger of added traffic to the curvy, narrow highway was mentioned, the DANC officials said they would fix it. Questions about ongoing monitoring of the water in rural wells, at the Rodman waterworks and in Adams, were answered with assurances that the DANC, and the DEC, would accept the responsibility (Meeting at Rodman Fire Hall, 1987). Homeowners' expressions of disappointment over the devaluation of their extraordinary homes, built into the picturesque countryside adjacent to the landfill site, were met with an offer from the DANC Executive Director to buy one of the most valuable ones as a home for the caretaker (Landfill Site, 1987).

The residents are concerned about this "shotgun" approach to planning. Promises are couched in vague language and the term "guarantee" is used to make points, but not in any legal sense. An officer of Pure Water for Life said, "Guarantees are more like what you get when you buy a car. You can take it to a mechanic and get it fixed. There is no way to fix a polluted aquifer" (Meeting at Rodman Fire Hall, 1987).

Several corporations have announced that they are no longer interested in using the proposed Tug Hill landfill for their solid waste. Champion International Corporation officials said the company wants to avoid being the "deep pockets" in possible future lawsuits (Hummel, 1989). The City Council of Watertown has asked the City Manager to "study what it would cost the city to build its own landfill or incinerator" and to review the contract it signed with the DANC in October, 1986 (City and the Landfill, 29 December 1988).

Preliminary hearings on the draft environmental impact statement prepared by the DEC will be held in Watertown (Jefferson County) on 6 December, during the afternoon and evening, and in Lowville (Lewis County) on 7 December, in the evening. Pure Water for Life members have formed telephone chains and are busy reminding the residents and other supporters to prepare their statements and come to the hearings.

Conclusion

Pure Water for Life members have taken a proactive, even creative approach to dealing with the environmental threat that is being forced upon them They are deeply committed to the protection of their water supply and the wildlife habitat and have kept their energies focused on these issues. The threat came at a time when the people were expecting change and local governments had signed contracts with the Development Authority of the North Country. The governments and residents assumed that the DANC would represent their combined interests during this time of transition.

On the one hand, Pure Water for Life has enjoyed the support of many environmental groups and some concerned scientists while, on the other, they have had to cope with the editor of the only local daily newspaper being a member of the governing board of the DANC. With hearing on the suitability of the Tug Hill site for the landfill project approaching, Pure Water for Life members are continuing to build their case and to pressure the DANC to admit the presence of the aquifer and its environmental sensitivity.

Works Cited

City and the Landfill. 1988. *Watertown Daily Times*. 29 December 1988, 4.

Commoner, Barry. 1987. "A Reporter at Large." *New Yorker*. 15 June 1985, 46-71.

Foy, Paul. 1988. "Norris: Authority Could Explode." *The Watertown Daily Times*. 7 September 1988, 1, 20.

Foy, Paul. 1988. "Sligar will Sally Forth to Slay Landfill Plans." *The Watertown Daily Times*. 6 December 1988.

Gamson, William A. 1975. *The Strategy of Social Protest*. Homewood: Dorsey Press.

Garbology. 1988. *The Economist 302:* February 1988, 82.

Gibbs, Lois. 1988. Interview. "Grassroots Leader, Lois Gibbs, Speaks Out on Contaminated Drinking Water." *Water Technology.* September 1988, 13-18.

Hamilton, Lawrence C. 1985. "Concern About Toxic Wastes: Three Demographic Predictors." *Sociological Prespectives* 28: 4, October 1985, 463-485.

Hummel, Scott E. 1989. "Mill Running Into Trouble on Landfill." *Watertown Daily Times.* 5 January 1989.

Jenkins, Craig J. 1983. "Resource Mobilization Theory and the Study of Social Movements." *Annual Review of Sociology 9:* 527-53.

Landfill Site. 1987. *Walking Tour,* video tape. Rodman, NY: Pure Water for Life.

Mazur, Allan. 1985. *The Dynamics of Technical Controversy.* Washington, DC: Communications Press.

McCarthy, John D. and Mayer N. Zald. 1973. *The Trend of Social Movements in America: Professionalization and Resource Mobilization.* Morristown: General Learning Press.

McCarthy, John D. and Mayer N. Zald. 1973. "Resource Mobilization and Social Movements: A Partial Theory." *American Journal of Sociology, 82:* May 1973, 1212-41.

Meeting at Rodman Fire Hall. 1987. *DANC Presentation* video tape, 14 January 1987, Rodman, NY: Pure Water for Life.

Oberschall, Anthony. 1973. *Social Conflict and Social Movements.* Englewood Cliffs: Prentice Hall.

Recycle Report. 1988. *Town of Rodman Recycle Report.* 9 September 1988. Rodman, NY: Town of Rodman.

Walker, A.D., C.V. Mrozek and A.J. Hoffman. 1987. *Tug Hill Tug of War* video tape. Syracuse, NY: Syracuse University Newhouse School of Communications.

Beth Degutis is a Ph.D. candidate in sociology at the University of Tennessee, Knoxville. After working for several years as a registered nurse, she earned degrees in health education and in public health. Currently her interest is in environmental sociology.

The Bitter Creek Appalachian Symposium

Garry Barker

Buddy and the Bootleg Bandits reverently played that old Appalachian folksong, "Get Martha White self-rising flour, the real all-purpose flour," and the music flowed happily. Clarence Whittimore led the way on his steel guitar, and Alfred Cox followed on creaky fiddle. Buddy tugged down the brim of his black ten-gallon hat, glared out from behind wraparound sunglasses, and sang in a nasal monotone.

Most of the crowd was already noisily drunk. Buddy grinned wolfishly and dragged the tune out two more verses. He finished with a flourish. "Thankee, thankee," Buddy growled into the microphone. "Ya'll a nice crowd. Real nice. We appreciate it."

The Third Annual Bitter Creek Humor & Folklore Society's Appalachian Symposium was in full swing. Buddy and the Bandits had already played "All My Rowdy Friends," "I Like Beer," and "Don't Let Your Babies Grow Up To Be Cowboys," and now were ready to do some authentic mountain music.

"We're gonna do a little thing for you now that my granddaddy learned me," announced Buddy. "Grandpa, he never did see the words wrote down. He just learned her by listening." Buddy grinned. "Now what Granddaddy was listening to, it was a stereo tape. Grandma's new microwave oven has got a digital alarm clock, a dual tape deck, and chimes that play 'My Old Kentucky Home.' Anyhow, this here is a old mountain song my grandpa picked up while he was out in the kitchen heating up a pizza. Ready, boys?"

"The Devil Went Down to Georgia" featured Alfred's frantic fiddlework and Buddy's busy vocals plus tight harmony on the "Fire on the Mountain" segment.

As the tune ended, to rowdy applause, George Peters was trying to locate a parking place outside The Maverick Club. George finally edged the silver Volvo into a slot between a jacked-up, four-wheel-drive pickup truck and a sleek yellow 1957 Chevy Bel Aire. "Here we are," George announced grandly. "The elegant Maverick Club, on the weedy outskirts of suburban Pikeville, Kentucky."

The tall woman sniffed suspiciously.

"That's Bud Wilson's fish fry," chuckled George. "Deep fried catfish and hushpuppies and french fries. You won't see a whole lot of yogurt and alfalfa sprouts at the Bitter Creek Symposium."

Dr. Amanda Coldiron, Ph.D in Rural Sociology and visiting professor in the University of Kentucky Appalachian Center, uncoiled gingerly from the big Volvo seat. "What have you done to me, George?" she asked with a half-smile. She cocked an ear to listen. "Are they handling snakes in there?"

George grinned. "Not yet."

Amanda shuddered. "Are you sure this is safe?"

"Just don't get near Lem Stephenson," cautioned George. "Lem thinks all outside women are like some of the girls who came here in the sixties with VISTA. Lem laid stoned, in bed for three years, and he still gets a glazed look about him when he hears a city accent."

"Very funny," said Amanda. She hesitated. "Which one is Lem?"

"He looks like Little Abner," grinned George, "and talks out of the corner of his mouth. Like Elvis."

"You're kidding." Amanda laughed nervously.

"Am I?" George grinned. "There's just one way to find out. Ready?"

As they walked closer to the Maverick Club the noises were even louder. Somebody was vomiting between two trucks, and giggles and groans came from inside a red and black Monte Carlo. "Don't look now," advised George, "but it sounds like Lem has met another anti-poverty worker." He led Amanda to the front door. "After you," George said gallantly, "and welcome to the Bitter Creek Appalachian Symposium."

Amanda stopped halfway inside. "My God," she whispered. George shoved her on in, and followed. Buddy looked up, stopped the music, and pointed. "Here he is, folks," bellowed Buddy. "The poet laureate of the Bitter Creek Humor & Folklore Society, George Peters."

George waved to Buddy and somebody stuck a bottle of beer in his hand. "We'll hear more from George later," promised Buddy. "He said he'd read us a poem. Bitter Creek Breakdown." There were groans and boos. "But first," continued Buddy, "let's turn Clarence loose on the steel guitar."

Buddy left the band on stage, shucked his guitar, and worked through the maze of cords and connectors to greet George and Amanda at their table. "Dr. Amanda Coldiron," announced George, "meet Dr. Edward Chase."

"Dr. Edward L. Chase?" asked Amanda, staring blankly.

"Buddy to my friends," he laughed. "How's the beer?" Buddy poured from a plastic pitcher. "The Maverick is fresh out of white wine."

Amanda sipped, still awed by Buddy's presence. "Dr. Chase, I've read all your books."

"The name's Buddy," said Buddy, "and I've read all of yours too, but that doesn't mean we can't be friends." Buddy drained his mug and beamed. "So, Dr. Amanda Coldiron, what brings you to Pikeville tonight?"

"I thought George was serious," Amanda said weakly, "when he told me about the Bitter Creek Symposium. He said to come here if I wanted to meet some real Appalachians." Amanda stiffened. "I didn't know I was coming to an orgy. What is this place?"

"A genuine redneck honky tonk," grinned Buddy. "One that nobody has put in a book yet, so a body can still come here and have some fun."

"But," stammered Amanda, "what kind of symposium is this?"

"According to Dr. Chase," explained George, "a symposium, in the original sense of the word, was a time when a lot of people got together and did a lot of hard drinking."

Amanda glared. "So it's all just one big, not very funny joke. The symposium, the Bitter Creek Humor & Folklore Society, and your presence here."

"Not exactly," laughed Buddy. "It's sort of a conditioned reaction. The Appalachian Studies Conference, the New River Symposium, the Appalachian Humor Festival, and Saturday Night in Eastern Kentucky all rolled into one. With lots of beer, music, dancing, and laughing right out loud."

"I should have expected something like this from George," sniffed Amanda. "But not from you, Dr. Chase, you're a very respected scholar and professor."

"That's the cross I must bear," groaned Buddy. "Don't hold it against me. Want some more beer?" Buddy called for another pitcher, refilled the mugs and leaned close to Amanda. "Dr. Coldiron, every person in this room is a native Appalachian. People from families who've lived here eight, maybe ten generations, people who've never read your books, or my books, who wouldn't know Harry Caudill if he fell through the door screaming. But they'd buy Harry a beer." Buddy smiled. "There's not one dulcimer player, Danish folk dancer, academic storyteller, or ballad singer in the building. Just truckers, clerks, waitresses, bankers, coal miners, farmers, schoolteachers, a few bootleggers, and not more than a dozen used car salesmen. Take a good look,

Dr. Coldiron. Like it or not, these are the people you study and write about."

Amanda looked around the room and sniffed distastefully. "Does anybody ever get killed during your symposium?"

"Not so far," said Buddy. "We've had some broken jaws, bloody noses, some food poisoning, and a few pregnancies."

"I understand now," said Amanda. "This is all research for you. You're going to put it all in a new book."

"No way," scowled Buddy. "That wouldn't be right. I leave that kind of writing to George, only he calls it fiction and the editors give him hell for not writing about believable characters. George's weirdest stuff is just the pure truth with the names changed."

"The Maverick Club is a beer joint," George said quietly. "That's all. It's like the ones I grew up in, a few counties over. Call it a settlement school for rednecks." He chuckled. "When I went off to college, I had to hunt all over for a place where I felt at home. I found the old White Horse Tavern over in Richmond, but then had to quit going there when the bartender shot a customer. After that they checked IDs, and a seventeen year old couldn't get in."

"Does everybody in Eastern Kentucky spend their time in places like these?" Amanda asked weakly.

"Lord no," George said quickly. "My mother would burn this place down. But, I'd say attendance here comes in a close second to church services." He shrugged and grinned. "Lots of the same people at both places, too." George smiled. "Here, they let Buddy bring his band and have some fun. Sometimes a student or two will wander in, but the Maverick is too rough for kids used to rock bars, so it's pretty much just the natives who come back."

"So why did you drag me up here?" asked Amanda.

"To round your education," grinned George. "The hillbilly bars in Lexington that you go to are patterned after places like this, but you needed to see the real thing. In person. This is pure, scholarly research."

"I'd better get back to the band," said Buddy. "They're slowing down." Back onstage Buddy brought Alfred and a wolfish young mandolin player up closer to the microphone. "We're going to do a number now for Dr. Amanda Coldiron," grinned Buddy. "This one's for you, doc. Ready, boys?"

The band leapt into a wailing, hard-driving bluegrass version of "Long, Lanky Woman."

George howled, and Amanda bristled. "I've certainly learned the truth about Dr. Edward Chase," she snapped. "Monday morning his books come off the reading lists for my classes."

"Settle down and have a beer," suggested George.

Amanda sipped numbly and stared out across the dimly lit cement block dance hall.

George chuckled. "You'll see more Kentucky Cluster diamond rings, polyester, pancake makeup, sideburns, and gold chains in here tonight than you could find back in New Jersey in a month of Sundays. And any one of those big trucks out there in the parking lot costs more than you paid for that Saab."

Amanda studied George, slumped happily back in his chair, and smiled. "You don't belong here," Amanda said triumphantly. "Your blow-dried hair and plain glasses are a dead giveaway. Not to mention that fifty dollar sweatshirt and the scuffed up sneakers." She smiled, a little drunk and evil. "You, George Peters, are a fake. You're no more Appalachian than I am."

George shrugged. "Once I open my mouth all is forgiven. Once a hillbilly, always a hillbilly. No matter what you look like."

"Don't you find the term 'hillbilly' degrading?" asked Amanda.

"From you I would," said George, "or from anybody else who meant it as a slur. But I was a hillbilly, and damned proud to be one, a long time before some scholars and bureaucrats decided I was an Appalachian."

"Then why don't you live here?" Amanda asked. "And why don't you have any sideburns down to your neck?"

"Couldn't make a living here," grunted George.

"You could work in the mines," persisted Amanda. "Sell mobile homes. Teach English."

George grinned. "But then I'd never get to meet people like you. Besides, I like my running water and central air."

"They've got that here now," argued Amanda. "Plus satellite television, VCRs, fast food, cocaine, and venereal diseases."

"True," grinned George. He drank again, and sighed. "We've been given that kind of progress in Eastern Kentucky. I grew up on a hillside farm with nine brothers and sisters, an outhouse, and a big old heatstove. The happiest day of my young life was when they ran electricity and my parents brought home a used cookstove. That meant I didn't have to split kindling and carry coal all summer. Now, the kids eat pizza and walk around with ear plug radios, drive Camaros, and work at Druther's. Half of them can't read or write above a third grade level, but they're overweight, healthy as horses, and sexually active from the time they're twelve."

"Weren't you?" smirked Amanda.

"I sure did want to be," George said mournfully. "I just couldn't get anyone to cooperate."

"Why did you leave?" asked Amanda. "Seriously, George, why didn't you just stay at home?"

"College, I guess." George swirled his beer and pondered. "I wanted to go to school some more. I figured there had to be more to life than driving a truck or growing a crop, and it seemed to me that the only way out was college. I had good grades and test scores, and scholarship offers, but I still couldn't afford school in Lexington, so I went to Berea."

"The school for Appalachians," smiled Amanda.

George grunted. "When I was there, most of the faculty tried to make me over into a midwestern missionary. They didn't like anything about the way I talked, acted, or thought." He poured more beer. "But there were some professors who liked me the way I was. One even let me write about Eastern Kentucky while everybody else was imitating J.D. Salinger."

"I've tried to read your fiction," said Amanda. "You use too much dialect, too much stereotype, and far too much crude humor."

"Thank you," said George. He signalled for more beer. "Drink up, Dr. Coldiron. You get graded on class participation."

"You're already drunk," said Amanda. "How are we going to get back to Lexington?"

"On the great Bert T. Combs Mountain Parkway," George said grandly. "We'll crash the Winchester Wall at about ninety then cruise on up I-64 to the beautiful city built by the people who moved away from Hazard."

"What's the Winchester Wall?" Amanda asked anxiously.

"The Winchester Wall," George said solemnly, "is the great invisible barrier which keeps Eastern Kentucky from polluting the sacred bluegrass. They don't dare bring the Japanese carmakers past the Wall. If they did, we might shoot them. Some of us haven't forgotten Pearl Harbor." George leaned closer. "The Winchester Wall, Dr. Coldiron, is the line the Kentucky politicians drew when it came to divide up the power and money. Eastern Kentucky gets the shaft. Always has, always will. We're outnumbered, outvoted, and outspent. New industry goes to the golden triangle, Lexington, Louisville, and Cincinnati, and our coal severance taxes help pay for getting them there."

"That's sort of a one-sided evaluation," smiled Amanda.

"I can be one-sided if I want to," mumbled George. "I'm a deprived minority."

Buddy and The Bootleg Bandits played "Blue Moon of Kentucky," and George sang along.

"You're very drunk," observed Amanda.

"Part of my heritage," grinned George. "I come from a long line of men who got very drunk now and then."

"Since you're so wound up," smiled Amanda, "what warped view of the future do you have? What comes next for Eastern Kentucky?"

"In a hundred years," George announced profoundly, "this place where we're sitting will be in the middle of a desert. Or a garbage dump. When the coal is all gone, we may become the refuse depository for all of the Eastern United States."

"My God," laughed Amanda. "Now you've turned morbid."

"A genetic defect," said George. "I'm descended from the scum of London, you know."

"Such a pessimist," said Amanda, smiling gently. "Don't you see any hope? Any changes that could make things different?"

George shrugged. "Schools. But that won't happen until parents and taxpayers decide to value education enough to foot the bills, and that's not likely until there are jobs here for the ones who do get educated. But we can't get the industry until we improve the schools, so it's sort of a hopeless, vicious circle." He sighed. "In my home county, unemployment runs about 25%. Half of the ones who do work commute. A hundred to two hundred miles a day, for low-end jobs. The counties themselves are a big part of the problem. Too many, too small and too poor to support good schools and services; too crooked to change."

Amanda grinned. "What about the welfare system? I assume you hate it too?"

"No," said George, "I don't. At least now nobody starves to death, or freezes, and thirty years ago that happened. I don't like the way the system penalizes the ones who want to work, but anything is better than the misery some people used to endure."

George rocked his chair back and continued. "I'll tell you what kills me. It's the hopelessness. You see so many people who've given up. They won't try any more. They've been whipped, then whipped again, and now they've quit. It all changed so fast, after World War II, that some families never did adjust. Up till then you could live pretty good without cash money. With enough kids to do the work, you could scratch a living out of a hillside farm. Grow or shoot your own food, order whatever else you had to have from the Sears & Roebuck catalog, and survive if you'd worked hard enough. That ain't so any more. You can work your butt off and still have to have help."

George drank more beer and stared morosely at his hands. "I'm one hell of a scholar. I preach doom, practicing raising cane. I love Eastern Kentucky but won't live here. I want it to change, but I want it to stay the same. I'm full of questions, but I don't have one single damned answer." George smiled wearily. "Welcome to the Bitter Creek Appalachian Symposium, Dr. Coldiron."

Amanda watched George, as he emptied the beer pitcher and signalled for one more. Buddy came back to the table. "Have you two solved all the ills of Appalachia, or have you said the hell with it and got crocked?"

Amanda had kicked off her sensible shoes, crossed her legs, and had opened the top buttons of her silk blouse. Buddy grinned. "Enjoying yourself, Dr. Coldiron?"

Amanda nodded and smiled sadly.

"I can tell. Old Lonesome George has been on the stump." Buddy chuckled. "Fill George full of beer and he'll preach until somebody stuffs a towel in his mouth. The drunker George gets, the more sense he makes. Or is it the drunker I get, the more sense he makes?" Buddy laughed. "Whatever. I guess George told you about the vast wasteland?"

"In detail," Amanda said thickly.

"George Peters is a walking contradiction," said Buddy. "He was too old to be a good hippie, and he's too young to be a proper mountaineer. George is smack-dab in between. About one more pitcher and he'll want to sing with the band. Did you ever hear a slobbery drunk try to sing 'Amazing Grace'?"

Amanda giggled. "Maybe we'll do a duet."

"A new George and Tammy," grinned Buddy.

"Who's that?" asked Amanda.

"You poor thing," grinned Buddy. "You just ain't been educated."

"Dr. Coldiron has led a very sheltered life," George said. "Until tonight she didn't even know about hillbillies."

"And she's learned from you?" Buddy snorted. "This man here," he told Amanda, "drinks beer for breakfast. He can shoot like Daniel Boone, but ain't killed a squirrel or rabbit in thirty years. He's got a 1959 Ford pickup and a new Volvo. He keeps a pack of red tick hounds out back of a house that came right out of *Architectural Digest*. George would die without air conditioning. He writes fiction. How could you believe a word George Peters says? He's about as much of a hillbilly as I am a cowboy, except I come closer because I at least got boots and a hat."

"I got a cap," protested George.

"And it says 'Eat More Possum' right across the front." Buddy grinned, and leaned close to speak softly to Amanda. "I've heard rumors that George Peters listens to classical music and goes to aerobics classes. I know for a fact that he drinks Perrier water and orders boots from L. L. Bean."

Amanda giggled.

George scowled.

"Have you seen George's bumper sticker?" Buddy asked. "The one that says 'Minor Regional Writer'?"

Amanda nodded.

"In George's case," said Buddy, "that sticker is the honest-to-God truth."

George nodded his agreement. "But it ain't my fault," he added, "that I write about such a minor region."

"My God," said Amanda. "I've stumbled onto the set of 'Hee Haw.' Where are the dancing pigs?" She stopped George. "Please don't answer that question." Amanda shook her head and sipped on the beer. "How," she asked, "are we ever going to get back to Lexington? George can't possibly drive, and I'm a little too drunk to try it."

"Just get a little drunker," grinned Buddy, "and drive like the natives do. Stop and shoot up a few road signs. Pull off on the ditch to puke and sleep it off. If the sheriff gets you all you have to do is spend the night in Pikeville jail."

Amanda grimaced.

"It ain't all that bad," shrugged George. "You get pork-and-beans twice a day and a shower once a week."

"How would you know?" asked Amanda.

"Research," grinned George. "Pure scholarly research. Working on a paper. 'Famous Kentucky Jailhouses I Have Known.' We'll get Appalshop to make the movie, with Ned Beatty." He yelled for more beer and studied Amanda. "Well, Dr. Coldiron, how do you like the real Appalachia? Will this change the way you teach?"

Amanda peered over her glasses at the two men who sat smiling at her. "Not really," she finally said. "But I might bring my class to your next Symposium."

"You do that," Buddy said wearily. "Bring the youngens to see the hillbillies up close. Have them write essays about how the mountaineers drink away their frustrations." Buddy drained his mug. "Ready, George?"

"Ready for what?" mumbled George.

"Your poetry reading," beamed Buddy. He shoved back his chair. "This here's the serious part, Dr. Coldiron. Literature. Classy stuff." Buddy wobbled to the stage, stopped the band, and bent to the microphone. "Here's what you've all been waiting for, folks," he said dryly. "It's time for George." Buddy waved away the groans. "Here he is."

George shuffled up to the mike, pulled a tattered paper out of his pocket, coughed, and blushed. "I'll make it fast," he mumbled. "This is 'Bitter Creek Breakdown'." George bent over close to the mike and read:

> Up here on Bitter Creek
> The water runs green and acid yellow
> Clogged by Pampers and Clorox jugs
> Refrigerators and shells of old Chevrolets.
>
> The government run us a water line
> In 1968, so we got a mobile home,

And Uncle John's Black Lung check
Pays the bills
Ever since we voted wet
And a body can't make a living no more
Bootlegging.

Cousin Jeff grows marijuana
Over on Poosey Mountain
But he says it's hard to make any cash money.
Last year some old boys from
Hazard stole half his crop
And this year the cows got in
And et it.

They give mighty good milk for a while,
Jeff said,
But then they got all sniffly and red-eyed
Went to wearing red bandannas
And writing poetry.

Brother Ben went to Vietnam
And come home a hippie.
Beard, hair
Old Army field jackets
And a strange look in his eyes.

But now they made him a memorial
Over in Frankfort
And the lottery, it's going to get Ben a hundred-dollar bonus
So I guess it's okay
That he still don't sleep at night
Can't hear out of one ear
Or hold down a job.

There's work up around Lexington, they say
If a body'll drive two hours each way
Build Japanese cars
Or sweep up floors for one of the coal companies
That owns most of this county.

No work here, though.
Mines are about shut down,

Timber's all cut,
And the government's idea of how to get us all back to work
Is to have us make quilts, whittle, spin and weave,
And peddle our stuff to the tourists.

Ain't no tourists here, though.

And factories, they say,
Won't come to the mountains.
Bad roads, bad water, and bad schools,
And we're all too damned ornery to work
When it's squirrel season.

So here on Bitter Creek
We got to go it on our own
Scrouge out a living somehow
Hang onto this hillside
And 80 acres of scrub timber.

You ask me why?

Why, this here land's been ours for 200 years.
Up in that graveyard they's markers
Ten generations that lived here
And died poor.

So I got to stay.
Got to keep the strip miners out
Of Grandpap's graveyard
Scratch out enough cash money
To send the youngens to school
And get 'em a little Christmas.

But don't you worry none.
When it's all over,
When the coal's give out,
The creeks is dry,
And the do-gooders have done
Give up and gone

We'll still be right here.

George folded up his paper, stepped back, nodded to the audience, and waited, uneasy in the sudden silence.

"Goddamn," Buddy finally growled. "You'd take the fun out of a funeral, George. Why'd you have to go and read that?" Buddy waved to the band. "Play," he ordered. "Give us a little bit of 'Foggy Mountain Breakdown.' George, get your skinny butt off of that stage."

As the band leapt into the driving music George walked slowly back to the table and sat down heavily. "Beer," he said. Dr. Amanda Coldiron poured.

"I think you need this," she said. "For what it's worth, George, I liked your poem."

"Me too," grinned Buddy, "but I couldn't let everybody stand around all embarrassed, and this bunch ain't much to show it when they get serious."

George shrugged. "Hey, it's a symposium, right?"

"Right," laughed Buddy. "We all came here to learn, didn't we?" He leaned closer to Amanda. "And what I want you to learn next is the words to a song. I want you to do a number with us."

"Me?" Amanda stared.

But, thirty minutes later, with George Peters swaying beside her singing harmony, Dr. Amanda Coldiron belted out a gutsy rendition of "It Wasn't God Who Made Honky Tonk Angels," and the Bitter Creek Appalachian Symposium was back in session.

The poem has been published in ***Appalachian Heritage****, **New River Free Press** (Appalachian Voices), and in **Bitter Creek Breakdown**.*

Garry Barker is assistant director and marketing manager of the Berea College Student Crafts Program in Berea, Kentucky. His published books include three short story collections—*Fire on the Mountain, Mountain Passage,* and *All Night Dog*—plus a novel, *Copperhead Summer.* His short fiction has appeared in *Appalachian Heritage, Grab-a-Nickel, The Mountain, Delta Scene,* and *The Mountain Spirit.*

A Bridge or a Barrier?: Assessing the Usefulness of Public Education for Individual Success in an East Tennessee County

Roberta Campbell and Alan J. DeYoung

During the past decade, business leaders, government officials, and national politicians have increasingly begun to view American children as "human resources" to be (better) developed in our schools in the pursuit for better "international competitiveness" (DeYoung, 1989). In addition to this national agenda for "improving" education via school reform, we are also witness in our own region to public calls for educational improvement, supposedly as an aid to increasing local economic development.

In rural America (as in our central cities), many politicians claim that declining local economies are a function of the inferior condition of rural schools. And much of the contemporary rhetoric regarding "what's wrong" with such schools begins with some reference to the supposedly inferior attitudes toward education held by students and their parents; with the inferior skills of classroom teachers; and/or with the inadequate financial resources available to schools in the region.

Predictably, national efforts to "improve" education have taken two directions to solving "problems" like those mentioned above. On the one hand, increased funding for education (for teacher salaries, better supplies, etc.) is being championed around the country at both local and state levels. Relatedly, a second strategy increasingly involves creating a higher "demand" for public schooling through publicizing hypothetical returns on educational investments for high school diplomas, and exhorting parents and community leaders regarding the "technological requirements for a post-industrial society."

Education for Appalachia

At the national level, there have been a variety of insightful critiques of the educational excellence "movement" and motives behind it from a multiple of sources (e.g., Aronowitz and Giroux, 1985; Spring, 1984). Many such criticisms take issue with the lack of analysis of social and cultural factors associated with educational "underperformance" in America, and go on to suggest alternative perspectives on this relationship and requirements for improving our schools,

Much of the national critique of efforts to "upgrade" our economi(es) via concentrating on school reform, however, has already been visible in the discourse of Appalachian scholars. Here, the importance of cultural factors in explaining the status of education has been discussed and debated for several decades, and rarely have discussions about the nature of schooling been reduced to discussions solely about cognitive skills acquisition and/or high school graduation rates, etc. (as important as they may be). As a number of regional and national educational sociologists and anthropologists have pointed out, the hidden or unadvertised features of formal and compulsory schooling are as, or more, important in understanding the mission of public instruction than is all the concern about its cognitive content of (e.g., achievement test scores, courses completed, etc.).

"Modernization" and the Public School

For example, while the concept of social/political/individual "modernity" has been rendered theoretically suspect both internationally and locally, the list of personal attributes associated with psychological modernity have been pointed out by many social scientists (not only those identified with modernization theory), as the most central cultural "teachings" of public education. Importantly, those who worked in this area when it was "in vogue" (during the 1970s) claimed that the public school (as sponsored by national governments in developing countries) was one of the most important (if not *the* most important) formal institutions for bringing about the individual modernity demanded for sociocultural and political progress.

A representative working list of modern personality characteristics ostensibly related to individual modernity and contributed to by participation in formal schooling is available in works like those of Alex Inkeles and his colleagues (Inkeles and Smith, 1974; Inkeles and Holsinger, 1974). For example, Inkeles et al. argue that "modern" individuals are (among other things): open to new experience; accepting and ready for social change; able to reflect on issues and form independent judgements; interested in acquiring information and facts; oriented toward the future as opposed to the past; have a sense of mastery over the environment; believe in the value of future planning; have an appreciation of technical skills; and have high educational and occupational aspirations.

According to those who argue for the utility of individual modernity perspectives, persons locked into more traditional societies are typically less interested in new experiences; uninterested in social change; more likely to form and hold opinions based on beliefs held by others in the tribe and/or kinship systems; uninterested in acquiring knowledge for its own sake; value the past more than the future; are more fatalistic than optimistic regarding the human ability to control future events; place less value on occupational specialization and competence; and have low educational and occupational aspirations.

Importantly for our purposes, "deficiencies" of psychological modernity like those listed above have also frequently been applied to Appalachians, who, it is believed, are unable to participate in middle-class culture because of a history of isolation and the tenacity of a traditional subculture. Mountaineers, in other words, culturally "lag behind" most other Americans, and this is the reason for their inability to assimilate into the mainstream. As Tyler (1919) once phrased it: "Shut up within these fastnesses they have stood still for a hundred years." Their "provincial" mentalities impede the acceptance of modern world advantages.

"Bridging the Gap" Through Education

Whether one agrees or disagrees with various tenets of the sociocultural modernization thesis, few social scientists tend to doubt the "modern" features and orientations of public schooling internationally or domestically; rather, they debate the desirability of becoming "modern," and/or the hidden stratification dimension concealed within most elaborations of the modernity thesis.

Adherents to a variety of "functionalist" views of social progress and the role of schooling in its evolution all tend to focus on the transmission of norms and values consistent with instrumentalism, impersonal authority structures, and future orientation as primary components of any formal schooling agenda (Dreeben, 1968; Jackson, 1968). Meanwhile, even the critics of such perspectives in Appalachia (and elsewhere) do not take issue with the list of attributes as suggested above, but rather emphasize the role of public schooling in reproducing the larger modern/urban/capitalist culture (Bowles and Gintis, 1976; Branscome, 1971; Whisnant, 1980).

Perhaps the most optimistic and sympathetic interpretation of the role public education could play in bridging the gap between the region and "The Great Society" was brought forward by Schwarzweller and Brown (1960). In this essay, the authors suggested (before it became fashionable) that the kinship, political and economic systems of Appalachia continued to instill character traits among the youth of the region which were inappropriate for their integration into the increasingly available outside world. The school, they argued, could indeed become a cultural bridge from this agrarian/kinship centered Appalachian subculture to "the great society," because the formal policies and practices of the school, coupled with the more cosmopolitan role models of university trained teachers, could provide for mountain youth an access to skills, values, and attitudes they needed to journey from an outmoded past into the future. According to these authors, since the school is an institutional complex situated within and supported by the local community but directly tied to the Great Society, it "is a natural and strategic center for the diffusion of Great Society norms" (Schwarzweller and Brown, 1960: 37).

According to the cultural bridge metaphor, schools in Appalachia provide the best mechanism for providing young people with the skills, values, and norms necessary for rational decision-making in the modern "great society," and thus the capability to "escape" the bonds of traditionalism. Illustrative of their hopes for the school would be "instruction" in processes of desired social change through evaluative thought.

For example, voting behavior may be influenced when children learn that "government in the United States is in many respects shaped by economic pressure groups," enabling students to become oriented to evaluating political issues, and, thereby, becoming more rational decision-makers (Schwarzweller and Brown, 1960: 371). Such teachings would counter, according to the authors, trends of traditional voting based on family loyalty, and on loyalty to the past (which theoretically renders political institutions less effective in solving current social problems in Appalachia).

Significantly, not only the teachings, but also the organization of instruction were touted by these authors (and others) as enabling mountain children to become more modern. For example, the transition from the non-graded and community based elementary school to the subject-matter oriented and impersonal high school signifies both the importance of academic knowledge and the organization of such knowledge into compartments of expertise. This social teaching of modern education and its theoretical link to the requirements of mainstream and modern society have been eloquently presented by structural functionalists like Parsons (1959) and Dreeben (1968).

As institutions tied importantly to the larger society, schools can perform modernizing functions which other important social institutions in the region cannot, according to Schwarzweller and Brown. For example, the local orientations of many Appalachian churches and extended families are more "insular" in the region, and (they claim) tend to perpetuate traditional norms.

To be sure, Schwarzweller and Brown suggest that other demographic and economic factors can affect the modernization process in desirable ways. For example, aspects of the modern organization of work in the mining communities of Appalachia can facilitate progress (as opposed to those still dependent upon declining agriculture), because mining is a more centrally organized industry and more integrated into the national culture.

Critiques of Modernization Theory and the Great Society

In essence, Schwarzweller and Brown echo ideas put forth in other works sympathetic to modernization theory, which contend that the "lagging" Eastern Kentucky subculture can catch up to the rest of America as great society linked institutions, like the school, socialize Appalachian students with the modern norms required for great society participation. The central point of the entire analysis is that Appalachia as a region is located somewhere in the progression to modernity, and institutions existing in the region with close ties to the modern world are the keys to a more rapid arrival date into the modern world.

Unfortunately, even though such arguments sound plausible (and to some, hopeful), there are several features of the cultural bridge metaphor which may be misleading and have proven erroneous and/or problematic. Furthermore, emphatic critiques of the "great society" and modernity perspectives have been authored since Schwarzweller and Brown developed their metaphor. Therefore, while we will soon present evidence with regard to the shortcomings of formal schooling to provide the "cultural bridge" in one Appalachian county, some attention to inadequacies of the entire progress to modernity perspective must be highlighted.

A variety of social scientists take issue with the key assertions and descriptions of "the great society," and/or other optimistic versions of modern society. Several basic fallacies of modernity theory, some claim, are the unquestioning acceptance of a continuum between traditional and modern cultures; that social change happens through linear stages; and that the transition automatically represents progress (Dickens and Bonanno, 1988; Gusfield, 1967).

For example, modernity theory clearly suggests that tradition is an obstacle to modernization. Yet, what evidence is there that some "traditions" have no utility within this process? The fact that such questions are rarely seriously considered by modernity theorists suggests the *ideological* character of modernization theory itself, according to various critics (e.g. Gusfield, 1967: 358). Furthermore, by reifying the distinction between "modern" and "traditional" individuals, any inequality brought about by unequal access to the (new) structure of opportunities inevitably leads to blaming the victims of unequal development for their own perceived social "backwardness."

Peter Berger (1977) also makes a compelling argument against the ideological nature of modernity theories. He points out five dilemmas of modernity which he argues are underestimated by would-be harbingers of "modern" society at home or abroad. And, in point of fact, the dilemmas he foresees in the modernization process are some of the very factors which modernist theorists champion as unilaterally progressive for the human species.

One dilemma with severe consequences for human social systems, according to Berger, is the loss of communit(ies) made necessary by abstract market and bureaucratic forces as they govern social interaction in modern societies. As he phrases it, "this destruction, of the concrete and relatively cohesive communities in which human beings have found solidarity and meaning throughout most of human history" (Berger, 1977: 72).

Secondly, Berger notes the *imprisonment* of humans in modern societies to the demands of time management and future orientations: clocks and watches dominate everyday life; individual biography is described as a "career," and societal institutions operate according to "plan" (Berger, 1977: 73). This dominance of futurity and weakening of community facilitates the abstraction of institutions and the *individuation* process which in turn increases the danger of anomie (Berger, 1977: 75-76). The dilemmas of futurity and individuation then result in the "underlying ambiguity of people wanting both individual autonomy...*and* communal solidarity" (Berger, 1977: 76).

In modern societies, fate takes a back seat and human beings can see choices: "One of the most seductive maxims of modernity is that things could be other than what they have been...Tradition is no longer binding; the status quo can be changed; the future is an open horizon" (Berger, 1977: 77). The dilemma of liberation is that in challenging tradition, collective life becomes uncertain. The price of liberty is the confusion between freedom *of* choice and freedom *from* choice. This is the "terror of chaos" (Berger, 1977: 77-78).

The last dilemma, according to Berger, concerns secularization. The challenge to religion by modern science and technology as well as the modernization process itself, whether one is religious or not, "frustrates deeply grounded human aspiration—most important among these, the aspiration to exist in a meaningful and ultimately hopeful cosmos." In other words, the process of modernization, of *rationalization*, not only confuses through liberation, but chops away at the transcendental escapes from pain and sorrow. However, the impact of secularization is shown in the strength of countermodernizing trends and movements characterized by religious faith and fervor (Berger, 1977: 79).

If Berger's assessment suggests equivocal and problematic aspects of modernization, different social theorists have taken issue with other benign assessments of modern capitalist society. Stephenson, for example, posited a typology of families in his study of Shiloh, based on their situation and "stages" of modernity (1968). Although his analysis does not decry the modernity thesis, he clearly suggests that "cultural lags" present in Appalachia might more appropriately be viewed as economic with unequal skills and resources.

A more direct "attack" on the cultural lag thesis of modernity theory appeared in the 1970s with the development of the internal colony model (i.e., Gaventa, 1980; Lewis, 1978; Melizia, 1973; Walls, 1978 and 1976). Based on Third World studies, especially dependence theory, this perspective charged that the experience of colonialism was still affecting the political processes and social organizations of those countries. Applied to Appalachia, this model claimed our region to be a "victim" of uneven capitalist relations, whereby the mineral wealth of Appalachia (the periphery) became appropriated by the industrialized north (the core). The model was attractive because of its powerful analysis of the destruction of indigenous culture by the dominators (Walls, 1976: 238), a practice that prevails internationally in core/periphery situations.

Relatedly, much recent scholarship on "uneven development" has looked at the specifics of cultural trends, class analysis and power relationships in hopes of explaining the dynamics of regional behavior (Eller, 1982; Waller, 1988; Whisnant, 1983 and 1980). For instance, Waller (1988) argues the violence that erupted among the feudists of Virginia and Kentucky in the late 1800s was a reaction to the frustrations of economic deprivation brought on by the influx of capitalism. Her analysis emphasizes the social relationships within the local community as well as the "modernized" society-at-large and makes class distinctions a central theme. In arguments like these, the existence of a unique Eastern Kentucky subculture is not dismissed outright, but its economic and political origins became the focus of discussion and analysis.

The Utility of "Tradition" in "Modern" Appalachia

If modernization poses the many dilemmas which theorists like these suggest, then perhaps any view which castigates the importance of traditional social institutions, like the extended mountain family and local churches, ought to be reconsidered. For example, when Stephenson (1968: 51-56) explored the effects of modernization on an Appalachian community, he noted the more fundamentalist nature of mountain churches which served some of the most marginal residents. It seems quite plausible that such institutions provided a shelter for those families less able (or welcome) to join "the great society." In fact, Stephenson's suggestion is that perhaps traditional norms should not be viewed automatically as artifacts, but a particular means of adapting, of hanging on to a sense of self in an encroaching modern world, a way of adjusting to a new situation which is superimposed and not part of a "natural progression." Furthermore, it could be said, were the problematic dilemmas of modernization realistically faced, perhaps dealing more directly and sympathetically with local institutions like mountain churches and families would be in order, rather than seeing such institutions as unequivocal hindrances to the modernization process.

Of course, if the various dependency theorists earlier mentioned are more accurate than those subscribing to modernity perspectives, much of the foregoing discussion is rendered moot. For, in order for "internal colonies" like much of Appalachia to become part of a larger empire, individuals and social institutions within the colonies need to accept and to internalize the ideologies, values and norms of external agents (and their local representatives) which enable the colonies to remain under absentee control. Thus, for example, learning to see the world as framed by outsiders, coming to accept external definitions of the nature of the world and social progress, and internalizing individual inadequacies as the reason locals are "backward," demands that the social teachings of the family and the local church must be diminished and replaced by external ideologies.

Class and Education in "Modern" Appalachia

As most readers will recognize, important theoretical and institutional aspects of the preceding discussion are readily available in a variety of sources, many of which are noted. However, our more particular task in this essay is to consider the status of the public school in Appalachia, particularly with reference to claims by Schwarzweller and Brown that such schools can and will provide the cultural bridge to the great society.

Unfortunately, and as much of the preceding discussion no doubt implies, in our view the cultural bridge metaphor as elaborated upon by these authors is much more problematic than it is laid out to be. In our view, there are several claims about the possibilities of public schooling in the region which are not confirmed by reference to the evidence available—at least with regard to the evidence we have for one Appalachian county/school district.

One of the major confessions evident in Schwarzweller and Brown's argument is with regard to the external allegiance of public education in the mountains. Unfortunately, while it *might* be true in developing nations that the public educational system is tied directly to a federal government, this is clearly not the case in America. Here, schooling has always been a local concern, and under the control of local agents. And, while aspects of the formal school curriculum have usually been dedicated to external teachings, it is unclear from the historical evidence that local populations have always equated the mission of the "school marm" with their own "educational" aspirations.

For example, counter to the pedagogical aims of generations of American educators, it appears that a variety of non-intellectual goals have been of concern (and remain of concern) in many rural areas of the U.S. Boy's sports activities (for example) have always dominated school life in Appalachia in the twentieth century, ostensibly because of the community pride (rather than individual success) which such programs generate locally. In the mountains, football and basketball programs and teams exist at virtually every grade level in even the smallest of schools. Not coincidentally, such aspects of rural schools have enraged and encouraged reform efforts of generations of urban based school reformers, once they began to infiltrate state departments of education throughout the land (Tyack, 1974).

Another "traditional" fact of life in most rural school districts concerns attendance patterns, where missed days of school and "tardiness" rates are epidemic compared to such patterns in metropolitan America. Anecdotal evidence from many Appalachian communities will confirm that the first week of hunting season, or planting/harvesting time for Purley tobacco drains 20-40% of all students in a district (mostly boys). And, while many school districts in the U.S. mandate that students repeat a grade for having as few as a week of unexcused absences per year, many rural Appalachian districts have no formally enforced attendance policy at all.

Not wishing to belabor the point, the point is that the social life of Appalachian schools has a variety of "traditional," "pre-modern," "counter hegemonic" (pick one) features which weaken any argument that Appalachian schools are automatically agents of the great society.

They have histories and social functions, in other words, independent of norms of the great society—and many of these norms may run counter to modernization interests.

Furthermore, as public schools in America are locally controlled, much of what transpires within the schools of many mountain counties is also a function of the local political mechanisms which dominate many aspects of formal life. It might even be argued that the political nature of schooling in Appalachia is less "modern" than many other features of Appalachia, given that state and federal monies directed to local school boards and superintendents is arguably the single greatest source of patronage there.

Economic and Occupational Conditions in One East Tennessee County

So far we have been suggesting theoretical and anecdotal problems and weaknesses in the cultural bridge which Schwarzweller and Brown suggest the school can provide between Appalachia and "the Great Society." At this point, we would like to document more precisely some of these problems with reference to an east Tennessee county school district in which we are currently doing fieldwork.[1]

Located in the northeastern section of Tennessee, Clinch County is one of the poorest counties in Tennessee, and among the poorest in the nation. Per capita income in 1984 for this county was approximately $5,300, 41% of the national average. The official unemployment rate in 1984 was reported to be 11.9%, yet since many of the rural poor are not actively seeking employment, this figure probably underestimates the number of individuals who would work were suitable employment available. Furthermore, jobs held by county residents are typically in neighboring counties, where minimum wage is the maximum for most Clinch Countians; where much of the employment is in the textile and furniture industries; and where one and two hour commutes to and from such unskilled and minimum wage employment "opportunities" are not uncommon.

During the past sixty years, unemployment and out-migration have been a fact of life on Clinch County. In 1940 the county had a population of over 11,000 people, and 86% of those "employed" earned a living through agriculture. Currently, the county contains approximately 6,000 residents, and agriculture accounts for less than 20% of employment there. While outmigration has somewhat stabilized during the past decade, the percentage of aged and disabled among those who remain has greatly increased.

Like many Appalachian counties, Clinch County has some history of timber and mineral exploitation but is recognized as having primarily an agricultural economic base. One of the impediments to industrial development noted by its citizens is the lack of major roads leading into the county. As well, no railroads, airports, or navigable waterways exist in Clinch County. And reliable telephone service there (outside of the county seat) is reputed to be a relatively recent invention.

The School Situation in Clinch County

A major oversight evidenced among those who write about public schools, without having worked within them, lies in the lack of appreciation for the large discrepancies between schools and school districts in this country. There are schools with ample funding, excellent academic programs and large amounts of parent involvement (all of which appear associated with successful academic school performance); and there are schools which clearly lack most of these (Howley, 1988).

So too, what many modernization theorists underestimate in their pronouncements regarding education and its relationship to economic development and social progress has to do with the real structure of opportunities in "modernizing" nations/regions. And according to some, the *competition* for better jobs in America usually is won by those with the better educational credentials, irrespective of how these credentials actually relate to job requirements/performance (Collins, 1979).

To move quickly to the point, the schools of rural Tennessee in general, and of Clinch County in particular, compare very unfavorably to those of many more affluent communities in the U.S. And unfortunately, this can be said not only with regard to school facilities and school funding, but also with regard to a variety of educational practices which do not exist in Clinch County but are taken for granted in most of metropolitan America.

For example, in 1980 Clinch County enrolled approximately 1400 students, of whom over 86% came from homes below the poverty line. Furthermore, even though residents of the district provide average tax *effort* in support of local schools, the taxes *generated* in the county are among the lowest in the state, since there is almost nothing of value (in terms of real property) for taxable purposes. In 1980, less than 12% of the money necessary to run Clinch County schools was generated from local revenues. Therefore, the bulk of money spent for education in the county is supplied from state and federal sources.

Since equalization formulas in Tennessee are geared to providing a "minimum foundation," it comes as no surprise that teacher salaries in Clinch County in 1980 were the third lowest in the state (of a total of 141 districts). Furthermore, the school facilities in the county are by current standards almost obsolete. While the state helped the county build a new high school almost thirty years ago, the other five remaining school buildings are at least fifty years old. The school most residents would claim to be "the best" in the county (in terms of programs) is a grim reminder of the fact that education has always been operated on a shoestring: for this building (in the county seat) was built in the 1930s as part of a WPA project.

While some might believe that Clinch County schools can operate effectively on state and federal aid, this appears clearly not the case at the present time. For example, the state legislature in Tennessee mandates that even the poorest districts must generate adequate funds to match various state level appropriations. Furthermore, the state mandates specific quotas for student/teacher ratios and for educational specialists without supplying additional funds for their salaries. And in 1986, the state raised all teacher salaries in the state by mandate, without providing all of the funds required to meet the payrolls.

Trying to meet these state guidelines is one of the main reasons the Clinch County school system faces a possible deficit of just under $400,000 for the 1988-1989 school year, according to the local superintendent. This point was brought home to local residents when he ordered that all school buses would cease operation following the 1988-1989 Christmas holiday. Recognizing the seriousness of the problem, a hesitant County Commission "donated" an additional $13,000 dollars to resume bus operation until new funds could be raised.

In Tennessee, school budgets are determined not by the school systems themselves, but rather by appropriate municipal/county governments. In Clinch County this has led to bitter contention between the county commission and the school superintendent. Because there is not enough money to provide for almost any of the services local citizens require, no county agencies get the money they request; all such agencies are forced to bargain with the county commission for funds; and since most commissioners in the county are elected on an "I won't raise taxes" platform, additional monies for running things like the local schools are always being sought.

Unfortunately, since there is no industry in Clinch County, since there is no state income tax, and since sales taxes on purchases by Clinch Countians are paid out of the county (where all the new malls and bigger shopping areas are), there literally is no source of new revenue for the county to attach.

The latest attempt by the county commission (supposedly undertaken to generate money specifically for Clinch County schools) involved contracting with first the state, and then with a private company from Washington D.C., to house hundreds of state and D.C. prisoners in a new county jail (being built specifically for such purposes in the only large population center in the county). Unfortunately for local schools (but perhaps fortunately for the general public), this possibility was scaled back substantially due to a loud public outcry against the most ambitious version of the prison construction plan. School funding problems have become so overwhelming in Clinch County that its problems have been highlighted in a current lawsuit filed by 66 rural school districts in the state. In essence, this suit charges that the present system of funding education in Tennessee is inequitable, and discriminates against the poor and rural children. (Similar lawsuits in Kentucky, Texas and West Virginia have found state funding systems unconstitutional.)

The Politics of Clinch County Schools

Funding inequities of rural and poor schools are not the only problems for achieving some of the modernizing goals which proponents hold out for Appalachian schools. Another is the serious patronage problem in the county with regard to the hiring and firing of local teachers and administrators. For example, based on interviews we have made in Clinch County, a typical "career pattern" of classroom teachers there involves attending a local teacher training program close to home, and then taking temporary employment in a local furniture factory until a relative or close political friend gets elected to the school board. From this point on, it behooves newly hired teachers to help his/her benefactor(s) on the school board to remain on the board until his/her tenure is achieved. Subsequently, the worst that can happen is that a tenured teacher can be moved (seemingly) arbitrarily from one school to another, or from one grade to another, without benefit of any review related to job performance. When asked how particular teachers get assigned particular duties within the system, the inevitable answer given is "it's political." And, contrary to hopes like those mentioned earlier, that the school can model "modern" rational and non-political decision making processes, most citizens (and children in the system) appear to learn quickly that such procedures are routine and inevitable.

Another example of the political nature of school district functioning in the county might be inferred from the highly politicized dispute during recent years between the county executive and the school superintendent. Clinch County is a Republican county, with two entrenched factions (going back for several generations, according to some sources). Furthermore, as the school superintendent is an elected official, his ability to run the schools in ways he would like depends upon the majority of the school board coming from the same faction as his. However, this has not been the case until just the past year (he has been superintendent for five years).

Furthermore, the (other) most powerful politician in the county is the executive of the county commission. Without dwelling on the matter, battles over the school budget alluded to above have been quite revealing during the past year, with the county executive typically complaining about personnel costs of the school system, at the same time the superintendent is blaming shortfalls on county and state appropriations. Not coincidentally, the county executive is fond of pointing out that two of the highest paid employees of the school system are the superintendent and his wife, who also works in the central office. According to him, this couple receives almost $100,000 from the county in combined salaries, which would be almost 15 times the average family income in Clinch County. Of course, the superintendent denies that he and his wife earn this much, but they are hesitant to share such "sensitive" information with either the county commission or the public at large.

Clinch County Academic Programs

Needless to say, the academic programs of the six schools in Clinch County are no model by national standards. The dropout rate for schools in Clinch County hovers at about thirty percent, although it has officially been over sixty percent within the last decade. The county superintendent claims, however, that all such figures are probably inaccurate, since officially reported data are sometimes mis-reported to the state where the statistics are tabulated.

With regard to academic achievement, Clinch County fell within the bottom five percent of all reporting districts in Tennessee in 1980 on high school achievement tests in reading, spelling, and mathematics. In fact, they came in dead last on several of these tests. And while the County seems to have improved its performance on standardized tests of late, the superintendent's candid comment that some (or most?) school data may be unreliable gives some pause for suspicion.

Stories of political intrigue and inadequate funding in Clinch County could no doubt provide a worthy subject of a Hollywood soap-opera for years. So, too, profiling the statistical inferiority of Clinch County schools, compared to more affluent and less politicized systems around Nashville and Knoxville, could occupy many pages of text. More central to the concluding section of this paper, however, is how such issues and/or problems get translated into educational opportunities and programs which might enable Appalachian students in this East Tennessee county to bridge the gap from "tradition" to modernity. Sadly, whether one truly believes that the public school can and should help children bridge the gap to modernity in Clinch County, the programs and policies evident there do not seem to provide such possibilities.

We have already suggested, for example, that being a "good" teacher (whatever this means) appears not of particular concern in the hiring and retaining of teachers in the county. So, too, since most teachers also farm and/or have other "non-professional" interests, little attention in the county to teacher "improvement" courses/workshops, etc., is evident there; at least it hasn't been during the year of our fieldwork.

As well, district philosophy at the high school level appears to be more in line with the school as a military outpost than an educational facility. Locks and chains on every door, and across the main corridors of the school are perhaps the most visible characteristic of the institution. And teachers, as well as students, are typically gone within minutes of the final bell each afternoon.

So, too, the principal of the high school is a young man with a good income-producing farm, and perhaps, some political future. His primary claim to school fame in the county is that he is a "good disciplinarian," meaning that he has a reputation for suspending or expelling any and all troublemakers from the school with the slightest cause. Other than discussion of financial woes, the only other predictable item on the agenda of Clinch County school board meetings has frequently to do with the list of expulsions requested by the principal.

Two other examples of the comparative marginality of school district operation have also become evident to us in our year working in Clinch County. One has to do with the growing national consensus that effective schools (in terms of academic programs) demand strong and innovative school leadership patterns, either as led by or facilitated by building principals. However, for a variety of reasons, such leadership is dramatically underdeveloped in Clinch County (except, perhaps, for the high school principal).

On the one hand, since money is so tight there, four of the six principals in the district are teaching principals; they teach multiple grades in addition to serving titularly as the administrative leaders of the school. Unfortunately, administration of the schools in each of these four schools primarily involves filling out free—and reduced—lunch forms, and selling soft drinks and candy after school to help generate funds for school supplies not supplied in the school board budget.

The other major activity of the four principals is in coaching the multiple basketball teams in each school. And this is no minor responsibility, as the basketball season runs virtually all year long in the county, and appears to be one of the most important activities of the school as far as the parents are concerned. Each of the four "elementary" schools has fewer than ninety students, yet manages to field two or three teams each for games in the county and in contiguous counties, two or three times a week, and which are typically held either right after school or during the school day itself.

Another primary reason why principals in the four smaller county elementary schools are not instructional leaders involves the fact that during the year of our study none of them had even taught in their schools before, and two of them had never taught before at all. In each case, assignments to the respective schools in question had been "politically" motivated. And, there is little guarantee at this writing that any of these four will still be in the same school this time next year.

This, of course, is not even to mention the rather rigid nature of school leadership already discussed at the high school, or that of the largest "elementary" school. In the latter case, the principal was "invited" out of retirement (from a non-education related business) to become principal of a school he had graduated from almost forty years earlier. Not surprisingly, the person who invited him was his "drinking buddy," the county superintendent; and the principal in early interviews with us confided he knew almost nothing about the job he had agreed to take, except that he "liked children."

A final educational anomaly worth mentioning here is in regard to district policies allowing/enabling students throughout the county to bypass the outlying small schools in order to attend the larger and age-graded consolidated school in the county seat. On the one hand, this has caused the more centrally located school to become seriously overcrowded. Even so, according to most educational personnel in Clinch County, the teachers, facilities, and students there are all better than they are in the outlying schools. According to some, this reputation causes both the more "professional" teachers and the more affluent county residents to prefer "Central," where not surprisingly, parent involvement is much greater (at least in athletic affairs). Meanwhile, the less affluent (meaning, in Clinch County, those in the most abject poverty and/or the furthest removed from town and/or those least able to request or demand improved school services) students and parents remain dependent upon the isolated, multigraded, and underfunded outlying schools, where politically motivated teaching assignments are routine and the bridge to the "great society" is not even in sight.

Conclusions

While most schools in the region have become more and more "modern" during the past decade (in terms of school consolidation, stricter certification requirements, etc.) under the auspices of state department of educations, many schools in Appalachia are by no means comparable to those in other parts of America. Based on the evidence in Clinch County, schooling as a means of bringing the mountaineer into "Great Society" (a term which we obviously believe is a misnomer), is extremely problematic. Due to a variety of historical and economic reasons, many Appalachian schools still do not function to counter the effects of other more "insular" institutions, assuming this is what they ought to do. Rather, they are inadequately funded, (still) locally controlled, frequently the focal point of county politics, and often viewed by parents as the site of community social life rather than as purely academic settings.

The reasons why schools in places like Clinch County appear as they do could no doubt lead to the same type of theoretical disputes presented earlier in this analysis. Modernity advocates, for example, might suggest that the reason learner outcomes in Clinch County appear as outlined is because those individuals and families with the most modern values and skills are the ones who have migrated out of the county, leaving more traditionally focused families behind. And, they would probably point out that state efforts to reform schools along criteria as listed above indicate good progress towards modernity in the region.

Those impressed with core/periphery explanations of local domination by external elites would no doubt focus on the transformation of Clinch County households from self-sufficient farming to low-income wage earners. Such an interpretation would probably argue that local schools and school personnel function as agents of external political and economic interests. The purpose of schools like those of Clinch County is to provide the minimum of cognitive skills necessary to work in minimum wage jobs, and the real task of the schools is to introduce time and authority structures to mountain children, making sure that students drop out of high school, and thus blame themselves for not being able to obtain better employment. The class standing, political location, attitude, and educational philosophy of the high school principal earlier profiled would perhaps provide a prototypical model of a local agent in service of external agendas.

Through our eyes, both and neither of such perspectives totally explain the educational status and/or the location of the public school in Clinch County. Schools have increasingly become more "modern," rational and bureaucratic there during the past three decades. Yet, much of the day to day life of children and teachers in Clinch County schools probably resembles school life earlier in the century. And given that learner outcomes in this County compare unfavorably to those from more affluent areas, it would be hard to argue that the modern schooling practices which have replaced more traditional ones have well served its children.

In our judgment, Clinch County schools probably function well as reproducers of social inequality in the County. Yet, while the school system seems clearly related to the stratification system there, social stratification mechanisms appear to have existed long before the public school became so central to county political life. Contrary to both modernity theory and to various conflict perspectives, small/community/elementary schools in most of the mountains had, and continue to have, social histories and non-academic functions carried over from an earlier era. Furthermore, the dilemmas of social change toward modern life which Peter Berger outlines appear in some ways mediated by these "non-rational" functions in some rural schools.

We have no easy answer as to how to solve social problems in the mountains, and we are hesitant to suggest that some natural progress towards a problematic "great society" will take care of the issues we raise here. However, to us it certainly seems that *assuming* that public schools can and/or should be a primary institution for unilaterally bringing about this process is in error. Rather, perhaps it is time to entertain the transitional possibilities of mountain schools, instead of insisting on "reforming" them by making them more "modern." Perhaps these institutions could be made more useful for the future of our region were the important non-instructional functions of mountain schools highlighted, and were the community importance of such schools developed into formal components of the curriculum. [Such an argument, of course, underlies much of what the Foxfire Project(s) of Eliot Wigginton are all about. See for example his *Sometimes a Shining Moment* (Garden City, New York: Anchor, 1985.)]

Works Cited

Aronowitz, Stanley and Henry Giroux. 1985. *Education Under Siege: The Conservative, Liberal and Radical Debate over Schooling.* South Hadley, Massachusetts: Bergin and Garvey.

Berger, Peter L. 1977. *Facing Up to Modernity: Exclusion in Society, Politics and Religion.* New York: Basic Books, Inc.

Bowles, Samuel and Herbert Gintis. 1976. *Schooling in Capitalist America.* New York: Basic Books.

Collins, Randall. 1979. *The Credential Society.* New York: Academic Press.

DeYoung, Alan J. 1989. *Economics and American Education: A Historical and Critical Overview of the Impact of Economic Theories on Schooling in the United States.* New York: Longman.

Dickens, David R. and Alessandro Bonanno. 1988. "Analyzing Development, Dependency, and Underdevelopment: Suggestions for an Alternative Approach." *Sociological Spectrum* 8: 169-186.

Dreeben, Robert. 1968. *On What is Learned in Schools.* Boston: Addison Wesley.

Eller, Ronald D. 1982. *Miners, Millhands and Mountaineers: The Industrialization of the Appalachian South,* 1980-1930. Knoxville: University of Tennessee Press.

First Tennessee Development District. 1985. "Facts." October, 1985. Johnson City, Tennessee.

Ford, Thomas R. (ed.). 1962. *The Southern Appalachian Region: A Survey*. Lexington: University of Kentucky Press.

Gusfield, Joseph. 1967. "Tradition and Modernity: Misplaced Polarities in the Study of Social Change." *American Journal of Sociology* 72: 1967, 351-362.

Hogan, David. 1982. "Education and Class Formation: The Peculiarities of the Americans." ed. Michael W. Apple. *Cultural and Economic Reproduction in Education*. Londen: Routledge and Kegan Paul.

Howley, Craig. 1988. *Synthesis of the Effects of School and District Size: What Research says about Achievement in Small Schools and School Districts*. ERIC Clearinghouse on Rural Education and Small Schools. Charleston, West Virginia, Appalachia Education Laboratory.

Keefe, Susan E., Una Reck and Gregory Reck. 1985. "Family and Education in Southern Appalachia." Berea, Kentucky: Appalachian Studies Conference.

Livingstone, D.W. 1985. "Class, Educational Ideologies, and Mass Opinion in Capitalist Crisis: A Canadian Perspective." *Sociology of Education* 58: January, 3-30.

Mulkey, David. 1988. Workshop, "Education Policy and Rural Development: A Perspective from the Southern Region." Southern Region Rural Development Policy. 3-5 October 1988. Birmingham, Alabama.

Parsons, Talcott. 1959. "The School Class as a Social System: Some of its Functions in American Society." *Harvard Educational Review* 29: 297-313.

Plunkett, H. Dudley and Mary Jean Bowman. 1973. *Elites and Change in the Kentucky Mountains*. Lexington: University of Kentucky Press.

Reck, Una Mae, Gregory Reck and Susan Keefe. 1987. "Teachers' Perceptions of Appalachian and Non-Appalachian Students." 20-24 April 1987. Washington, D.C., Annual Meeting of the American Educational Association.

Schwarzweller, Harry K. and James S. Brown. 1962. "Education as a Cultural Bridge between Eastern Kentucky and the Great Society." *Rural Sociology* 27: 4, 357-373.

Sher, Jonathan P. 1987. "Making Dollars by Making Sense: Linking Rural Education and Development in Appalachia." Proceedings of the University of Kentucky Conference on Appalachia.

Spring, Joel. 1984. "Education and the Sony War." Phi Delta Kappan. April 1984, 534-537.

Stephenson, John B. 1968. *Shiloh: A Mountain Community*. Lexington: University of Kentucky Press.

Tennessee Department of Economic and Community Development. 1986. "Economic Statistics." 4 March 1986. Authorization #330244.

1988. "Education". February 1988. Authorization #330324.

1986. "Population." March 1986. Authorization #330112.

Tennessee Department of Education. 1987. State of Tennessee: "Annual Statistical Report of the Department of Education for Scholastic Year Ending June 30."

Tyack, David. 1974. *The One Best System*. Cambridge, Mass: Harvard University Press.

Tyler, J.W. 1919. *Our Appalachian Cousins*. The Executive Committee of Home Missions. Presbyterian Church of the United States. Atlanta, Georgia.

Waller, Altina L. 1988. *Feud: Hatfields, McCoys and Social Change in Appalachia, 1860-1900*. Chapel Hill: University of North Carolina Press.

Whisnant, David E. 1983. *All That is Native and Fine: The Politics of Culture in an American Region*. Chapel Hill: University of North Carolina Press.

Whisnant, David E. 1980. *Modernizing the Mountaineer: People, Power and Planning in Appalachia*. Boone, North Carolina: Appalachian Consortium Press.

Wigginton, Eliot. 1985. *Sometimes a Shining Moment*. Garden City, New York: Anchor.

Footnote

[1] This work has been partially facilitated by the Appalachia Educational Laboratory of Charleston, West Virginia. The views represented within this document, however, are those of the authors' and do not necessarily represent those of the Lab.

Roberta Campbell is a doctoral candidate and teaching assistant in the sociology department at the University of Kentucky majoring in Appalachian Studies.

Alan DeYoung is a professor in the department of educational policy studies and evaluation at the University of Kentucky. His most recent book is *Economics in American Education: A Historic and Critical Overview of the Impact of Economic Theories on Schooling in the United States*.

"Never Met a Man who Made a Basket ... Never Saw My Daddy Cane a Chair"

Bobby Ann Starnes

A study by Jake Kroger found that only nine of the sixty-one sixth grade students who comprised the class of '84 at the Oyler Elementary School in Cincinnati, Ohio, were still in school on graduation day six years later (Kroger, 1984).

The findings of Kroger's study are sobering. Yet, they do not come as a surprise to the urban Appalachian population of Cincinnati. Parents, community leaders, and researchers have long recognized the dropout rate, low student achievement, and student alienation as symptomatic of the failure of the school system to meet the educational needs of students of Appalachian heritage (Appalachian Advocate, 1984; Wagner, 1974; Berlowitz and Durand, 1977). Experience in and with the public school system has led many of us to believe that teachers, for the most part, are unaware of Appalachian history and culture, include nothing in their curriculum to support the development of a healthy identity, and often consider urban Appalachian students to be less able than other students. Word of mouth assessments, as well as studies with parents and students, have indicated that they think teachers, schools, and curricula are insensitive to children of Appalachian heritage. No directed study, however, was done earlier with teachers to actually determine their attitudes; this paper is based on that study. It is my belief that an understanding of teachers' opinions and attitudes is vital to guide the development of methods and materials to improve the quality of urban Appalachian children's educational experiences. The study consisted of questionnaires and follow-up interviews, and was conducted in three predominantly urban Appalachian elementary schools in Cincinnati. It posed the following questions: do teachers value the inclusion of Appalachian history and culture? would they use materials if they existed? how do teachers view their students of Appalachian heritage? and, what expectations do teachers have for students of Appalachian heritage?

In this paper, study findings will be discussed only briefly. Additional discussion will be featured in the upcoming *The Advocate*, a publication of the Urban Appalachian Council.

For the most part, the findings are not surprising. Participant teachers do have low expectations for the children of Appalachian heritage. For example, when asked to rate students on a scale of 1 to 5 in 29 academic-related traits, teachers consistently rated urban Appalachian students lacking in almost all areas; for example: social skills, ability to understand abstract concepts, ability to concentrate, reading skills, and writing skills. They further claimed that "Appalachian people do not seek to do well," and, "Appalachian students have short attention spans." Urban Appalachian students are, as one teacher put it, "the broom pushers" of tomorrow. "As they get older they [will] value education less. They will get pregnant and drop out" or "only 3 of 90 will graduate." A teacher of first graders says she "knows" that most of her students will be unprepared and undisciplined. And on the section of the questionnaire that asked teachers to list the strengths of their urban Appalachian students, only such traits as "loving nature" were listed.

Views expressed in questionnaires were supported in follow-up interviews; three themes emerged in teacher responses: teachers have a sense of frustration, confusion, ineffectiveness, and powerlessness; teachers' values are in conflict with community values (often stated as class conflict); and, teachers blame parents for poor achievement. Although these themes are complex and intertwined, I will attempt to discuss them only briefly here. It should be understood, however, that in the life and culture of the classroom, each theme would support others, creating an almost indistinguishable cycle.

Teachers consistently identified a class difference between themselves and their students, as though to be urban Appalachian is to be poor. In most cases, they saw this difference as making it impossible for them to understand how urban Appalachian parents and students understand the world, what their goals are, or why they make the choices they make in their daily lives. This class difference led to both confusion and frustration as demonstrated by comments such as:

> ... My family has ... money. I drive a big ... car ... my Mom and Dad bought it for me. There are just some things I can't understand about these people. I will never be able to ... I just have to do the best I can to make a place where my values and theirs can be together ... Sometimes ... I impose my values ... I know I do ... I feel guilty, but I think I'm right ... I think my way is better ... makes more sense ...

Each of the teachers made similar comments about value differences. When discussing these differences, teachers generally used the terms "poor" and "Appalachian" interchangeably. The effects of such culture confusion are played out in a number of ways that affect students' educational program, opportunities, and chances of success.

Having acknowledged that they do not understand their students or their families, or the values they hold, teachers expressed frustration, confusion, and hopelessness. They talked about their ineffectiveness with urban Appalachian students and, at the same time, expressed feelings that they were powerless to change the way things are in their schools.

Although I went into this study expecting that teachers would care little about their students of Appalachian heritage, I was moved by the concern expressed by these teachers. While they are, I believe, ill-informed about Appalachian history and culture, miseducated with regard to appropriate ways to teach children not of the middle-class dominant culture, and unwilling to either accept or respect the values of urban Appalachian students, much of their frustration and their feelings of powerlessness rise out of their sincere desires to help their students to, as they put it, "break the cycle of poverty."

It seems clear, then, that at least some teachers want to be more effective with their students. They know they are failing to teach, and, while they blame others, they also blame themselves. They seem to be grasping for ways to make sense out of a culture and class that they do not understand. For example, I would suggest that, while some teachers do label urban Appalachian children, they might do so in order to mentally construct an understanding of their students and how they might help them. The use of the label—though actually quite harmful—may make students seem less mysterious and the situation seem less out of control.

While the tendency to blame parents for students' lack of academic success is a serious obstacle, using the study to understand teachers, rather than blame or judge them, makes this tendency quite valuable as a sort of "roadmap" for effecting change at least in individual classrooms where teachers are struggling—without much success—to improve their teaching and to help their students succeed. It is highly possible that frustrated but well-intentioned teachers can be assisted in ways that would meet their need to feel less frustrated and ineffectual and, at the same time, and more importantly, increase students' chances of success.

Clearly, however, change will not come easily. Any one of these findings has implications that require a massive commitment to rectify. Still, important as each seems, they are, I believe, secondary. The first thing we must address is the teachers' perceptions of what it means to be of Appalachian heritage—what is our culture and what is our history. Because *these* perceptions shape the instruction, expectations, and opportunity afforded to urban Appalachian students, any reform that does not first redefine the perceptions of Appalachian history and culture currently being presented in schools is doomed to failure. The balance of this paper will focus on these perceptions and how we might go about redefining them.

So, although teachers say they believe it is important to include Appalachian history and culture in their classrooms, we must ask what is the history and culture they would include, and is it the history and culture we think worth including?

Currently, teachers in this study are presenting Appalachian history and culture in two primary ways: art crafts (i.e., doll making, baskets, and quilts), and performance crafts (i.e., music, dance, and storytelling). Therefore, almost all of what is currently being presented as the history and culture of Appalachia is craft related.

This indicates that teachers' current perceptions of Appalachian history and culture are superficial. However, they are not *only* superficial. For at least two reasons, they are dangerous. First, as we recall from the studies of the effects of stereotyping on black students, such a narrow list of cultural activities conveys a message to children which limits their options (See Fenton, 1970, and Roth, 1969, for example). And second, such superficiality trivializes the culture.

By presenting primarily craft activities as strengths of the culture, urban Appalachian students are consistently sent a message that, as members of their cultural group, their talents lie in working with their hands rather than in more academic areas. The results of this study offers evidence that teachers have accepted this limited view of their students and of their cultural roots. To them, Appalachians as a people, and, therefore, their students, are somehow inherently talented with their hands, but not talented intellectually. One teacher put it this way:

> What we have to understand about Appalachian people is that they are right-brained. They can cane chairs. They can make quilts, and they can make baskets, but they just can't get the academics ... We have to realize that these will be the broom pushers and cash register operators ... and we have to educate them for that ... We have to teach them how to make change ... and apply for jobs ... We have to be realistic, set realistic goals ...

Also disturbing was the fact that teachers who were of Appalachian heritage themselves seemed to need to distance themselves from the culture as much as possible. We must seriously address this issue because of the messages it sends to our children and to the mainstream population. For example, one teacher became quite angry about having to identify himself.

> My paternal grandfather was from the Blue Ridge of Virginia—near Washington D.C. ... [Students] do not identify themselves as Appalachians. I don't think this school body in general identifies as Appalachians and neither do I. I do not consider myself Appalachian. I personally resent being tagged an Appalachian because one grandparent whom I never knew was from there. I think its wrong for a government office to arbitrarily identify people in this way. I'm more Anglo-German than anything else and so are many who happen to have an Appalachian ancestor. I also have an American-Indian ancestor, but I'm not considered Indian.

It is here then that we must begin our attack. First, I believe we must actively disclaim a crafts identity. It is not only the focus of the school on crafts, but also our own that is limiting and false. We must, at every occasion, point out its falseness. And we must say what it is about us and about our heritage that is at the core of our identity. There is more to us, and we must learn to say what it is. It is, of course, far easier for us and others to point to a quilt and say, "there, that is what our culture is about." It is concrete. It can be held in our hands and we can see the beauty, skill, and hard work in it. Perhaps we ourselves understand what else that quilt tells us about the person who made it and about our people. Perhaps not. However, teaching about our heritage almost exclusively through such concrete topics as storytelling, music, or quilt making, without teaching the social, economic, and political contexts in which the stories, music, or quilts were created, misses the abstract aspects of the culture which gave rise to the crafts. To learn the words to bluegrass music, for instance, without, at some point, discussing their meaning or why they were written—or failing to note the complexity and sophistication of the music itself—is to trivialize the art form and, possibly, the culture itself.

Many urban Appalachians know this difference, though they may not have explained it to outsiders. For example, Thomas Owens, an urban Appalachian born in Baptist Bottom, Kentucky, and currently a computer programmer at MIT, believes that emphasis on mountain craft misses the heart of his culture. Like many of us, he:

> ... never met a man who made a basket. Never saw my Daddy cane a chair. But Daddy wouldn't sell land as long as he lived ... said "Owenses don't sell land," and we don't ... There is something more basic than crafts that identify us. Crafts are just how we entertained ourselves or carried our eggs from the hen house. Who we are as a people, and the history we've lived, goes much deeper than that.
>
> ...[In Floyd County] I knew lots of people who made corn cribs and houses and foot bridges, but I never met anybody who made a basket. Our people worked. They worked in the mines, and they worked in the fields ... We have will ... stamina. We know how to sacrifice for the family ... and [back home we] knew how to get by—and be happy—without material things... I remember Dad talking about trying to [build] a $500 car out of a $200 car for $1.50 in parts. We had to know how to get by ... to take care of ourselves and take care of our families ... Those are the things I want my kids to know [about the culture] ... If they learn to quilt, that would be nice, but I wouldn't say they were more Appalachian for it.

So, if not crafts, what do we want to tell our children and the children of non-Appalachians about our history and culture? To answer this question, we must know more about ourselves and the effects of our unique cultural identity—that of city dwellers with roots that run deep into the mountains.

Recently, talking with my Aunt Polly, a sturdy mountain woman well-versed in traditional mountain skills, I explained that my city friends think that because I am from the mountains I know all about mountain cooking and canning. My aunt was surprised. "Why you're not *from* the mountains. You're a city girl." Aunt Polly's response and the response of my city friends is typical—to mountain people, urban

Appalachians are city dwellers, and to city dwellers, they are hillbillies. And, as the situation currently exists, as much as we might wish otherwise, some urban Appalachians are uncertain about who they are and where their "home" is. Teachers in this study who call themselves "kind of" Appalachian demonstrate this uncertainty. And there is reason for it. We are no longer Appalachians; we were never urbanites. Many of us find that our hearts are in the mountains, but our lives are in the cities. I believe our experiences have created a new culture and history—neither Appalachian nor urban—and it is this that we must come to understand. Long-range research addressing the following questions should help to define who urban Appalachians are and what traits we have in common across class and race lines with Appalachians and with native urbanites—and which traits are purely urban Appalachian.

Who are Urban Appalachians?

A very large number of migrants achieved mainstream success. Many descendants of these migrants can no longer be identified as hillbillies by their accents, where they live, or what they do for a living, but who are they? What do they value? What Appalachian traditions have they maintained? What values do second or third generation middle-class urban Appalachians have in common with first-generation urban Appalachians. What do they have in common with poor or working class urban Appalachians still living in the inner city? How do the value systems and traditions of middle-class urban Appalachians differ from their non-Appalachian counterparts? How are the traits, values, traditions, and culture of urban Appalachians similar to and different from rural Appalachians? Have they hidden their identity? If so, why?

What of black urban Appalachians? What traits do they have in common with urban Appalachian whites? How does their "double minority status" (Turner and Cabell, 1985) affect their identity? Do they perceive themselves as black, as urban Appalachian, or as urban Appalachian black? How did their Appalachian roots affect their assimilation in the city?

How Do Class and Culture Differ?

Teachers in this study seem to believe that white poverty in Cincinnati is limited to Appalachians and that Appalachians are limited to poverty. Urban Appalachian must be defined in a way that separates class from ethnicity. What are the traits, values, and culture of poor urban Appalachians which are separate and distinguishable from the traits, values and culture of poor whites in general? At the very least, the culture of poor whites should be compared to the culture of poor urban Appalachians through a study of the literature.

What Can be Learned from the Stories of Urban Appalachians?

Little is known about the experiences of urban Appalachian migrants. And, unless their stories are known, statistics and other forms of research seem of little real value. More important than knowing how many students drop out of school, is knowing the experiences of those who dropped out, not through someone else's interpretation, but through stories told in their own words. We can better explain why urban Appalachian parents have certain attitudes toward school when their own school experiences are known. This known, programs can be more effectively planned and the urban Appalachian community will be better able to advocate for change. I am, therefore, suggesting extensive research to collect the stories of black and white, adult and child, male and female urban Appalachians from the poor, the working, and the middle classes. This research is, I think, both the most important and the most neglected.

Action for Change in the Classroom

First and without compromise, urban Appalachian children must acquire the skills necessary to gain access to educational, occupational, and financial opportunities. Students must also be taught in ways that instill pride, create a sense of personal power, and provide a variety of successful experiences. The use of any approach should be decided by how well it attains these goals. What educates with pride and power should be used. What does not should be replaced. The current traditionalist approaches have not proven effective with urban Appalachian children. I believe these approaches are so class- and majority-culture oriented that it is unlikely that any recommendations based on their use will prove successful. Instead, I suggest that access, pride, power, and successful experiences are most apt to occur when teaching methods are grounded in, but not limited to, a cultural base.

The recommendations I make in this section are based on the findings of this study, particularly the teacher interviews, and on my experiences as an urban Appalachian and as a teacher. To a large degree, they are approaches developed over a period of years working with urban Appalachian children and with a culturally diverse school population. Some aspects are similar to those used by Eliot Wigginton in his *Foxfire* curricula. It is important to note, however, that these recommendations are not intended as solutions, but as directions and alternatives to be explored. They are based on the assumptions that students are capable of achieving; that education is important in success outside of school; and, that teachers want to help their students achieve. I have suggested that two major actions to be carried out simultaneously: creating a culture-based curriculum, and providing support for teachers. In this paper I will discuss only the creation of a curriculum.

Creating a Curriculum

While "Appalachian Week" activities, folk singers, or bulletin board displays are probably favorable to excluding Appalachian awareness from the curriculum, they are, as I have said earlier, often superficial in their approach. Here I will discuss ways Appalachian history and culture may be integrated into the curriculum and their definitions broadened.

One of the things I find most exciting about curriculum development is the opportunity to design with multiple layers, each layer offering different possibilities and meeting different objectives. I suggest that two strands be woven into a curriculum for white urban Appalachian children. The first strand should be directed at presenting the cultural traits that "go deeper" than crafts. A second strand should address race issues. This is especially important considering the implementation of a desegregation plan that requires cross bussing between the predominantly black and urban Appalachian enclaves. White urban Appalachian students tend to be fearful in integrated situations (Wagner, 1975) and black students tend to be more nervous around poor or working class whites than middle-class whites (Delpit, 1988). The desegregation plan is apt to result in racially tense situations for many participating black and white Appalachian students. Curriculum developed with this in mind could teach basic skills and, at the same time, contribute to a reduction in racial tension.

Topics, materials, and classroom speakers could be chosen to demonstrate the diversity of the Appalachian region and to highlight examples of blacks and whites working together in Appalachia. One example of such a topic is a study of the coal mining industry, focusing on the creation of the first multiracial union resulting from alliances between black and white miners. Or, younger children could be told stories about life in the mountains that focus on the positive racial relationships there (see Starnes, 1988, and Corbin, 1985, for example). And, when the Underground Railroad is studied, the significance of the contributions of white mountaineers, normally not mentioned, could be emphasized. Appalachian diversity could also be illustrated by including stories of Appalachian Native Americans, and of immigrants who came to the mountains during the mining boom.

In addition, ways can be found to teach mandated social studies skills, at least to some extent, through Appalachian history. Books about and by Appalachians can be integrated into English and reading curricula, not only for the urban Appalachian population of Cincinnati; but for the population in general. Both black and white Appalachians can be included as speakers and as role models for students—role models who have come out of the mountains or the inner city to become successful in mainstream society, but have not sacrificed their roots in the process. If carefully chosen, role models could serve more than one purpose. For example, Harriet Marsh-Page is a Cincinnati civic leader involved in the arts and education and is the daughter of a black coal miner from West Virginia. Identifying herself as a black Appalachian woman, Harriet tells engaging stories with important messages for urban Appalachian students of today—black or white. Such a curriculum could provide role models and options quite different from those provided by the crafts person.

Though the language of Appalachia and of the urban Appalachian have an undeniable beauty and have meanings that cannot always be accurately translated into mainstream English, those who are able to express themselves in the language of the majority are more apt to have access to opportunities. Therefore, curricula must emphasize the development of fluency in this mainstream language. However, attaining *fluency* must not require students to sacrifice or devalue their culture or their own language. Since many urban Appalachians speak a language foreign to those in the mainstream, their language need not be considered "substandard," but rather a second language. Teaching mainstream English to urban Appalachian children then becomes a matter of using techniques that have proven successful with other language minority or bilingual groups. Such methods can teach the language of the dominant culture without stigmatizing students for using their first language.

These are only a few of many ways that a creative curriculum can instruct both those who are and those who are not of Appalachian heritage. The possibilities are almost limitless. In addition, the inclusion of a *Foxfire*-like program that would teach basic skills through a study of the community would help students to identify their personal histories and to celebrate their culture—in the city—as well as to identify and celebrate the history and culture their parents or grandparents brought with them from the mountains.

Conclusion

In this study, I set out to gather information on teachers' attitudes toward their students of Appalachian heritage. The study yielded that and much more.

Dealing with the education of urban Appalachian children, or any cultural minority for that matter, is not an easy task. The ingredients of low school achievement are so intertwined and deeply rooted that change can not be expected when any one of the actors—the parents, teachers, children, Appalachian activists, or school power structure—is working in isolation. I am suggesting, therefore, that since teachers apparently do have negative attitudes toward their urban Appalachian students, they will need assistance to change their attitudes and practices. It is not only logical that assistance should come from the urban Appalachian community, it is necessary. Part of that assistance will come from identifying our cultural traits, learning our history, and helping teachers to include these in their curriculum. If we believe that change is required, we must work with teachers, not policy makers, to bring about change at a grassroots level.

Without these changes, we are all victims. Some of us are victims because we are denied access to the quality education we are entitled to. Others of us are victims because we are forced to give up, or deny, our culture in order to achieve mainstream success. For me, the value of this study is not that it provides concrete examples of teachers who have low expectations or who are biased or insensitive (though it certainly does provide those examples). It is, rather, valuable because it points out so clearly that people do not know who we are, and that many of us do not ourselves know who we are. We must be vigilant in identifying ourselves, and in finding ways to inform others. We must learn to say what it is about us, regardless of race, class, or education, that sets us apart from the mainstream. We must then celebrate that difference and help others to celebrate with us. I am not really sure what all of those difference are, but I am sure that they are not crafts. I am also sure that we must not let others define who we are, what is important or valuable in our history and culture, or what our children should be taught.

Bringing about the kind of change I have suggested in this paper would not be a small task. It is, however, a task worthy of our time and energy. And we must act quickly. Classrooms in Cincinnati and other urban settings are filled with children waiting for our action.

Works Cited

Appalachian Task Force for Reducing Racial Tension. 1984. Cincinnati Public Schools, Stuart Faber, Chairman. March-April, 1984. Unpublished meeting notes.

Berlowitz, Marvin J. and Henry Durand. 1977. "School Dropout or Student Pushout? A Case of Possible Violation of Property Rights and Liberties by Defacto Exclusion of Students from Public Schools." Working Paper, No. 8. Cincinnati: Urban Appalachian Council.

Delpit, Lisa. 1988. "The Silenced Dialogue: Power and Pedagogy in the Education of Other People's Children." *Harvard Educational Review*.

Fenton, D. 1970. "Crispus Attuks is Not Enough." *National Association of Secondary School Principals.* April 7-14, 1970.

Fouts, Arnold. 1988. Personal Communication. July, 1988.

Kroger, Jake. 1985. "Lower Price Hill Community School Fights Dropout Rate with Adult Education." *Appalachian Advocate.* March 4-5, 1985.

Roth, Richard. "Effects of Black Studies on Negro Fifth Graders." *Journal of Negro Education* 38: 435-9.

Starnes, Bobby Ann. 1988. "Two Urban Appalachian Families: Down but not Out." Unpublished manuscript.

Starnes, Bobby Ann. 1988. "The Education of Blacks in the Coal Camps 1935-1958: Social Integration, Educational Segregation, and Economic Oppression." Unpublished manuscript.

Wagner, Thomas. 1975. "Report of the Appalachian School Study Project." Working paper, No. 4. Cincinnati: Urban Appalachian Council.

Wagner, Thomas. "Urban Schools and Appalachian Children." *Urban Education* 12: 283-295.

Bobby Ann Starnes is in the Harvard graduate school of education, Cambridge, Massachusetts.

Appalachian Studies Association Members

Adams, Lynn
Pikeville College
Box 26
Bypro, KY 41612
606-452-4842

Adams, Marty
Pikeville College
PO Box 492
Pikeville, KY 41501
606-432-9253

Adkins, Roy
Pikeville College
200 Winston Creek Rd
Pikeville, KY 41501
606-432-0649

Akers, Ellen
New River
Community College
PO Drawer 898
Wytheville, VA 24382
703-228-6611

Anglin, Mary
Lenoir-Phyne College
Dept. of Sociology
Hickory, NC 28603
704-328-7232

Anglin Kuhne, Sharon
109 Wing Road
Bakersville, NC 28705
704-688-4810

Arcury, Thomas A.
University of Kentucky
365 Patterson Off. Tw
Lexington, KY 40506
606-257-5851

Arnow, Pat
East Tenn. State Univ.
Box 19180A
Johnson City, TN 37614
615-929-5348

Asbury, Jo Ann
Radford University
515 Newbern Road
Pulaski, VA 24301
703-980-5036

Asbury, Sr., Roger
Pulaski High School
515 Newbern Road
Pulaski, VA 24301
703-980-5036

Askins, Justin
Radford University
Rt. 1, Box 215
Radford, VA 24087
703-831-5494

Athey, Lou
F & M College
Dept. of History
Lancaster, PA 17604
712-299-3482

Austin, Sonya
Radford University
PO Box 6082
Radford, VA 24142
703-731-7292

Badgett, Ken
Appalachian State Univ.
Rt. 4, Box 491
Dobson, NC 27017
919-374-4698

Baker, Moira P.
Radford University
Dept. of English
Radford, VA 24141
703-831-5352

Banker, Mark
Webb Sch. of Knoxville
PO Box 70
Kingston, TN 37763
615-376-6485

Barker, Garry
Berea College
CPO 2347
Berea, KY 40404
606-986-9341

Bartholomew, Betsy
301 Thompson Street
Stanton, VA 24401
703-885-0233

Bashaw, Carolyn
233 University Drive
Athens, GA 30605

Baxley, Robert E.
East Tenn. State Univ.
Box 21130A
Johnson City, TN 37614
605-929-6738

Bell, John
Western Carolina Univ.
Dept. of History
Cullowhee, NC 28723
704-227-7243

Benson, Randy
Wake Forest University
2213 Queen Street
Winston-Salem,
NC 27103
919-750-0474

Bently, Donna
Pikeville College
Box 180
Hellier, KY 41534
606-986-3204

Best, Bill
Berea College
CPO 42
Berea, KY 40404
606-986-3204

Best, Irmgrad
Berea College
CPO 42
Berea, KY 40404
606-986-3204

Bickers, Doyle
West Georgia College
147 Griffin Drive
Carrollton, GA 30117
404-836-6416

Bickers, Phyllis
West Georgia College
147 Griffin Drive
Carrollton, GA 30117

Black, Kate
University of Kentucky
Appalachian Collections
Lexington, KY 40506
606-257-8634

Blackeney, Anne
E.K.U.
Wallace 109
Richmond, KY 40475
606-622-3300

Blaustein, Richard
East Tenn. State Univ.
PO Box 19180A
Johnson City, TN 37614
615-929-5348

Blee, Kathy
University of Kentucky
Dept. of Sociology
Lexington, KY 40506
606-257-4418

Blethen, Tyler
Western Carolina Univ.
Cullowhee, NC 28723
704-227-7129

Blevin, Margo
Davis & Elkins College
Elkins, WV 26241
304-636-1903

Bowen, Rich
Wake Forest University
1251 W. 4th Street
Winston-Salem,
NC 27101
919-748-0287

Boyd, Tom
Berea College
CPO 65
Berea, KY 40404
606-986-9341

Bradford, Elinor
42 West Street
Morgantown, WV 26505
304-296-6304

Braswell, Maria
Appalachian State Univ.
Rt. 4, Box 559
Newland, NC 28657
704-733-0747

Brosi, George
Appalachian Mt. Books
123 Walnut Street
Berea, KY 40403
606-986-1663

Browder, Amy
Wake Forest University
Reynolds Station
Winston-Salem,
NC 27109
919-750-1295

Brown, Alice
University of Kentucky
641 So. Limestone
Lexington, KY 40506
606-257-8269

Brown, Harry Neil
Eastern Kentucky Univ.
English Department
Richmond, KY 40475
606-622-2102

Brown, Jane
Western Carolina Univ.
Rt. 3, Box 225
Sylvia, NC 28779
704-227-7268

Brown, Jo Baily
West Virginia University
PO Box 6069
Morgantown, WV 26505
304-293-7185

Buxton, Barry M.
Appalachian
  Consortium, Inc.
University Hall
Boone, NC 28608
704-262-2064

Byer, James
Western Carolina Univ.
Cullowhee, NC 28723
704-227-7264

Byer, Judy P.
The Hill Lorists
Rt. 1, Box 150C
Bristol, WV 26332
304-366-5387

Cable, Stephen
Radford University
PO Box 7244
Radford, VA 24142
703-731-7018

Caldwell, Derek
Wake Forest University
2213 Queen Street
Winston-Salem,
NC 27103
919-750-0474

Campbell, W. Charles
Wake Forest Univ.
2213 Queen Street
Winston-Salem,
NC 27103
919-750-0474

Carpenter, Claire
University of Kentucky
Appalachian Center
641 So. Limestone
Lexington, KY 40506
606-257-4852

Carucci Goss, Rosemary
Virginia Tech.
Rt. 1, Box 342 AA
Blacksburg, VA 24060
703-961-4784

Catron, Rhonda K.
Radford University
603 Madison Street
Radford, VA 24141
703-639-3528

Cheek, Edwin R.
Mars Hill College
PO Box 502
Mars Hill, NC 28754
704-689-2172

Cheek, Pauline B.
Earlham School of Religion
PO Box 502
Mars Hill, NC 28754
704-689-2172

Christensen, Amy
Pikeville College
211 Kentucky Avenue
Pikeville, KY 41501
606-437-6563

Clelland, Donald
9520 Kingston Pike
Knoxville, TN 37922
615-691-9896

Cloud, Lewis
PO Box 188
Cullowhee, NC 28723

Collins, Timothy
University of Kentucky
Dept. of Social Science
Lexington, KY 40546
606-272-2958

Cooper, Leland
Appalachian State Univ.
Boone, NC 28608
704-264-9186

Councill, Rebecca S.
Watauga Co. Hist. Soc.
310 Brookside Drive
Boone, NC 28607
704-262-1348

Covey, Mary
Concord College
PO Drawer A
Athens, WV 24712
304-384-5369

Covey, Winton
Concord College
PO Drawer A
Athens, WV 24712
304-384-5238

Cox, Ricky
Radford University
Rt. 2, Box 135
Willis, VA 24380
703-789-4145

Cox, Jr., John David
Appalachian State Univ.
Appalachian Studies
Boone, NC 28608
704-262-4087

Crews, P. Ann
Radford University
PO Box 441
Radford, VA 24141
703-731-4124

Crissman, James
Ill. Benedictive College
Lisle, IL 60532
312-690-1436

Crouch, Jerry
Univ. Press of Kentucky
663 So. Limestone Street
Lexington, KY 40506
606-257-2951

Cunningham, Rodger
Sue Bennett College
London, KY 40741
606-864-4178

Davidson, Jan
Western Carolina Univ.
Mt. Heritage Center
Cullowhee, NC 28723
704-227-7129

Davis, Donald
7901 Collier Road
Powell, TN 37849

Davis, Peggy E.
Pikeville College
306 Spilman
Pikeville, KY 41501
606-432-5013

Defoe, G. Mark
West Virginia Wesleyan
28 Dentral
Buckhannon, WV 26201
304-472-0667

Degutis, Beth
7920 Embercrest Tr.
Knoxville, TN 37938
615-922-0334

DeYoung, Alan
University of Kentucky
College of Education
Lexington, KY 40506
606-257-3846

Dickerson, II, Lynn C.
PO Box 81
Richmond, VA 23173

Dickstein, Carla
West Virginia University
511 No. High Street
Morgantown, WV 26506
304-293-2896

Dietz, Dennis
Mt. Memories Books
216 Sutherland Drive
S. Charleston, WV 25303
304-744-5772

Dorgan, Howard
Appalachian State Univ.
Communication Arts
Boone, NC 28608
704-262-2403

Drake, Richard
Berea College
Box 2283
Berea, KY 40404
606-986-9341/X6337

Duke, David C.
Marshall University
History Department
Huntington, WV 25701

Dunn, Durwood
Tenn. Wesleyan College
Dept. of History
Athens, TN 37303
615-745-0296

Edwards, Grace
Radford University
Box 5917
Radford, VA 24142
703-831-5366

Edwards, Mike
Radford University
Rt. 1, Box 81
Woodlawn, VA 24381
703-731-1875

Elledge, Barry
Appalachian State Univ.
Economic Department
Boone, NC 28608
704-262-6121

Eller, Ron
University of Kentucky
641 So. LImestone
Lexington, KY 40506
606-257-4851

England, Rhonda G.
University of Kentucky
129 Taylor Ed.
Lexington, KY 40506

Evans, David K.
Wake Forest University
1926 Faculty Drive
Winston-Salem,
NC 27106
919-724-0187

Fannon, Brian
Wake Forest University
3714 No. Cherry Street
Winston-Salem,
NC 27105

Farago, Laszlo
West Virginia University
Regional Research
Morgantown, WV 26506
304-293-2896

Farr, Sidney
Berea College
109 High Street
Berea, KY 40403
606-986-9685

Faulkner, Gavin
Rowan Mountain Press
2010 Broken Oak Drive
Blacksburg, VA 24062
703-961-3315

Feely, Michael
PO Box 1854
Alexandria, VA 22313
703-836-4324

Feldhake, Charles
111 Walnutview Drive
Beaver, WV 25813 304
-252-9494

Fisher, Steve
Emory & Henry College
PO Box BBB
Emory, VA 24327
203-044-3121

Fletcher, Juliet
Appalachian State Univ.
Appalachian Consortium
Boone, NC 28608
704-262-2064

Fortney, Lindalee
Univ. of Tenn. Press
293 Comm. Bldg.
Knoxville, TN 37996
615-974-3321

Frazier, Kitty B.
West Vir. State College
English Department
Institute, WV 25112

Fulp-Parker, Gloria
Appalachian State Univ.
Appalachian Studies
Boone, NC 28607
704-262-8724

Garvin, Margaret
PO Box 474 WOB
West Orange, NJ 07052

Gayheart, Willard
Pencil Artist
PO Box 605
Galax, VA 24333
703-236-5890

Ginn, Linda W.
Western Carolina Univ.
Box 2106
Cullowhee, NC 28723
704-227-7415

Glen, John
Ball State University
Department of History
Muncie, IN 47306
317-285-8729

Goldman, Pam
131 Burnett
Lexington, KY 40505
606-254-4755

Goode, Elizabeth
Wake Forest University
811 Gales Avenue
Winston-Salem,
NC 27103
919-777-1556

Gooden, Randall
West Virginia University
202 Woodburn Hall
Morgantown, WV 26506
304-293-2421

Goodwin, Sara
The River Foundation
2629 Longview Avenue
Roanoke, VA 24014
703-345-1295

Graves, Glenna H.
University of Kentucky
3515 Danada Drive
Lexington, KY 40502
606-271-0886

Gray, Angela L.
Wake Forest University
Box U762
Winston-Salem,
NC 27109
919-761-6731

Gray, Debby
9 Elm Manor
Berea, KY 40403
606-986-1402

Greene, Janet
New York University
Bobst Library
New York, NY 10012
212-998-2637

Greene, Mary C.
Appalachian State Univ.
Boone, NY 28607
704-262-3117

Gross, Carol J.
Appalachian State Univ.
Chappel Wilson Hall
Boone, NC 28608
704-262-6398

Gunter, Jr., Charles
8 Okeechobee Drive
Johnson City, TN 37604
615-926-6788

Gupta, Veena
West Virginia University
511 No. High Street
Morgantown, WV 26506
304-293-2896

Hager, Beth
Huntington Mus. of Art
Hega, WV 25701
304-529-2701

**Hallam Peterson,
   Hallie**
Rollins College
Winter Park, FL 32789
407-646-2502

Halpin, Mary E.
West Virginia University
41 Meade Street
Buckhannon, WV 26201
304-472-5145

Hamilton, Evelyn
209 Williams Street
Abingdon, VA 24210
703-628-9504

Hariow, Barbara
Asheville, NC 28804
704-251-6415

Haskell Speer, Jean
Virginia Tech.
2088 Derring Hall
Blacksburg, VA 24061
703-231-5874

Hassler, Kassandra
Tenn St. Lib. & Archives
403 7th Avenue No.
Nashville, TN 37219

Hatcher, Wilma
Bluefield High School
2312 Spring Garden
Bluefield, WV 24701
304- 325-9116

Hawker, Ginny
Augusta Heritage Ctr.
Rt. 1, Box 132
Cox's Mill, WV 26342
304-462-8427

Hayden, Jr., Wilburn
Western Carolina Univ.
Dept. of Social Work
Cullowhee, NC 28723
704-227-7112

Hennen, John
West Virginia University
Morgantown, WV 26506
304-293-2896

Henry, Abbe
Pikeville College
229 Straight Fork
Pikeville, KY 41501

Henry, Charles
Pikeville College
229 Straight Fork
Pikeville, KY 41501
606-639-6298

Herrin, Roberta
East Tenn. State Univ.
Box 22990A
Johnson City, TN 37614

Higgins, Jr., Ray
Emory & Henry College
Emory, VA 24327

Hiles, Delores
Univ. Press of Kentucky
663 So. Limestone
Lexington, KY 40506
606-257-8442

Hill, Brandon
Wake Forest University
Box 9525
Winston-Salem, NC 27109
919-761-6727

Hill, Doug
Augusta Heritage Ctr.
Davis & Elkins College
Elkins, WV 26241
304-636-1903

Hines, Percy W.
Archives and History
13 Veterans Drive
Asheville, NC 28805
704-298-5024

Hinson, Carolyn
Radford University
PO Box 403
Newbern, VA 24126
703-831-5953

Holliman, Mary C.
Pocahontas Press
2805 Wellesley Ct.
Blacksburg, VA 24060
703-951-0467

Howell, Benita
U.T.-Knoxville
7225 Wellswood Lane
Knoxville, TN 37909
615-584-0538

Howley, Aimee
Univ. of Charleston
306 20th St. S.E.
Charleston, WV 25304
304-357-4877

Howley, Craig
Eric/Cress
PO Box 1348
Charleston, WV 25304
304-347-0463

Hsiung, David
University of Michigan
1586-15 Murfin Avenue
Ann Arbor, MI 48105
313-747-1545

Humphreys, Betsy
305 Lebanon Avenue
Morgantown, WV 26505

Huntley, Joy
12485 Peach Ridge Road
Athens, OH 45701
614-592-5741

Inscoe, John
University of Georgia
Department of History
Houston, TX 77098
713-527-6039

Jennings, Judi
Appalshop
306 Madison Street
Whitesburg, KY 41858
606-633-0108

Jenrette, Jerra
West Virginia University
Morgantown, WV 26506
304-293-2896

Johnson, Jennifer
Pikeville College
399 Hambley Blvd.
Pikeville, KY 41501

Johnson, Mary
West Virginia University
1056 Van Voorhis K-8
Morgantown, WV 26505
304-293-5548

Jones, Loyal
Berea College
Appalachian Center
Berea, KY 40404
606-986-9341

Joyner, Nancy
Western Carolina Univ.
Department of English
Cullowhee, NC 28723
704-293-5290

Karr, Carolyn
Marshall University
400 Hal Greer Blvd.
Huntington, WV 25701
304-696-2962

Keefe, Susan
Appalachian State Univ.
Anthropology Depart.
Boone, NC 28608
704-262-6384

Kessler, Clyde
PO Box 3612
Radford, VA 24143
703-639-5076

Kester, Jr., Tom
Wake Forest University
PO Box 8241
Winston-Salem, NC 27109
919-761-6411

Kline, Michael
Western Carolina Univ.
Mt. Heritage Center
Cullowhee, NC 28723
704-227-7129

Lapresto, Brigitte
Pikeville College
399 Hambley Blvd. 401
Pikeville, KY 41501
606-432-9241

Lapresto, Craig
Pikeville College
399 Hambley Blvd.
Pikeville, KY 41501
606-432-5970

Lawson, Garlene
Pikeville College
Pikeville, KY 41650

Lefler, Lisa
Western Carolina Univ.
PO Box 662
Dillsboro, NC 28725
704-586-9313

Leftwich, Christi
Radford University
201 Madison Street
Radford, VA 24141
703-731-4845

Leonard, Phillip
Virginia Central
  Community College
1309 Grove Road
Lenchburg, VA 24502

Lewis, Helen
Highlander
Rt. 1, Box 270
Dungannon, VA 24245
703-476-2240

Lewis, Ron
West Virginia University
Department of History
Morgantown, WV 26506
304-293-2421

Lightfoot, William E.
Appalachian State Univ.
English Department
Boone, NC 28608
704-262-1050

Lindberg, Laurie
Pikeville College
Humanities Division
Pikeville, KY 41501
606-432-9379

Little, Pat
Pikeville College
PO Box 2265
Pikeville, KY 41650
606-452-2729

Lloyd, James
University of Tennessee
Hoskins Library
Knoxville, TN 37996
605-974-4480

Lohmann, Roger
West Virginia University
709 Allen Hall
Morgantown, WV 26506
304-293-3501

Lohr, Karen
Appalachian
  Consortium, Inc.
University Hall
Boone, NC 28608
704-262-2064

Looney, Donna
Box 246
Breaks, VA 24607
703-531-8269

Lushko, Rene
Western Carolina Univ.
PO Box 1794
Cullowhee, NC 28723
704-293-3663

Lyday-Lee, Kathy
Elon College
Box 2202
Elon College, NC 27244
919-584-2274

MacDonald, Frederick
736 Norton Drive
Kalamazoo, MI 49001
616-349-6135

Mackey, Karee
Appalachian State Univ.
Box 13740
Boone, NC 28607
704-262-1132

Maggard, Sally Ward
University of Kentucky
6701 Greenwish Pike
Lexington, KY 40511
606-299-2906

Maholland, Roslyn
Pittsburgh School of
  Social Work
313 Winston
Pittsburgh, PA 15207

Maiden, Emory
Appalachian State Univ.
Boone, NC 28608
704-262-2320

Maloney, Michael
134 Kinsey Avenue
Cincinnati, OH 45219

Martin, Miles
1 Blair Road
Plattsburg, NY 12901
518-561-0844

Mayer, Henry C.
Appalachian Center
7187 Blenheim Road
Louisville, KY 40207
502-896-4780

Mc Donald, C.E.
West Virginia University
74 Pierce Street
Westover, WV 26505
304-292-8854

Mc Griff, John
Union College
Box 408
Barbourville, KY 40906
606-546-4151

McAvog, Rogers
West Virginia University
608 Allen Hall
Morgantown, WV 26505
304-293-3879

McCehee, Stuart
Eastern Regional Coal
Archives
600 Commerce
Bluefield, WV 24701
304-325-3943

McCrumb, Sharyn
Rowan Mountain, Inc.
PO Box 10111
Blacksburg, VA 24062
703-961-3315

McCulloh, Judith
Univ. of Illinois Press
54 E. Gregory Drive
Champaign, IL 61820
217-244-4681

McCutchen, M. Gene
University of Tennessee
Department of P.E.
Knoxville, TN 37996
615-974-2104

McDonald, Tana
Univ. of Tennessee Press
293 Comm. Bldg.
Knoxville, TN 37996
615-974-3321

McKenzie, Roberta
University of Kentucky
424 Linden Walk #1
Lexington, KY 40508
606-252-8676

McKinney, Gordon
Western Carolina Univ.
History Department
Cullowhee, NC 28723
704-227-7243

McMillan, Greg
Emory & Henry College
Emory, VA 24327

Miller, Danny
Northern Kentucky
  University
2624 Jefferson Ave. # 1
Cincinnati, OH 45219
513-221-7492

Miller, Jim Wayne
West Kentucky Univ.
IWFAC 272
Bowling Green,
KY 42101
502-745-5904

Miller, Wilbur R.
Suny-Stony Brook
374-11th Street
Brooklyn, NY 11215
718-499-1037

Milnes, Gerry
Augusta Heritage Ctr.
Davis & Elkins College
Elkins, WV 26241
304-636-1903

Mobbs, Rebecca P.
Rt. 1, Box 332
Ocoee, TN 37361
615-338-220

Moore, Ms. Warren
1800 No. Elm. St. #A2
Greensboro, NC 27408

Moore, Phyllis
101 Morgan Street
Clarksburg, WV 26301

Morefield, John
East Tenn. State Univ.
PO Box 22990A
Johnson City, TN 37614
615-929-4347

Moretz, Ray
Unc-Chapel Hill
Rt. 2, Box 514
Boone, NC 28607
704-264-1989

Moser, Ann H.
Radford University
Rt. 2, Box 251
Blue Ridge, VA 24604
703-977-1579

Moser, Joan
Warren Wilson College
312 Wilson Cove Road
Swannanoa, NC 38778
704-298-8971

Moser, Mabel Y.
310 Wilson Cove Road
Swannanoa, NC 28778
704-298-1640

Mullins, Mike
Hindman Settlement
  School, Inc.
Box 844
Hindman, KY 41822
606-785-5475

Nance, Nanci T.
Watauga High School
Hwy 105
Boone, NC 28607
704-264-2407

Nance, Paula
Wake Forest University
2735 Henning Drive
Winston-Salem,
NC 27106
919-761-8928

Nelson, Ken
Mayland Com. College
PO Box 547
Spruce Pine, NC 28777
704-765-7351

Nichols, Betty Marie
Pikeville College
KC 67, Box 485
Philips, KY 41553
606-456-3047

Noble, David
Ohio University
110 Carnel Road
Wheeling, WV 26003
614-695-1720

Nordeen, Elizabeth
Marshall University
Rt. 1, Box 422
Chesapeake, OH 45619
304-696-2357

Norris, Monica L.
Appalachian
   Consortium, Inc.
University Hall
Boone, NC 28608
704-262-2064

Obermiller, Phillip
Northern Kentucky
   University
Highland Hgt, KY 41076
606-572-5259

Oliver, Scot
Appalshop, Inc.
306 Madison Street
Whitesburg, KY 48158
606-633-0108

Olson, Eric
Appalachian State Univ.
Appalachian College
Boone, NC 28608
704-262-4041

Palmer, Nikki
Pikeville College
CPO Box 518
Pikeville, KY 41501
606-437-3429

Palmer, Tersh
Spartanburg Dist School
311 McEntire Rd.
Tryon, NC 28782
704-863-2129

Parker, R. Clinton
Appalachian State Univ.
Academic Affairs
Boone, NC 28608
704-262-2070

Parson, Delra
827 Beaumont
Charleston, WV 25314
304-348-0070

Pendleton, Susan
Radford University
PO Box 725
Radford, VA 24141
703-731-4124

Perry, David
Univ. of N. C. Press
PO Box 2288
Chapel Hill, NC 27515
919-966-3561

Peterson, Thomas
Rollings College
Winter Park, FL 32789
407-646-2397

Pollard, Roger G.
Radford University
PO Box 95
Lindside, WV 24951
304-753-4504

Poore, Dawn
Avery High School
Rt. 2, Box 389
Newland, NC 28657
704-733-9792

Porter, Julia D.
1601 Spring Garden
Philadelphia, PA 19130

Puckett, Anita
University of Texas
Anthropology Depart.
Austin, TX 78712
512-471-4206

Pudup, Mary Beth
West Virginia University
Regional Research
Morgantown, WV 26505
304-293-2896

Quinn, Edythe A.
University of Tennessee
8724 Pedigo Road
Powell, TN 37849
615-922-0291

Randolph, John H.
West Vir. Heritage Ctr.
Jackson's Mill
Weston, WV 26442
304-269-6681

Rasmussen, Barbara
West Virginia University
Department of History
Morgantown, WV 26506
304-293-2421

Ratliff, Phillip
Pikeville College
HC 65, Box 440
Belcher, KY 41513
606-754-5835

Ready, Milton
UNC-Asheville
History Department
Asheville, NC 28804
704-251-6415

Reed, Jeannie
Western Carolina Univ.
PO Box 181
Cherokee, NC 28719
704-497-6952

Reed, Maureen
629 Adams Street
Riverton, IL 62561
217-629-8402

Reiman, Bob
Appalachian State Univ.
Geography & Planning
Boone, NC 28608
704-262-2651

Riley, James
214 Bank Street
Pikeville, KY 41501
606-437-4041

Roberts, Gerald
Berea College
Berea, KY 40404
606-986-9341

Roberts, Sam
Tenn. Wesleyan College
Athens, TN 37303
615-745-7504

Robertson, Tom
West Virginia University
Morgantown, WV 26506
304-293-2896

Rose, Anita
Western Carolina Univ.
17 Clairmont Avenue
Asheville, NC 28801
704-251-6588

Ross, Charlotte
Appalachian State Univ.
Boone, NC 28608
704-262-2282

Salstrom, Apul
Marshall University
728 W. 2nd Street
Huntington, WV 25701
304-525-3404

Salvati, Janet S.
Fairmont State College
Fairmont, WV 26554
304-367-4121

Samples, Joyce
802 Hillman Hwy.
Abingdon, VA 24210
704-628-9504

Sayre, Greg
West Virginia University
Regional Research
Morgantown, WV 26506
304-293-2896

Scancarelli, Janine
University of Kentucky
English Department
Lexington, KY 40506

Schneider, Ernie
Oxford Graduate School
PO Box 474
Tunnelton, WV 26444
304-568-2194

Schweiker, Carol A.
Salem College
Art Department
Salem, WV 26426
304-782-1341

Sellers, Bettie
PO Box 274
Young Harris, GA 30582

Shirley, Patricia
University of Tennessee
1431 Cherokee Trail
Knoxville, TN 37920
615-573-5081

Shook, Jane G.
Appalachian
 Consortium, Inc.
University Hall
Boone, NC 28608
704-262-2064

Simpkins, Chris
New River Com. College
PO Drawer 1127
Dublin, VA 24084
703-674-3607

Smalley, Lorraine
PO Box 1174
Cullowhee, NC 28723
704-497-9151

Smith, Barbara
1815 Hash Ridge Road
Barboursville, WV 25504
304-733-2253

Smith, Betty N.
475 Bluff Road
Hot Springs, NC 28743
704-622-3381

Smith, Denise
University of Kentucky
710 Hambrick Ave., #3
Lexington, KY 41508
606-253-1081

Speer, Allen
Hemlock & Balsams
Literary Mag./Box 128
Banner Elk, NC 28604
704-898-5241

Spiker, J. Scott
West Virginia University
117 Kingwood Street, #2
Morgantown, WV 26505
304-291-5249

Squibb, Joyce
East Tenn. State Univ.
Rt. 2
Jonesborough, TN 37659
615-753-8645

Stanwitz, Sandra L.
Rt. 1, Box 821
Max Meadows,
VA 24360
703-699-6490

Starnes, Bobby Ann
Harvard University
36 Walker Street, #1
Cambridge, MA 02139
617-354-2314

Stevens, Timothy E.
4436 Blackwood Drive
Montgomery, AL 36109
205-277-0870

Steward, Troy
Maarshall University
Huntington, WV 25701
304-696-2766

Stiltner, Carl
Pikeville College
PO Box 35
Steele, KY 41566
606-835-2034

Stiltner, Denise L.
Pikeville College
PO Box 1104
Elkhorn City, KY 41522

Stinton-Glen, Kathy
State of Indiana
1409 W. Washington
Muncie, IN 47303
317-282-0976

Stipes, Karen
Montgomery Co. Schools
216 Givens Land
Blacksburg, VA 24060
703-552-0487

Stokes, Doris M.
Cincinnati Public
  Schools
230 E. 9th Street
Cincinnati, OH 45202

Sturgill, Carolyn
Appalshop
306 Madison Street
Whitesburg, KY 41858
606-633-0108

Sullivan, Ken
Depart. of Culture
  & History, W.V.
Capitol Complex
Charleston, WV 25305
304-348-0220

Sutton, David
Appalachian State Univ.
Appalachian Studies
Boone, NC 28608
704-262-4089

Sutton Cahoon, Jane
Quinn Publishing Co.
PO Box 9452
Asheville, NC 28815
704-298-5318

Taylor, John C.
Union College
Box 463
Barbourville, KY 40906
606-546-4151

Tenney, Noel W.
Fort New Salem
Salem College
Salem, WV 26426
304-782-5245

Thomas, Norma
East Tenn. State Univ.
Box 22450A
Johnson City, TN 37614
615-929-6991

Thompson, Edgar H.
PO Box 34
Emory, VA 24327
703-944-5600

Thompson, Vanessa R.
335 Ellison Avenue
Beckley, WV 25801
304-252-7679

Tipton Gray, Amy
Caldwell Com. College
1000 Hickory Blvd.
Hudson, NC 28638
704-724-4323

Tipton, Jeff
Brown University
Music Dept./Box 1924
Providence, RI 02912
401-863-3234

Trevino, Diana
Withrow High School
7304 Scottwood Ave.
Cincinnati, OH 45237
513-761-9195

Tribe, Deanna L.
Ohio State University
017 Standpipe Road
Jackson, OH 45640
614-286-2177

Tribe, Ivan M.
Rio Grande College
Rio Grande, OH 45674
614-245-5353

Tyner, Martha
Augusta Heritage Ctr.
Davis & Elkins College
Elkins, WV 26241
304-636-1903

**Vance Cantrell,
  Patricia**
Radford University
Box 5767
Radford, VA 24142
703-831-5108

Vest, Makaia
Radford University
Rt. 2, Box 28
Blacksburg, VA 24060
703-951-3827

Wagaman, Gena D.
West Virginia University
744 Snider Street, #4
Morgantown, WV 26505
304-291-3175

Wagner, Melinda
Radford University
Radford, VA 24142
703-831-5157

Waller, Altina
Suny Plattsburgh
Department of History
Plattsburgh, NY 12901
518-564-5220

Ware, Kathy
Augusta Heritage Ctr.
Davis & Elkins College
Elkins, WV 26241
304-636-1903

Watkins, Charles A.
Appalachian State Univ.
Appal. Cultural Ctr.
Boone, NC 28608
704-262-3117

Watson, Steve
Radford University
1908 Shadow Lake Road
Blacksburg, VA 24060
703-831-5614

Weaver, Hank
Appalachian State Univ.
Appalachian Studies
Boone, NC 28608
704-262-4089

Weaver, Joseph H.
Allegany Com. College
Cumberland, MD 21502
301-724-7700

Weaver, Sallie
Appalachian State Univ.
Appalachian Studies
Boone, NC 28608
704-262-4089

Webb, James W.
Appalshop, Inc.
306 Madison Street
Whitesburg, KY 41858
606-633-0108

Webb, Judy
Pikeville College
314 Grapevine Road
Phyllis, KY 41554
606-835-4377

Weingartner, Paul
University of Kentucky
Lexington, KY 40507
606-257-6897

Weiss, Chris
PO Box 2125
Charleston, WV 25328
304-345-1298

Wellington, Bill
Augusta Heritage Ctr.
Davis & Elkins College
Elkins, WV 26241
304-636-1903

Wheeler, Cecilia
PO Box 1141
Oxford, NC 27565
919-693-9281

Wheeling, Teresa
Radford University
Rt. 2, Belspring
Radford, VA 24141
703-731-1519

White, Blair H.
East Tenn. State Univ.
Carroll Reece Museum
Johnson City, TN 37614
615-929-4392

White, Gregory
June Appal Recordings
306 Madison Street
Whitesburg, KY 41858
606-633-0108

Whittemore, Barry
Southern Seminary
College
Buena Vista, VA 24416
703-261-8400

Wiggins, Eugene
103 Jones Circle
Dahlonega, GA 30533

Williams, David
Valdosta State
Department of History
Valdosta, GA 31698
912-333-5800

Williams, Dean
Appalachian State Univ.
Appalachian Studies
Todd, NC 28684
704-877-5803

Williams, Mary
802 Hillman Highway
Abingdon, VA 24210
703-628-9504

Williamson, Jerry
Appalachian State Univ.
Appalachian Journal
Boone, NC 28608
704-262-4072

Wilson, Larry
Highlander
Rt. 2, Box AA68
Middlesboro, KY 40965
606-248-8213

Wilson, Shannon H.
Berea College
Special Collections
Berea, KY 40404
606-986-9341

Wood, Curtis
Western Carolina Univ.
Mt. Heritage Center
Cullowhee, NC 28723
704-227-7219

Wood, Sharon
7815 Conner Road, NE
Copperhill, VA 24079

Woods, Geoff
West Virginia University
Regional Research
Morgantown, WV 26506
304-293-2896

Workman, Mike
West Virginia University
Morgantown, WV 26506
304-293-2896

Worley, Bethany
Emory &Henry College
Emory, VA 24327

Yamazaki, Hiroe
West Virginia University
511 H. High Street
Morgantown, WV 26506
304-293-2896

Yang, Heather
Wake Forest University
Reynolds Station
Winston-Salem,
NC 27109
919-750-1332

Yarrow, Michael
Ithaca College
407 Hancock Street
Ithaca, NY 14850
607-272-4943

Young, Lisa
Wake Forest University
PO Box 7543
Winston-Salem,
NC 27109
919-723-0626

Zahorik, Pamela
East Tenn. State Univ.
Depart. of Family Med.
Johnson City, TN 37614
615-929-6738

Journal of the Appalachian Studies Association
Subscriptions and Order Form

Detach, Fold and Staple this Form, and Mail to:

Appalachian Consortium
University Hall
Boone, NC 28606

Please make checks payable to the **Appalachian Consortium**.

No. of Copies	Issue	Price	Total
_____	Journal of the Appalachian Studies Assoc./Vol. 2, 1990 "Transformation of Life and Labor in Appalachia"	$10.95	$_____
	Back Issues		
_____	Journal of the Appalachian Studies Assoc./Vol. 1, 1989 "Mountains of Experience"	$10.95	_____
	Proceedings of the Appalachian Studies Conference		
_____	(10) "Rememberance, Reunion, Revival"	$10.95	_____
_____	(9) "Contemporary Appalachia"	$10.95	_____
_____	(8) "The Impact of Institutions in Appalachia"	$10.95	_____
_____	(7) "The Many Faces of Appalachia"	$10.95	_____
_____	(6) "The Appalachian Experience"	$10.95	_____
_____	(5) "The Critical Essays"	$10.95	_____

                              Subtotal $_____
5% N.C. Sales Tax
(NC residents only)   _____
Handling $ 2.00
Shipping is $1.00 per copy   _____

Total Enclosed $_____

Name _____
Address _____
_____
Phone _____

_____ Please enter my name on the Subscriber's list. I understand that Subscriptions for the *Journal of the Appalachian Studies Association* are available through the Appalachian Consortium. The cost is $13.95 per copy, which includes shipping and handling. I understand that orders will be kept on file and automatically shipped and billed once each year unless cancelled by written correspondence.

Return Address

Stamp

Appalachian Studies Association Journal
Appalachian Consortium Press
University Hall
Boone, NC 28608

www.ingramcontent.com/pod-product-compliance
Lightning Source LLC
Chambersburg PA
CBHW051053160426
43193CB00010B/1164